CCBA® and CBAP® Certifications Study Guide

Expert tips and practices in business analysis to pass the certification exams on the first attempt

Esta Lessing

BIRMINGHAM - MUMBAI

CCBA® and CBAP® Certifications Study Guide

Commissioning Editor: Ravit Jain
Acquisition Editor: Ashitosh Gupta
Content Development Editor: Aamir Ahmed
Senior Editor: Martin Whittemore
Technical Editor: Deepesh Patel
Copy Editor: Safis Editing
Project Coordinator: Kinjal Bari
Proofreader: Safis Editing
Indexer: Rekha Nair
Production Designer: Jyoti Chauhan

First published: May 2020

Production reference: 1210520

Published by Packt Publishing Ltd.
Livery Place
35 Livery Street
Birmingham
B3 2PB, UK.

ISBN 978-1-83882-526-3

www.packt.com

I dedicate this book to my parents, who always made me believe I could do anything; to my husband, who catches me when I fall; and to my brother and sister, who are my cheerleading squad.

– Esta Lessing

Packt.com

Subscribe to our online digital library for full access to over 7,000 books and videos, as well as industry leading tools to help you plan your personal development and advance your career. For more information, please visit our website.

Why subscribe?

- Spend less time learning and more time coding with practical eBooks and Videos from over 4,000 industry professionals

- Improve your learning with Skill Plans built especially for you

- Get a free eBook or video every month

- Fully searchable for easy access to vital information

- Copy and paste, print, and bookmark content

Did you know that Packt offers eBook versions of every book published, with PDF and ePub files available? You can upgrade to the eBook version at www.packt.com and as a print book customer, you are entitled to a discount on the eBook copy. Get in touch with us at customercare@packtpub.com for more details.

At www.packt.com, you can also read a collection of free technical articles, sign up for a range of free newsletters, and receive exclusive discounts and offers on Packt books and eBooks.

Contributors

About the author

Esta Lessing is a passionate professional business analyst and educator who helps to transform business analysis teams to meet the increasing demand for up-to-date skills and capabilities. She founded her company, Business Analysis Excellence Pvt Ltd, in 2013 and her primary focus is to provide education solutions to enable business analysts globally to effectively deliver business value in constantly changing environments.

Esta was one of the first to achieve a CBAP® designation in Australia and New Zealand and served as a Certification Role Delineation Committee member for the **International Institute of Business Analysis (IIBA®)**. She has a strong background in business analysis, including having completed multiple **British Computer Society (BCS)** business analysis certifications and finishing her BCom (Hons) Informatics degree at the University of Pretoria and London School of Economics. She has worked as a business analyst in South Africa and the United Kingdom, and she is currently based in Australia. She has also been closely involved with building the business analysis community of practice teams in different organizations. Esta's most recent achievement is developing an innovative strategic planning and analysis methodology that engages team creativity and delivers strategic roadmaps for achieving a team's future vision.

I would like to acknowledge the very supportive staff and editorial team at Packt Publishing. They have all been patient with me as a first-time author; they are a highly talented team who guided me through this journey. Thank you so much for giving me this opportunity to become a published author. Special thanks to all of my peers and business analysis students for their direct and indirect contributions to my career experiences, business analysis knowledge, passion for education, and ultimately for helping me start and complete this study guide.

About the reviewer

Adedayo Idowu, CBAP, is a certified business analyst with expertise in process analysis, process improvement, and automation who has been leveraging business analysis knowledge and experience to drive business transformation and operational excellence projects with the aim of achieving business objectives and moving organizations from their current state to their desired state. Having worked in the financial and social media industries, she has been able to hone her problem-solving, innovative, analytics, and collaborative skills and use them to recommend solutions to meet different business needs.

She currently leverages her business analysis skills to help small and medium business owners identify and meet their business needs.

Packt is searching for authors like you

If you're interested in becoming an author for Packt, please visit `authors.packtpub.com` and apply today. We have worked with thousands of developers and tech professionals, just like you, to help them share their insight with the global tech community. You can make a general application, apply for a specific hot topic that we are recruiting an author for, or submit your own idea.

Table of Contents

Preface

Business analysis is one of the most rewarding and diverse business-focussed careers, because not only can it be practiced within almost any industry but it focuses on finding opportunities to help every type of business grow and improve. Once you embark on a business analysis career, you are on a journey of continuous learning and problem-solving.

This book, *CCBA® and CBAP® Certifications Study Guide*, aims to take you on a practical journey through the BABOK® v3 Guide. The goal is to bring the concepts in the BABOK® v3 Guide into the real world with examples in order to assist you in preparing to take the IIBA® CCBA® and CBAP® exams. This guide includes some background of my personal career journey and how the CBAP® designation has supported my career. It discusses a few study approaches and includes some ideas that you could incorporate into your own study plans. This guide outlines the exam requirements as they are stipulated by the International Institute of Business Analysis (IIBA®).

As you work through this study guide, you will be taken through all the knowledge areas, their tasks, and the elements to consider. Each of these chapters will include practical real-world examples to assist you in fully understanding the context, reasons, and practical application of the BABOK® v3 Guide's concepts. The book takes a unique perspective on the BABOK®v3 Guide's techniques chapter by describing each technique, summarizing its purpose, key elements, and the different business analysis task contexts it could be applied in. Each chapter ends with a knowledge quiz based on a real-world scenario as well as key concepts covered during the chapter. At the end of the journey through the BABOK® v3 Guide's knowledge area discussion chapters, I finish with additional mock exam-style questions that include theoretical and scenario-based questions to test your knowledge with. The last chapter in this book takes you into the future, to a time after you have achieved the CCBA® or CBAP® designation, and not only gives you advice on how to ensure that you maximize your confidence as a professional business analyst, but also outlines advice on how to make sure you also achieve a better position or salary outcome as a result of your achievement.

The Knowledge Area chapters (*Chapters 5 -11*) in this study guide contains content similar to the course *BABOK® v3 Core Practitioner Course*. However, we have included some different examples, element descriptions, and some different questions

Who this book is for

This study guide is aimed at business analysts who want to undertake the CCBA® or CBAP® certification exams and need a more practical view on the content of the BABOK® v3 Guide. It is for people who are seeking guidance and advice on how to achieve a successful exam result. This guide is also suitable for everyday use by practicing business analysts in the workplace who would like to ensure that they fully understand and apply business analysis tasks at work.

What this book covers

Chapter 1, *Planning for Success*, is where I will be sharing what I have learned are important steps to ensure that you give yourself the best chances of exam success.

Chapter 2, *Exam Application Requirements*, outlines the IIBA® exam application requirements that you need to meet before you can sit the exam. It also includes some tips about the application process.

Chapter 3, *Study Tools*, discusses the BABOK® v3 Guide structure and how you navigate and make sense of this guide both during your exam preparation activities and in your everyday practical work life.

Chapter 4, *What to Expect From the Exam*, describes the IIBA® exam blueprints as well as shedding some light on what types of exam questions you can expect to encounter when you take the CCBA® or CBAP® exams.

Chapter 5, *Business Analysis Foundation Concepts*, starts with the study material by outlining the foundational concepts that you should understand before attempting the rest of the knowledge area concepts.

Chapter 6, *Business Analysis Planning and Monitoring*, is where I discuss the Business Analysis Planning and Monitoring knowledge area in terms of its purpose, intent, and tasks, by describing elements to consider using straightforward language and practical examples. This chapter finishes with a real-world case study-based knowledge quiz.

Chapter 7, *Elicitation and Collaboration*, is where I discuss the Elicitation and Collaboration knowledge area in terms of its purpose, intent, and tasks, by describing elements to consider using straightforward language and practical examples. This chapter finishes with a real-world case study-based knowledge quiz.

Chapter 8, *Requirements Life Cycle Management*, is where I discuss the Requirements Life Cycle Management knowledge area in terms of its purpose, intent, and tasks, by describing elements to consider using straightforward language and practical examples. This chapter finishes with a real-world case study-based knowledge quiz.

Chapter 9, *Strategy Analysis*, is where I discuss the Strategy Analysis knowledge area in terms of its purpose, intent, and tasks, by describing elements to consider using straightforward language and practical examples. This chapter finishes with a real-world case study-based knowledge quiz.

Chapter 10, *Requirements Analysis and Design Definition*, is where I discuss the Requirements Analysis and Design Definition knowledge area in terms of its purpose, intent, and tasks, by describing elements to consider using straightforward language and practical examples. This chapter finishes with a real-world case study-based knowledge quiz.

Chapter 11, *Solution Evaluation*, is where I discuss the Solution Evaluation knowledge area in terms of its purpose, intent, and tasks, by describing elements to consider using straightforward language and practical examples. This chapter finishes with a real-world case study-based knowledge quiz.

Chapter 12, *Underlying Competencies*, is where I discuss the core competencies that every business analyst should develop throughout their career, as outlined in the BABOK® v3 Guide, using practical examples. This chapter finishes with a knowledge quiz.

Chapter 13, *Techniques (Part 1)*, covers each of the BABOK® v3 Guide techniques by summarizing their purpose and key considerations. It then also describes each technique in terms of the knowledge area tasks it applies to in order to bring it into the different contexts it is used in.

Chapter 14, *Techniques (Part 2)*, covers each of the BABOK® v3 Guide techniques by summarizing their purpose and key considerations. It then also describes each technique in terms of the knowledge area tasks it applies to in order to bring it into the different contexts it is used in.

Chapter 15, *Mock Exam Questions: Case Studies*, includes exam-style questions based on a series of four different real-world case studies. It aims to test your knowledge and ability to consider scenarios as part of your reasoning.

Chapter 16, *Mock Exam Questions: Theory*, includes exam-style questions based on the theoretical content you have covered during the study guide chapters and the context of the BABOK® v3 Guide.

Chapter 17, *Your Future with a Success Mindset,* takes you into the future, when you have already achieved your CCBA® or CBAP® designation, and provides you with advice on progressing your career as a result of your recent achievement.

To get the most out of this book

You can achieve a good level of knowledge and understanding of the BABOK® v3 Guide simply by studying the content of this study guide. However, in order to get the most out of this study guide and your exam preparation efforts, I do recommend that you also refer to the BABOK® v3 Guide as part of your study activities.

Prior business analysis experience would be highly beneficial when reading the content of this study guide; even so, if you are new to the business analysis profession, you will still get a lot of value from the practical examples covered in this study guide.

Conventions used

 Warnings or important notes appear like this.

 Tips and tricks appear like this.

Get in touch

Feedback from our readers is always welcome.

General feedback: If you have questions about any aspect of this book, mention the book title in the subject of your message and email us at customercare@packtpub.com.

Errata: Although we have taken every care to ensure the accuracy of our content, mistakes do happen. If you have found a mistake in this book, we would be grateful if you would report this to us. Please visit www.packtpub.com/support/errata, selecting your book, clicking on the Errata Submission Form link, and entering the details.

Piracy: If you come across any illegal copies of our works in any form on the Internet, we would be grateful if you would provide us with the location address or website name. Please contact us at copyright@packt.com with a link to the material.

If you are interested in becoming an author: If there is a topic that you have expertise in and you are interested in either writing or contributing to a book, please visit authors.packtpub.com.

Reviews

Please leave a review. Once you have read and used this book, why not leave a review on the site that you purchased it from? Potential readers can then see and use your unbiased opinion to make purchase decisions, we at Packt can understand what you think about our products, and our authors can see your feedback on their book. Thank you!

For more information about Packt, please visit packt.com.

Planning for Success 1

As a **CCBA®** (**Certification of Capability in Business Analysis**) or **CBAP®** (**Certified Business Analysis Professional**) aspirant, you may have wondered about how to prepare for the CCBA® or CBAP® exams in a way that is effective and comprehensive, to guarantee that you can pass the exams. This chapter ensures you are clear and confident about your goals in relation to achieving the CCBA® or CBAP® designations, and outlines an approach and plan framework to guide you on how you can make sure you are successful when sitting for the exam.

At the end of this chapter, you will have learned the following:

- Writing clear reasons for embarking on this journey
- Listing all the benefits of certification for my career
- Applying the visualization technique to guarantee success
- Creating a plan framework using key concepts
- Customizing your plan to your needs
- Applying techniques to encourage consistent plan execution

This study guide covers the breadth of the **Business Analysis Body of Knowledge** (**BABOK®** Guide **version 3 (v3)**) in a way that is easily digestible and exam-focused, using applied examples and scenarios to help bring concepts into the real world of analysis. It is important for you to understand the way the *BABOK® Guide v3* has been put together so that you can make optimal use of this study guide while aligning your knowledge with what is captured in the *BABOK® Guide v3*.

This study guide will provide you with a knowledge assessment at the end of each chapter so that you can practice exam-style questions as you progress through your study plan.

Don't skip any content or explanatory sections in this study guide. Read each chapter carefully in conjunction with the *BABOK® Guide v3*, and only once you have done that should you attempt the end-of-chapter assessment. We have included a large number of exam simulation assessment questions in this guide, but we know that the CCBA® and CBAP® exam questions will be different from what we have here. Make sure you study each part of this guide carefully before attempting to do the exam.

We'll cover the following topics in this chapter:

- Benefits of the CCBA® or CBAP® designations
- Visualization as a powerful study tool
- Key concepts for creating a good study plan
- Your study plan framework
- Your custom study plan

"Life is like a combination lock; your job is to find the right numbers, in the right order, so you can have anything you want."

-Brian Tracey

Benefits of the CCBA® or CBAP® designations

A great way to get motivated to get started with your study plans for any exam is to focus on all the benefits you will receive once all the hard work is done. As a CCBA® or CBAP® aspirant, you will have some ideas of why you believe it is a good idea to achieve one of these designations. There will be a core reason or belief about what you think you will achieve by taking the time, putting in the effort, and sitting the exam. *Right*?

You may have seen others take the exams and achieve positive results, or perhaps you simply know that doing a professional certification in your chosen field of work—being business analysis, in this case—can only be of benefit to your career. There are certainly many good reasons for embarking on this journey, and the job market is certainly one of these reasons because employers are asking for the CCBA® and CBAP® certification more and more often.

Perhaps you would like to hear some of the benefits I experienced (and I'm still experiencing) ever since I passed the CBAP® exam in 2007.

Improved confidence

I gained a lot of confidence in my knowledge and abilities as a business analyst. I mention this benefit first because I believe that this is what led to me experiencing all the other, more measurable, benefits in my career. Once I obtained the CBAP® designation, I simply felt more confident in my ability as a business analyst, and this gave me the confidence to consider and choose from multiple job opportunities within the city I was working in at the time, rather than just taking the first job that came along. I also felt more confident to speak up about business analysis best practices within my workplace, which enabled me to make a difference in the way we worked as a business analysis team at the time. This led to the next direct benefit I experienced…

Recognition in the workplace

Once I had the qualification, I started to actively improve the business analysis practices we followed at the company in which I was working. This led our team and management to recognize my level of knowledge and skills a lot more. I started to develop a strong reputation as the person to go to about any business analysis-related questions or issues. My peers started to trust my knowledge and came to seek guidance more and more often. Over a period of time, this led to the next key benefit….

Better career opportunities

I was promoted within a few months of expressing more confidence and improving the business analysis best practices in our company, to become a team leader. This also opened up opportunities to get involved to work directly with the **International Institute of Business Analysis (IIBA®)** to review and design the next-level-down certification exams for the CCBA®. This highlighted to me another perspective on how I could use my CBAP® designation to make a difference. It reawakened my passion for education.

An entirely new career focus

I embarked on a career focus where education became central to my life. I re-certified as a CBAP® professional a number of times since then while building a thriving education business, helping other business analysts achieve great career success through CCBA® and CBAP® certification paths.

Regardless of where you would like to eventually take your business analysis career, the CCBA® and the CBAP® certifications have very specific and clear career benefits attached to them, and, in my personal experience, the CBAP® certification is the primary reason I achieved great career success. The benefits are tangible and exciting and are the path to a great career.

Visualization as a powerful study tool

Have you considered what it will be like once you have achieved your CCBA® or CBAP® designation? If you haven't yet, then now is a great time to do that.

Do this small experiment with yourself and see what comes up for you:

Imagine you finished the exam and you receive the passing score of the CCBA® or CBAP® exam. What does that feel like for you? When you go back to the office and tell your colleagues that you are now a CBAP® or CCBA® professional, in your mind's eye, see them congratulate you. They might shake your hand or give you a wide smile while they say things such as: "Wow, that is awesome!", "I am so impressed with you!", or "Well done, I wish I could do that!". See the certificate you received from the IIBA® to confirm your achievement—is it displayed on a wall at home? Imagine the pride you will feel when you tell your boss about your achievement or when you apply for your next role. Imagine colleagues approaching you for advice because you are now a certified business analyst.

I recommend you create a visualization of these types of positive results you will experience once you pass the CCBA® or CBAP® exam. Revisit this mental picture every day for a couple of minutes. This will go a long way toward telling your subconscious mind what you want, and then, before you know it, it will be what you have.

You get what you focus on

What on earth do I mean with "you get what you focus on"?

You know all those really successful people that we read about, hear about, and even see within our own organizations? They all have one important thing in common. They all have an *end goal* they are working toward. They have a vision of where they want to end up and what they want to achieve along the way. They also have a clear plan of how they will achieve that outcome or end goal.

To have a successful business analysis career, you must do what they do. So, let's have a look at how you go about creating your vision or end goal, and what steps you need to take to ensure you reach your goal.

Setting your certification goal

You are reading this study guide because you have at least one clear goal right now: to achieve a successful outcome when you take the CCBA® or the CBAP® exam.

The goals you set for yourself are the "map" for reaching your business analysis career outcome or vision. It lays out the milestones or "cities" you need to get to on your "map" to be moving closer to your vision or outcome.

As with any goal, you must set your goals with the end goal in mind—so, in this case, your end goal is to have passed the exam. The goals (or cities on your map) you define can consist of short-term (next week, next month, or in 3 months), medium-term (6 months to 2 years), and longer-term goals (2 to 5 years). The idea is for you to start with the end goal in mind; keep your focus on that while you achieve the smaller goals to get there.

In the context of your goal to pass the exams, you should visualize the end goal and create your study plan with shorter-term goals to achieve and measure successful progress. These goals could take the form of completing study sessions successfully and executing your study schedule consistently.

The ideal timeframe for preparation

A very common question is: "How much time do I need to set aside to prepare for the exams?" While this is a valid and important question, it is also a question that has many different potential answers. Let us look at a few factors for you to consider when determining how much time *you* might need to set aside for *your* studies.

How familiar are you with the BABOK® Guide v3 today?

If you are used to referring to the *BABOK® Guide v3* as your reference guide at work, then you will be familiar with the terminology, structure, and overall content coverage of the guide. This will reduce the time you need to prepare for the exams. However, if you are brand new to the *BABOK® Guide v3*, you will need to allow time to get familiar with the structure, terminology, and general content. This will inevitably have an effect on the amount of study time you would need to plan for.

What is your preferred learning style?

Some of us like to study under pressure and in a condensed timeframe, whereas some of us need to study in a more systematic way and at a slower pace. Naturally, this has an impact on how much time you allow for preparing yourself to sit the exam.

Are you a confident learner or a conservative learner?

Everybody has their own unique level of confidence in their ability to learn and apply new concepts. Some of us are very detailed and conservative and will turn a concept over many times before we feel confident that we will be able to interpret and apply the concept in real-world exam questions. However, some of us only need to consider a concept once to feel confident that we know enough to apply that concept to an exam scenario. So, depending on your personal style of learning, you will need more or less time to prepare.

Have you done a lot of business analysis study before?

Another real consideration is how much academic or professional development business analysis training you have done in your career. In my own case, I was lucky to have completed a university degree as well as a series of professional development certifications in my career prior to attempting the CBAP® exam. This helped me tremendously in terms of understanding the concepts in the *BABOK® Guide v3* really quickly, and this had a direct impact on the amount of time I needed to study for the exam. I am also a short-term, under-pressure type of learner, which meant my preparation was intense but over within a couple of weeks.

Average preparation time—considering these primary factors—would be between 4 weeks and 12 weeks. This is based on my own experience, but also on my experience after speaking to a wide variety of different people over a long period of time. My advice is that you consider these factors, spend some time to get familiar with the size of the *BABOK® Guide v3*, and prepare a plan for your studies. In the next section, I provide you with some ideas for how to create a good study plan to suit your own personal circumstances and learning style.

Key concepts for creating a good study plan

Many of the business analysts that I have worked with in the past who have achieved their CCBA® or CBAP® designations have told me that they had a specific study plan and an approach drafted before they started. Not everyone followed the exact same approach, yet everyone took the time to decide what they believed would be practical and realistic for their individual circumstances and their own preferred learning styles.

Some of the key considerations when creating your study plan are as follows:

#1 Working backward

Your first step is to decide when you want to sit the actual CCBA® or CBAP® exam. Is it 3 months from now, 6 weeks, or perhaps a full year into the future? Once you know when you want to sit the exam, you will have a starting point to work out what it will take to achieve that date, and then schedule some time to study every week. It is important to agree on a date with yourself or your certification coach and then stick to this date.

#2 Knowing your own learning style

Each of us has an idea of how we learn most effectively. Some of us like to study months in advance, and some of us like to study under a bit of time pressure. Some of us prefer lots of mock tests, case studies, and discussion, whereas others like to focus on the detail in a systematic, step-by-step fashion. Some of us like visual aids, and others prefer audio tools; and, finally, some of us would like to study a little every day, and others would like to take a block of time and focus just on the study. There is no one right way to study, just as there are no two people who are exactly the same. You will, however, help yourself a great deal if you think about which learning style you prefer and which would make you feel the most productive. Don't blindly try to follow how someone else studied—take it on board, and then adjust that method by focusing on your own study preferences.

#3 Being practical and choosing a routine activity

One of the first and often most challenging aspects of embarking on the CCBA® or CBAP® exam preparation pathway is that of finding time to study. Most business analysts have very busy work and home lives and have to find time in between all of this to get ready for the exams. Some ideas that have worked well for others include the following:

1. If you commute on the train or bus to work, use this time to study.
2. If you like getting up early (or even if you don't!), consider getting up 1 hour earlier a couple of days every week, and revise using this study guide or other materials.
3. What about a lunchtime study session with colleagues? Share the responsibility to ask each other quiz questions or discuss specific topics covered in the *BABOK® Guide v3* or this study guide.
4. Evenings can work for study too, especially if you are the kind of person that lights up after work and feels energized.
5. Although weekends are sacred to most of us, perhaps commit to studying for a few hours on a Saturday and/or Sunday for a few weekends.

#4 Limiting the scope of study during each session

Regardless of when you choose to study, I recommend you define exactly which part of the content you will study in any given study session. If you don't have a specific plan that outlines the exact sections upfront, perhaps tell yourself you must study X number of pages per session. Don't do more or less than that part of the content. For example, if you decide to study the knowledge area around Elicitation and Collaboration during a session, perhaps agree with yourself to focus only on understanding the key tasks involved and the main techniques that can be applied during that hour and for those tasks. You might agree with yourself to do the knowledge quiz to test yourself on those tasks and techniques; however, once you completed that section, honor your agreement with yourself, and take a break. This way, you learn to trust yourself to achieve a specific study goal and don't feel as though you need to keep pushing each session's scope with more and more content. This way, you will also not feel guilty about whether you have studied enough or not! Be kind and fair to yourself.

#5 Having the right materials and study tools

Before you embark on your regular study sessions, you should make sure you have all the materials and tools ready to go! If your primary material is this study guide and the *BABOK® Guide v3* itself, then that is all good. You may also like to use flashcards or additional courses to help you study. Try your best to choose all these aids before you start. This will go a long way to building your confidence that if you focus on these tools and materials, you will be alright to pass the exams. If you keep changing the tools and materials you will use, you will indirectly be doubting yourself and your ability to pass the exams the first time.

#6 Having goals and measuring progress

The final ingredient for creating a solid study plan and approach is to have some clear, measurable goals for your study plan. We started this section talking about knowing when exactly you plan to sit the CCBA® or CBAP® exam. Now that you know when and you know when during the day you will make time to study, and you have your materials and tools worked out, you are ready to create a specific plan with milestones, dates, and tasks to complete. You are ready to convert those plans, dates, and tasks into measurable goals to achieve.

Your study plan framework

Now that you have considered your broad timeframes and which materials you plan to use, and you have determined your own preferred learning style, you are ready to draft your study plan using the framework outlined in this part of the chapter. This is a straightforward way to ensure you have a plan with clear steps to follow, and a visual way to demonstrate your study progress to build confidence within yourself. This is also a great way to manage your exam jitters too!

You should follow a framework similar to the one outlined here. Include these elements for each exam preparation session you include in your overall study plan:

Session topic

Describe the topic you plan to study here. Typically, this could be a knowledge area or a subset of techniques.

Chapter and/or sections

Reference the *BABOK® Guide v3* and this study guide's chapter and sections you plan to finish during a session.

Date

Allocate the date when you plan to do each study session.

Measure/s

How do you plan to measure whether you understand the topic well enough and have successfully finished the session (for example, pass a quiz)?

Status

Check this off as "complete" if you have done this day's session of study successfully.

Creating your custom study plan

The next step is for you to sit and draft your own custom study plan.

You should use this study guide as a guideline when developing your own custom study plan by following the chapters and sections outlined in this book. I do recommend you also incorporate specific references to the *BABOK® Guide v3*, and review that as you progress through each chapter of this study guide.

Here are two examples of potential entries for a typical 1-hour study session. You may choose to prepare multiple entries similar to the ones in the following table for one study session if you have more time available to spend during one session:

Date	Session topic	Chapters and/or sections	Measure/s	Status
July 4	Elicitation and Collaboration	Read *Chapter 3* of the *BABOK® Guide v3—Sections 3.1* and *3.2* Read *Chapter 7* of the study guide	Measure 1: Pass Study Guide Quiz	Completed
			Measure 2: Explain these tasks to a colleague, with a practical example	Not started
July 5	Elicitation & Collaboration	Read *Chapter 3* of the *BABOK® Guide v3— Sections 3.3, 3.4,* and *3.5* Read *Chapter 7* of the study guide (repeat)	Measure 1: List all key tasks of the knowledge area	Not started
			Measure 2: Describe the purpose of each task to a colleague & how it is applied in a real-world scenario.	Not started

Figure 1: Example study plan

Tips for when you draft your plan

A key tip when preparing your study plan is to include some specific types of sessions that measure your progress and encourage you to follow the plan. You should include these types of days/sessions upfront when you first draft your custom study plan.

Baseline days

A baseline day is a day you dedicate to completing a mock or simulation exam covering the entire scope of the *BABOK® Guide v3*. Ideally, you should build a baseline day into the start, the middle, and the end of your study plan. This way, you are able to assess where you are starting from (your baseline knowledge), determine how you are progressing with your knowledge and understanding (complete another mock exam in the middle of your study plan), and confirming you have a strong understanding and knowledge of the entire *BABOK® Guide v3* by completing a mock or simulation exam at the end of the study plan. This study guide includes mock-style exam questions that you can use to help you establish your baseline at the different intervals of your study plan.

Revision days

Always ensure you have a few planned study sessions that are dedicated to revising the previous chapter or session's content. This is a good way to ensure your knowledge of the *BABOK® Guide v3* content remains fresh and embedded in your memory and understanding. It also enhances your deeper understanding of the more difficult concepts.

Rest days

You should also plan specific days into your study plan that are meant to be rest days. On these days, you don't have to study, and you can use the time slot to do something more relaxing or perhaps simply spend a few minutes visualizing your success.

Ready to get started

Once you have a draft version of your study plan, make sure you place this plan somewhere where you can review and mark your progress on a daily or weekly basis. It is also a good idea to incorporate your study plan into your online calendar, which sends you reminders for when your next session is due. Share your study plan with your work colleagues and/or family to make sure they know that you are allocating time to study and cannot be disturbed.

Now, it is time to get excited about this outstanding learning opportunity ahead of you!

Summary

During this chapter, you have learned about some key principles and techniques to apply to ensure you are successful in your CBAP® certification goals.

The following are the key learnings we covered during this chapter:

- Benefits of certification
- Visualization as a study tool
- Key concepts when you create a study plan
- Your study plan framework

Make sure you revise these key learnings before completing the knowledge quiz at the end of this chapter.

Benefits of certification

During this chapter, we discussed some of the key benefits that you can expect to achieve as a result of achieving success in the CBAP® certification exam. These benefits include an increase in your professional confidence in your role as a business analyst, which leads to more career opportunities and recognition. You also learned that CBAP® certified individuals earn 16% more on average, and therefore you can expect to achieve a higher salary if you pursue this goal.

Visualization as a study tool

You have learned how to apply visualization as a technique to focus on the positive outcomes once you have achieved CBAP® certification success. You learned that this is done by creating mental pictures and focusing on them in your mind's eye on a regular basis.

Key concepts when you create a study plan

During this chapter, you learned how you can create your own study plan by considering different aspects, such as: working backward (starting from the end date) in your planning, understanding your own learning style, being practical by choosing to incorporate learning sessions into routine activities, limiting the scope of each study session, preparing all materials and tools in advance, and actively measuring your study progress.

Your study plan framework

During this part of the chapter, you learned which attributes to include when you draft your own custom study plan framework. You also learned to plan for specific types of days: baseline days, revision days, and rest days.

During the next chapter, we will look at the detailed CBAP® exam application requirements and how to ensure you meet all the requirements prior to submitting your application.

Knowledge quiz

Complete the knowledge quiz to see how well you understood the content of this chapter.

Question 1:

I should try to do as much study as possible in every study session.

Is this statement true or false?

> A. True
>
> B. False

Question 2:

It is a good idea to visualize the end goal of achieving the certification prior to starting my study for the exam.

Is this statement true or false?

> A. True
>
> B. False

Question 3:

When I create my study plan, I should include specific study sessions for the purpose of setting a baseline of knowledge. Select all the ideal times to do a baseline session:

    A. At the start of my study plan

    B. In the middle of my study plan

    C. At the end of my study plan

    D. During the third session in my study plan

Question 4:

When I create my study plan, I should include measurable actions I can take during each study session so that I can know whether I have completed the session successfully or not.

Is this statement true or false?

    A. True

    B. False

Question 5:

It is a good idea to regularly change the study materials I use during each study session because this will build my confidence in taking the exam.

Is this statement true or false?

    A. True

    B. False

Answers

Questions	Answers
1	B
2	A
3	A, B, C
4	A
5	B

2
Exam Application Requirements

In this chapter, you will learn about what the **International Institute of Business Analysis (IIBA®)** is and its role within the wider global business analysis community. This chapter also outlines how you should approach your application for the exam and provides key hints and information to ensure that your application gets approval from the IIBA®. Each exam's practical experience hours are explained, with a method for calculating how many experience hours you can claim per knowledge area requirement.

You will also learn what the CCBA® and CBAP® application requirements are, and we will provide some handy tips on what to consider when you complete your application. Each exam's practical experience hours will be outlined, and we will describe the minimum requirement for experience hours you can claim per knowledge area requirement. You will also learn about the exam application process itself. This chapter will be split into the following sections:

- About the IIBA®
- The competency-based certification model
- CCBA® experience requirements
- CBAP® experience requirements
- The exam application process

By the end of this chapter, you will have learned about the following:

- The role of IIBA® in the industry
- How to assess your experience in terms of IIBA® competency levels
- How to calculate your experience to meet CCBA® experience requirements

- How to calculate your experience to meet CBAP® experience requirements
- How to apply for the CCBA® or CBAP® exam based on meeting the requirements

We'll first talk about the body that produces and regulates the exams you'll be taking. Then we'll look at exactly what is required for your application.

The IIBA® is the International Institute of Business Analysis. It is a nonprofit professional organization that supports and promotes the discipline of business analysis. The IIBA® supports and helps business analysts develop their skills and further their careers in different ways. Two of the most visible ways in which the IIBA® helps you to develop and excel in your career is through the provision of the Business Analysis Body of Knowledge Guidelines, referred to as the BABOK® v3 Guide.

The second way the IIBA® promotes and supports your career progression is by establishing internationally recognized certifications, namely the CCBA® and CBAP®, among others. The IIBA® organization consists of a global organization with a head office based in Ontario, Canada, and was founded in October 2003. They also consist of a worldwide network of local IIBA® chapters that promote and develop the profession of business analysis in cities around the world.

A competency-based certification model

The IIBA® has developed the certification exams in a way that is based on a competency model developed by industry business analysts and coordinated and delivered by the IIBA®. The reason that the competency-based approach is followed is to demonstrate to employers that business analysts who have the CCBA® or CBAP® qualification have the required skills, knowledge, and experience in business analysis. It evaluates your understanding and ability to apply business analysis skills, tasks, tools, and techniques, and also validates your key competencies.

CCBA® application requirements

The CCBA® certification is targeted at mid-level experienced business analysts who would like to formalize their knowledge and capabilities with an internationally recognized professional business analysis certification.

Applicants who want to take the CCBA® certification exam must meet specific experience and education requirements. During the application process, you must demonstrate your competencies across a broad range of business analysis knowledge and practical skills. After your application has been reviewed and accepted, you will be eligible to take the exam.

The CCBA® certification exam is 3 hours in duration and consists of 130 multiple-choice questions.

You need to complete an online application process in which you are required to document proof of the following requirements:

A minimum of 3,750 hours of business analysis work experience aligned with the Business Analysis Book of Knowledge (BABOK® Guide v3) in the last 7 years of your career.

This requirement equates to 2.5 years of full-time business analysis work done within the last 7 years of your career, or you could potentially have done 50% of business analysis work during the last 7 years of your career. It is important to know that your practical experience must align with the BABOK® Guide's areas of knowledge, with a minimum of 900 hours in 2 of the 6 knowledge areas **or** 500 hours in each of 4 knowledge areas.

You must consider the following when you work out your project experience hours that you plan to include in your CCBA® or CBAP® application:

Be conservative when you calculate and document your project experience hours: do not claim more than 1,500 hours per year, even if you feel you have worked more than that. On average, an individual works about 1,500 hours per year. This takes into consideration annual leave, sick leave, and a normal workweek of no more than 40 hours. If you claim more hours in a 12-month period, you may prompt the IIBA® to perform an audit on your application.

CBAP® application requirements

The CBAP® designation is ideal for experienced business analysts with more than five years of practical experience. In the context of a general business analysis career, this certification is the most advanced level that you can achieve in terms of professional certifications offered by the IIBA®.

Applicants who want to take the CBAP® certification exam must meet specific experience and education requirements. During the application process, you must demonstrate your competencies across the breadth of business analysis knowledge and practical skills. After your application has been reviewed and accepted, you will be eligible to take the exam.

The CBAP® certification exam is 3.5 hours in duration and consists of 120 multiple-choice questions.

You need to complete an online application process in which you are required to provide documented proof of the following requirements listed:

A minimum of 7,500 hours of business analysis work experience aligned with the Business Analysis Book of Knowledge (BABOK® Guide v3) in the last 10 years of your career.

This requirement equates to 5 years of full-time business analysis work done within the last 10 years of your career, or you could potentially have done 50% of business analysis work during the last 10 years of your career. It is key to know that your practical experience must align with the BABOK® Guide's knowledge areas, with a minimum of 900 hours in 4 of the 6 knowledge areas.

Your job title doesn't have to be 'business analyst' in order for you to be able to claim work experience that directly aligns with the BABOK® Guide v3 knowledge areas.

The more practical and directly aligned to the BABOK® Guide v3 your experience is, the better you will be able to document it as part of your application!

A minimum of 35 hours of professional development in the past 4 years.

This requirement can be met by attending an IIBA®-endorsed training course, either in person or online. If you are unable to attend an IIBA®-endorsed training course, you can also include nonendorsed courses or workshops as part of your professional development, as long as they are directly relevant to the topic of business analysis training. If you choose to include non-endorsed training (an example could be an internal training workshop you attended at work that relates to business analysis), you will need to ensure that you have at least 70 hours of nonendorsed training mentioned in your application.

Additional requirements for CCBA® and CBAP® applicants

Two references from a career manager, client, or CBAP® recipient.

As part of your application, you must provide two professional references. One of those references must be a current contact you have, meaning that you are in contact with this person on a regular basis. These references can be from a career manager (line manager), a client, or a Certified Business Analysis Professional recipient. You must have known your references for a period of at least 6 months. Your references will receive an email with a link to a reference check form, where they will be asked to answer a few questions about the work you have been performing for them. These questions are high-level and reasonably general, so they don't need to know the low-level details of your day-to-day tasks.

 Make sure that both of your references know that they will receive this email request and make sure that they know you are dependent on their completion of this online form for your CCBA® or CBAP® application will be approved.

Signed Code of Conduct

You will be asked to complete and sign a code of conduct form in order to apply to take the CBAP® or CCBA® exam. This form contains your agreement to act ethically, professionally, and responsibly in your business analysis work.

The exam

The IIBA® has documented the sequence of steps to follow when applying to sit the CCBA® and CBAP® exams very comprehensively. Although we urge you to review the IIBA®'s documentation in detail, we will provide you with a short summary of the key facts here. You will also learn some key facts about exam question types and breakdown, which will assist you in formulating an idea of what to expect on your exam day.

Application process

Step 1: Meet the criteria

To apply for the CCBA® or the CBAP® certification exam, you must make sure that you have met the aforementioned key requirements. If you are unsure about your eligibility, you should head over to the IIBA®'s website and read their CCBA® or CBAP® certification handbooks. They have documented every step of the application process thoroughly, and it is well worth reading prior to embarking on the application process itself.

Step 2: Apply to the IIBA®

If you feel that you satisfy all the certification application criteria, then you should go to the IIBA®'s website (www.IIBA.org) and submit your application directly to them. Once you have submitted your application and paid your application fee, their certification team will assess your application and confirm your eligibility to sit the exam.

If they have any questions or require an audit to be performed on your application, you will be notified and asked to either make amendments or resubmit your application at a later date. Be sure to complete your application thoroughly and correctly.

Step 3: Sit the exam

Once your application is approved, you have 12 months to schedule and sit the exam. There are approved test centers in all major cities around the world where you can take the exam. You also now have the option to take the exam online.

Summary

During this chapter, you learned what the CCBA® and CBAP® application requirements are and how to apply for these certification exams.

The following are the key concepts that we covered in this chapter:

- Competency-based certification model
- CCBA® application requirements
- CBAP® application requirements
- Additional CCBA® and CBAP® requirements
- The exam application process

Make sure that you revise these key pieces of information before completing the quiz at the end of this chapter.

Competency-based certification model

You now understand that the exam is based on a competency-based model that aims to demonstrate to employers that business analysts who have the CCBA® or CBAP® certification designation have the required skills, knowledge, and experience in business analysis.

CCBA® application requirements

During this chapter, you learned what the requirements are that an individual should meet prior to applying to sit the CCBA® exam with the IIBA®. You learned that some of the primary requirements involve the number of years of practical work experience, as well as a minimum of 21 professional development hours accrued during the last 4-year period.

CBAP® application requirements

During this chapter, you learned what the requirements are that an individual should meet prior to applying to sit the CBAP® exam with the IIBA®. You learned that some of the primary requirements involve the number of years of practical work experience, as well as a minimum of 35 professional development hours accrued during the last 4-year period.

Additional CCBA® and CBAP® requirements

You also now know that there are some overarching requirements to meet in terms of application references and that every application requires a signed a code of conduct.

Knowledge quiz

Go through the following questions and complete the mini mock exam based on this chapter:

Question 1

In order to be able to claim business analysis work experience hours as part of the CCBA® or CBAP® application, you must have gained that experience while working with a verifiable job title of 'Business Analyst'.

Is this statement true or false?

> A. True. You must have an official job title of a Business Analyst to claim the experience.

> B. False. You only need to be able to verify business analysis experience aligned to the BABOK® Guide and don't have to be called a business analyst to claim experience hours.

Question 2

How many years into the past are you able to record and claim practical work experience for if you apply for the CBAP® exam?

> A. 7 years

> B. 10 years

> C. 5 years

> D. 20 years

Question 3

For how many years into the past are you able to record and claim practical work experience if you apply for the CCBA® exam?

> A. 7 years

> B. 10 years

> C. 5 years

> D. 20 years

Answers

Questions	Answers
1	B
2	B
3	A

Study Tools 3

In this chapter, you will learn about the Business Analysis Body of Knowledge, better known as the BABOK® v3 Guide. This is the standard set by the IIBA® as the ultimate definition of, and guidelines for, what the business analysis profession entails. Both the CCBA® and CBAP® exam questions are based predominantly on what is covered in this body of knowledge, which makes this an essential study tool for you. This chapter outlines the unique structure of the BABOK® and acts as an essential foundation for navigating the BABOK® Guide. We will cover the following topics:

- BABOK® Guide sections
- Knowledge areas
- Underlying competencies, techniques, and perspectives
- How to use this study guide

By the end of this chapter, you will be able to do the following:

- Navigate through the main sections of the BABOK® Guide
- Define what each knowledge area is intended for and describe the composition of the content
- List the underlying competencies, techniques, and perspectives
- Use this study guide

BABOK® v3.0 Guide structure

The Business Analysis Body of Knowledge, better known as the BABOK® v3 Guide, is the complete definition of what business analysis entails from the perspective of the International Institute of Business Analysis (the IIBA®).

The BABOK® v3 Guide is used across the business analysis industry as the guideline for best practice and can be used to apply effective analysis across different types of organizations for a wide variety of reasons. In this section, we will outline the guide's content in terms of its structure and high-level sections. This guide is the primary source of information for all business analysis knowledge areas and techniques.

The BABOK® v3 Guide comprises of the following types of content:

- **Core content:** This comprises business analysis tasks organized into six knowledge areas.
- **Extended content:** The extended content helps guide business analysts to better perform their jobs, and includes the following topics:
  - Business analysis key concepts
  - Underlying competencies
  - Techniques
  - Perspectives

We will start by explaining briefly what is described by each of the listed types of content. We will follow the same sequence of content as it is outlined in the BABOK® Guide itself so that you can easily follow the summaries of what is contained in the BABOK® Guide, as shown in *Figure 1*:

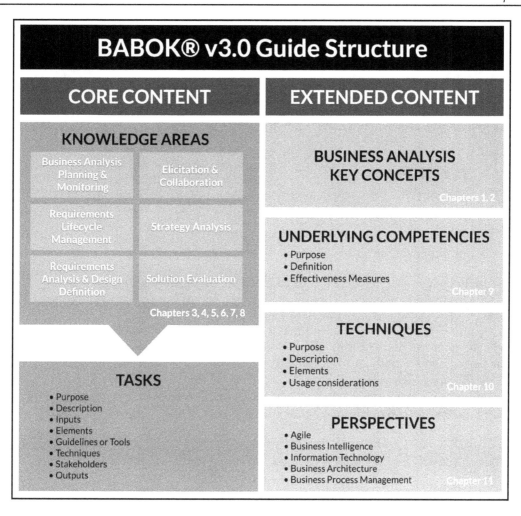

Figure 1: BABOK® v3.0 Guide structure

Business analysis key concepts

The first two chapters in the BABOK® Guide cover the key concepts that you need to understand before attempting to digest the other chapters in the guide. These introductory chapters are important because they introduce you to the key terms used in business analysis, the standard definition of how requirements are classified. It outlines the most common stakeholder types that a business analyst engages with and outlines the relationship between the concepts of a *requirement* and a *design*.

Knowledge areas

The knowledge area chapters in the BABOK® v3.0 Guide are considered the *core content* of business analysis, and cover specific areas of expertise within the business analysis domain.

The six knowledge areas include the following:

- Business analysis planning and monitoring
- Elicitation and collaboration
- Requirements life cycle management
- Strategy analysis
- Requirements analysis and design definition
- Solution evaluation

Each knowledge area is related to one or more of the other knowledge areas in the BABOK® v3.0 Guide and should always be considered within that context. None of the knowledge areas can stand completely in isolation.

Knowledge areas are divided into *tasks*. A task is described as a discrete piece of work that may be performed formally or informally as part of business analysis. The BABOK® v3.0 Guide defines a list of business analysis tasks for each knowledge area. A business analyst may perform other tasks in conjunction with the defined business analysis tasks, but those may not be considered part of business analysis.

In the BABOK® v3.0 Guide, each knowledge area consists of a set of specific tasks. Each *task* in the BABOK®® v3.0 Guide is defined according to the following key attributes:

- Purpose
- Description
- Inputs
- Elements
- Guidelines or tools
- Techniques
- Stakeholders
- Outputs

It is important that you consider each task individually and understand the key attributes as they are defined in the BABOK® v3.0 Guide. We will cover each aspect of the knowledge areas in this study guide.

Underlying competencies

The BABOK® v3.0 Guide has identified a certain set of characteristics, behaviors, skills, and knowledge that is believed to be part of a successful and effective business analyst's profile. These are referred to as the **underlying competencies** that a business analyst needs to exhibit while performing their role. Take note that the underlying competencies are not unique to the business analysis profession.

The underlying competencies are described in terms of their *purpose*, their *definition*, and the *effectiveness measures* used to determine whether they are present in a given situation. We cover the underlying competencies in this study guide.

Techniques

A large portion of the BABOK® v3.0 Guide describes a wide range of different techniques that can be applied in different situations. It also states that you should not limit yourself to these techniques or feel that you can't change or adapt a technique to fit a particular situation.

Each technique has been described using the following attributes:

- Purpose
- Description
- Elements
- Usage considerations

We encourage you to get familiar with each technique and truly understand what type of situation each technique can be used for. We cover the techniques in this study guide.

Perspectives

Some common perspectives or contexts in which business analysis is most often performed have been defined within the BABOK® v3.0 Guide. These are not the only perspectives that business analysis can be applied from, but they are the most common.

The perspectives include the following:

- Agile working
- Business intelligence
- Information technology
- Business architecture
- Business process management

Perspectives are also not mutually exclusive, and therefore an initiative can employ more than one perspective at different stages in the process.

Summary

During this chapter, you learned about the BABOK® v3.0 Guide and how to navigate through it and this study guide. You also explored a summary of each chapter in the BABOK® Guide. You are now ready to actively start using this study guide to get prepared for the CCBA® and CBAP® exams.

The following are the key topics that were covered in this chapter:

- Navigate through the main sections of the BABOK® Guide
- Define what knowledge areas are intended for and describe the composition of the content
- Understand the intent of the underlying competencies, techniques, and perspectives

Make sure you revise these key learnings before completing the knowledge quiz at the end of this chapter.

Navigating through the main sections of the BABOK® Guide

The BABOK® v3.0 Guide comprises of the following types of content:

- **Core content:** This comprises of business analysis tasks organized into six knowledge areas.
- **Extended content:** The extended content helps guide business analysts to better perform their jobs and includes the following topics:
    - Business analysis key concepts
    - Underlying competencies
    - Techniques
    - Perspectives

Knowledge areas

The knowledge area chapters in the BABOK® v3.0 Guide are considered the *core content* of business analysis and cover specific areas of expertise within the business analysis domain.

The six knowledge areas include the following:

- Business analysis planning and monitoring
- Elicitation and collaboration
- Requirements life cycle management
- Strategy analysis
- Requirements analysis and design definition
- Solution evaluation

Underlying competencies, techniques, and perspectives

In this chapter, you learned that the part of the guide dealing with underlying competencies describes a certain set of characteristics, behaviors, skills, and knowledge that is believed to be part of a successful and effective business analyst's profile. You also now learned that a large portion of the BABOK® v3.0 Guide's content has been dedicated to describing a wide range of different analysis techniques, which can be applied in different situations. You also learned about the common perspectives or contexts that business analysis is most often performed in and that these are described in the guide as well.

Knowledge quiz

Complete the following knowledge quiz to see how well you understood the content of this chapter:

Question 1:

The BABOK® v3.0 Guide is the primary source and reference from which business analysts should draw knowledge; they should also use it to apply techniques within the field of business analysis.

Is this statement true or false?

> A. True

> B. False

Question 2:

How many core knowledge areas are described in the BABOK® v3.0 Guide?

> A. 4

> B. 5

> C. 6

> D. 10

Question 3:

The BABOK® v3.0 Guide recommends that the business analyst only use techniques as they are described in the guide and not change or adapt the technique to fit a particular situation.

Is this statement true or false?

    A. True

    B. False

Question 4:

The BABOK® v3.0 Guide has identified a certain set of characteristics, behaviors, skills, and knowledge that is believed to be part of a successful and effective business analyst's profile.

Which of the following terms are used to describe this in the guide?

    A. Core competencies

    B. Underlying competencies

    C. Competency characteristics

    D. Analysis competencies

Question 5:

The BABOK® v3.0 Guide has a specific structure that it uses to describe tasks that fall within a given knowledge area. Which of the following aspects are used to describe what a task in the BABOK® v3.0 Guide consists of?

    A. Purpose, description, inputs, elements, guidelines/tools, techniques, stakeholders, and outputs

    B. Purpose, description, inputs, essentials, guidelines/tools, techniques, stakeholders and outputs

    C. Summary, description, inputs, elements, processes/tools, techniques, stakeholders, and outputs

    D. Purpose, description, inputs, elements, processes/tools, techniques, stakeholders, and outputs

Answers

Questions	Answers
1	A
2	C
3	B
4	B
5	A

What to Expect From the Exam

4

In this chapter, you will learn what to expect in terms of the CCBA® and CBAP® exam distribution of questions coming from each part of the BABOK® Guide. You will also get insights into the different types of questions to expect from the respective exams. This chapter will also describe the main differences between the CCBA® and CBAP® exam question styles.

We will cover the following topics in this chapter:

- CCBA® and CBAP® exam blueprints
- Types of exam questions

At the end of this chapter, you will be able to do the following:

- Know what percentage of questions come from which parts of the BABOK® guide for each exam
- Know what to expect from the different types of exam questions

Exam blueprints

You will be wondering what exactly you should study to be sure you have covered all the relevant materials that are included in the exams. The CCBA® and CBAP® exams are predominantly based on the BABOK® v3 Guide's content, and although it is important for you to study the entire BABOK Guide's content (using this study guide alongside the BABOK® v3 Guide), it is useful to understand the distribution of questions by reviewing the exam blueprints. Let's take a look:

 Note that each knowledge area mentioned here also includes the techniques associated with the knowledge area, and therefore you should take care to include this in your studies.

Knowledge Area	CBAP® Exam % of Questions	CCBA® Exam % of Questions
Business Analysis Planning and Monitoring	14%	12%
Elicitation and Collaboration	12%	20%
Requirements Life Cycle Management	15%	18%
Strategy Analysis	15%	12%
Requirements Analysis and Design Definition	30%	32%
Solution Evaluation	14%	6%

Figure 2: IIBA® Exam blueprints

Source: International Institute of Business Analysis®

 Although this breakdown of exam question coverage gives you some indication of where the emphasis of questions will lie, it should just be used as a rough indication and should not influence your focus of study too much. It is more important that you focus on the knowledge areas where you know you need a deeper knowledge and understanding rather than focusing your time on the exam blueprint's distribution.

Question types

You might be wondering what types of questions you can expect in the exam. Having been part of the exam IIBA® delineation committee and having been through the CBAP® exam itself, I can confidently say that the exam question types are varied throughout the exam. It tests your ability to recall specific facts, interpret facts, solve problems, recognize patterns, analyze material, and draw sensible conclusions. There are a number of questions expecting you to draw conclusions from specific case studies or scenarios.

The CCBA® exam will have slightly fewer question types expecting you to respond to case studies; however, these questions do exist in this exam, as well as in the CBAP®. These are often viewed as the harder questions that require you to apply your practical experience and knowledge in a cohesive manner.

This study guide includes mock questions of all these questions types, and you should make sure you review and practice answering all the different types of questions in preparation for the exam. This will enable your mind to absorb a sense of what to expect on exam day, as well as prepare and synthesize the specific knowledge you need in order to pass the exam on the day.

Summary

In this chapter, you learned what to expect from the CCBA® and CBAP® exams in terms of the IIBA® exam blueprints and the types of exam questions to expect.

Now you should know what percentage of questions comes from which parts of the BABOK® guide for each exam in the form of exam blueprints, and you should know what to expect from the different types of exam questions.

Make sure you revise these key learnings before completing the knowledge quiz at the end of this chapter.

Exam blueprints

During this part of this chapter, you learned what the distribution percentages are of questions coming from the different sections of the BABOK® v3 Guide for both the CCBA® and the CBAP® exams. This provided you with an idea of where you may need to focus and what you can expect in terms of question content.

Question types

You have learned that the exam question types are varied throughout both the CCBA® and the CBAP® exams. They test your ability to recall specific facts, interpret facts, solve problems, recognize patterns, analyze material, and draw sensible conclusions. There are a number of questions expecting you to draw conclusions from specific case studies or scenarios, and hence it is vital that you are able to relate each concept you learn about in this guide back to a practical workplace scenario that you have personally experienced during your career and/or be able to relate to the provided examples in this study guide.

Knowledge quiz

Complete this knowledge quiz to see how well you understood the content of this chapter.

Question 1:

I don't need to relate any theoretical concepts to practical scenarios or experiences I have had in my own work-life as part of my study.

Is this statement true or false?

     A. True

     B. False

Question 2:

The CCBA® exam only contains theory or recall type questions, so I don't need to prepare myself to be able to answer any practical scenarios.

Is this statement true or false?

     A. True

     B. False

Question 3:

It is a good idea to do mock tests, as outlined throughout this study guide so that I know what to expect on exam day and learn through measure and practice.

Is this statement true or false?

    A. True

    B. False

Answers

Questions	Answers
1	B
2	B
3	A

Business Analysis Foundation Concepts

5

This chapter is the basis for the business analysis knowledge and concepts to follow. It covers the core concept model of business analysis and also includes the industry definitions of business analysis, the requirements classification schema, stakeholder types, and key terms. This chapter is the entry point into the knowledge areas that will follow and is an essential introduction to establish a firm foundation of understanding.

We will cover the following topics in this chapter:

- Understanding business analysis
- The Business Analysis Core Concept Model™
- Key terms
- Stakeholders
- Requirements classification schema
- Requirements and designs
- Test your knowledge

By the end of this chapter, you would have learned the following:

- How to define what business analysis is and who is the business analyst
- How to apply the Business Analysis Core Concept Model across all business analysis tasks
- How to define all terms and stakeholder types
- How to define all types of requirements according to the requirements classification schema
- How to outline the differences between requirements and designs
- How to do a micro exam-style assessment

Understanding business analysis

Business analysis is the practice of understanding business needs and enabling change, including the recommendation of solutions. Business analysis can deliver value before, during, or after a project or business initiative. Initiatives, where business analysis is applied, can be tactical, strategic, or operational in nature. Business analysis is often used to understand the business's current state and future desired state.

According to the BABOK® Guide, business analysis can also be performed using a variety of different business perspectives. These perspectives include the following:

- The agile perspective
- The business intelligence perspective
- The information technology perspective
- The business architecture perspective
- The business process management perspective

It is important to note that these perspectives do not include the full range of potential contexts in which business analysis can be applied.

Who is a business analyst?

Any person in the organization who performs the tasks that are described within the BABOK® Guide is considered to be a business analyst

The BABOK® v3 Guide describes business analysts as follows: *"Business analysts are responsible for discovering, synthesizing, and analyzing information from a variety of sources within an enterprise, including tools, processes, documentation, and stakeholders. The business analyst is responsible for eliciting the actual needs of stakeholders – which frequently involves investigating and clarifying their expressed desires – in order to determine underlying issues and causes."*

So, if we consider this very broad definition of who the business analysts are in the organization, we would most likely recognize that many projects or product-related roles within the organization could be considered as playing a business analysis role to a certain extent.

Examples of roles that often include a variety of business analysis tasks would be as follows:

- The business architect
- The business systems analyst
- The data analyst
- The enterprise analyst
- The management consultant
- The product owner
- And the list goes on….

You probably get the picture that business analysis stretches across many different roles, perspectives, and areas within the enterprise.

The Business Analysis Core Concept Model™

The first content chapter in the BABOK® v3 Guide covers the key concepts that you need to understand before attempting to digest the other chapters in the guide. This chapter will describe the newly introduced Business Analysis Core Concept Model™, the key terms used, the standard for requirements classification, and the stakeholders and their relationship between requirements and design.

The purpose of this model is to describe what business analysis is without any regard for which perspective, industry, methodology, or level in the organization it is being performed from.

The Business Analysis Core Concept Model™ consists of six terms, all of which are intended to represent each concept in the model and should be used as common terminologies to aid with understanding within the profession:

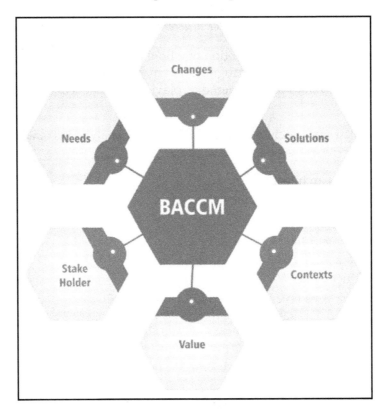

Figure 5.1: Business Analysis Core Concept Model

The six terms or concepts are as follows:

- Change
- Need
- Solution
- Stakeholder
- Value
- Context

Let's consider each of these concepts in turn to understand their meaning.

Change

The BABOK® v3 Guide describes this term as follows:

> *"The act of transformation in response to a need."*

This really reflects that the role of the business analysis is to facilitate the change to improve upon or to address a specific business need with specific activities and measures.

An example here could be **when a new initiative is started to implement an automated payroll calculator. One of the change aspects could include business analysis activities that focus on business processes that need to be changed to facilitate the automated calculation rather than using the existing manual business processes.**

Need

The BABOK® v3 Guide describes this term as follows:

> *"A problem or opportunity to be addressed."*

A need can cause a change to be triggered by stakeholders taking action. In the payroll calculator example, the need could have been originating as a result of payroll calculation errors with the existing process. Due to this, the stakeholders have initiated a project to implement a payroll calculator, which, in turn, caused business process changes to take effect.

Solution

The BABOK® v3 Guide describes this term as follows:

> *"A specific way of satisfying one or more needs in a context."*

A solution satisfies a need after stakeholders identify it. **In the payroll calculator example, the payroll calculator software is solving the need to have a reliable and accurate payroll calculation process in place.**

Stakeholder

The BABOK® v3 Guide describes this term as follows:

> *"A group or individual with a relationship to the change, the need, or the solution."*

A stakeholder is a person who is impacted by a business need, a change, or a solution.

In the payroll calculator example, the payroll manager will be identified as a stakeholder who is directly impacted by the solution, the change, and the need.

Value

The BABOK® v3 Guide describes this term as follows:

> *"The worth, importance, or usefulness of something to a stakeholder within a context."*

The value has a relationship with the stakeholders' perspective, the change, and the solution. The value can be tangible or intangible and is often different based on a point of view.

In the payroll calculator example, the value, as seen by the payroll manager, will be reflected in the reduction of errors occurring and penalties that may now not be payable as a result of implementing this solution.

Context

The BABOK® v3 Guide describes this term as follows:

> *"The circumstances that influence, are influenced by, and provide an understanding of the change."*

The context describes the situation and environment in which a change is being introduced. This could include culture, people, legislation, goals, processes, products, and any other aspects to consider when introducing a change. The context that change is introduced to is a determining factor of how that change will be realized.

In the example of the payroll calculator, the organization had many employees who belonged to a union, and every change that affects any union members has to be reviewed and approved by the union. So, if the organization wanted to make any change to the way a salary is calculated for a union member, they would need to consider the context of the union when introducing this change and incorporate their rules and agreements they have in place with the company.

Important questions for a business analyst to ask

As a business analyst performing your role, you should always ask the following questions to ensure you address all the core concepts while planning your tasks:

- What are the kinds of changes we are making?
- What are the needs we are trying to satisfy?
- What are the solutions we are creating or changing?
- Who are the stakeholders that are involved?
- What do stakeholders consider to be of value?
- What are the contexts that we and the solution are in?

Key terms

There is a core set of key terms used within the business analysis profession that has been defined in the BABOK® v3 Guide. It is important for you to understand and learn the meaning of each of these terms.

Here, will define and explore the meaning of the following terms that are used in the BABOK® Guide:

- Business analysis
- Business analysis information
- Design
- Enterprise
- Organization
- Plan
- Requirement
- Risk

Let's learn more about them in the following sections.

Business analysis

As we have already stated, *"business analysis is defined as the practice of enabling change in an enterprise by defining needs and recommending solutions that deliver value to stakeholders."*

Business analysis information

This term refers to all types of information that a business analyst uses to perform business analysis tasks. Each defined business analysis task has inputs and outputs of business analysis information.

Examples include requirements elicitation results, requirements, designs, and solution scope, to name but a few.

Design

Design, in the context of business analysis, refers to any usable representation of a solution. The design could take many different formats, depending on the specific situation, and essentially depicts how value can be realized with a solution.

Examples of design in this context could include a screen mockup, a process model, or a sketch of a dashboard.

Organization

We are all familiar with the meaning of the term organization. In this context, it is defined as a group of people working to achieve a common set of goals.

Organizations are continuously operating to achieve the goals they have set, while in the case of a project, the project will be disbanded when the goals have been met.

An example of an organization is a retail clothing company that sells a particular brand of clothes.

Enterprise

The BABOK® v3 Guide defines the term enterprise as a system of one or more organizations and the solutions they use to pursue a shared set of common goals.

The solutions being referred to in this definition can include processes, tools, or information. An enterprise can be a number of organizations, governments, or any other type of organization.

An example of an enterprise could be a large banking corporation that consists of many different smaller companies operating under the same umbrella company – local banks, investment banks, insurance companies, and so forth could all be part of the same enterprise.

Plan

The BABOK® v3 Guide defines the term "plan" as a proposal for doing or achieving something.

The term "plan" describes tasks to be performed, resources and materials required to execute the tasks, any dependencies and sequencing of tasks, as well as dates and expected outcomes. It also outlines the stakeholders involved in executing the plan successfully.

An example of a plan could simply be the project plan for the implementation of a customer relationship management solution.

Requirement

The BABOK® v3 Guide defines the term "requirement" as a usable representation of a need. Requirements focus on understanding what kind of value could be delivered if a requirement is fulfilled.

An example of a requirement could be a document describing the specific needs of a sales management solution in an organization.

Risk

Risk is the uncertainty around what is expected as an outcome. In the context of business analysis, this means that the risks need to be analyzed in terms of their priority to the business stakeholders and to collaboratively find ways to mitigate or decrease the likelihood of a risk eventuating. There are different types of risks that should be understood by the business analyst.

There are project-specific risks that affect the ability of the project team to deliver as expected. Then, there are also operational or business risks that exist as a consequence of the proposed solution or change introduced by the project or initiative. These risks need to be addressed in alignment with the proposed solution and changes to ensure the risks identified are acceptable and managed according to the wider organizational risk appetite.

An example of project risk is as follows: Due to additional and unexpected scope in the functionality required for the solution, there is a risk that the project team cannot deliver by the originally agreed delivery date.

An example of business risk is as follows: A risk has been identified in that highly skilled employees may leave the organization because their roles are being changed by the implementation of the new sales management solution.

Now that we have discovered the key terms used and their meanings, it is time to explore who the key stakeholders are that play an active role within the projects we deliver as business analysts.

Stakeholders

There are stakeholder roles you should be aware of and be able to define and interpret in the context of exam questions. Here, we'll take each of these stakeholder roles and understand what part they play within the realm of business analysis.

The different stakeholder roles you should be familiar with when working within the business analysis domain are as follows:

- Business analyst
- Customer
- Domain subject matter expert
- End user
- Implementation subject matter expert
- Operational support
- Project manager
- Regulator
- Sponsor
- Supplier
- Tester

Let's learn more about them in the following sections.

Business analyst

As you would imagine, the business analyst is responsible and accountable for the execution of **all** business analysis activities. In some cases, the business analyst may also be responsible for performing other stakeholder responsibilities.

An example of this role is a project business analyst who is responsible and accountable to deliver all the stakeholder and solution requirements for the project.

Customer

The customer is probably the most important stakeholder because they are the ones who will use products or services produced by the project, the organization, or the enterprise as a whole.

An example of a customer is a banking customer who uses the bank's credit card facility as a product.

Domain subject matter expert

This role is the individual who has an in-depth knowledge of the specific topic area where a business need or solution scope is being analyzed. There are many types of roles in the organization that can also play the role of a domain subject matter expert.

Two examples of the domain subject matter expert role include the Payroll officer in a new payroll solution initiative and a sales consultant where a new sales process is being implemented.

End user

The end users are the stakeholders who will be using the business solution that is being implemented. This could include a new business process and/or a specific product or system solution.

An example of an end user is a call center operator who uses the call center software package to perform their role.

Make sure you understand the difference between a customer and an end user. The customer can also be an end user when they are the end user of the system and the customer for a particular solution. For example, an online banking customer is a customer and an end user of online banking software. However, in a call center scenario, the end user of the call center software is the call center agent and the customer is the person who is being served by the call center agent who is using the software.

Implementation subject matter expert

These types of stakeholders are the individuals who are subject matter experts within a certain aspect of an implementation of business processes or software solutions.

Some roles that are considered implementation subject matter experts include change manager, solution architect, configuration manager, database administrator, usability analyst, and trainer.

Make sure you understand the difference between an implementation subject matter expert and a domain subject matter expert.

Operational support

This stakeholder group is responsible for the day-to-day management and maintenance of a system or a product.

Examples of these stakeholders include helpdesk staff, release managers, operations analysts, and product analysts.

Project manager

This stakeholder role is responsible for managing the work that is required to implement the solution that was defined to meet the business needs. The project manager must manage the project in terms of scope, budget, schedule, resources, quality, and risk.

Other stakeholder roles, which often play the project manager role within different situations, could include the team lead role, the product manager role, the technical lead role, or the project lead role.

Regulator

Many enterprise initiatives are subject to specific regulations. The regulator plays the role of enforcing specific standards across different industries and sectors. Examples of these standards include legislation, corporate governance standards, and audit standards.

Some example roles of regulators include the government, regulatory bodies, or an auditor.

Sponsor

The role of the sponsor is to initiate and support the efforts required to analyze a business need and to find and establish a solution for that need. The sponsor acts as the authorizer of all activities, and also controls the budget for the initiative. Other role titles for sponsors include executive or project sponsors. *For example, in a payroll initiative, it would be typical for the payroll executive to be the initiative's sponsor.*

Supplier

The role of this stakeholder sits outside the boundary of the enterprise or organization. The supplier provides products and services to support any business initiative and can often form an integral part of the solution. The supplier stakeholder, therefore, has a contractual and, in some cases, moral obligation toward the organization.

An example of a supplier could be the software vendor who has been selected to provide a new call center software solution as part of a business initiative.

Tester

Finally, the role of the tester is to define and establish a process to verify that the solution that is being implemented meets the requirements. The tester stakeholder will also be responsible for establishing a certain quality standard to be adhered to by the solution. The role of the tester is also referred to as the role of a quality assurance analyst.

An example of one of the responsibilities of a tester would be to write test scripts to match the business requirements to be tested using an agreed-upon test procedure.

Each business initiative requires all these roles to be present in order to be complete and well rounded. It is essential for the business analyst to consider and understand the roles of all these stakeholder types when planning the requirements approach and engagement activities.

Requirements classification schema

There are four main types of requirements defined by the BABOK® Guide v3.0. These are fundamental to business analysis and require you to fully understand each classification entirely. They include the following:

- Business requirements
- Stakeholder requirements
- Solution requirements
- Transition requirements

Solution requirements are also further defined into two subtypes: functional requirements and non-functional requirements (also known as quality of service requirements).

In order to implement the BABOK® v3 Guide Requirements Classification Schema, you will need to assess and map the levels of requirements to your existing requirements processes and the resulting requirements documents.

Now, let's consider the different types of requirements in more detail and understand what that means for your real-world requirements by looking at an example of each.

The following diagram summarizes the different types of requirements described in the requirements classification schema:

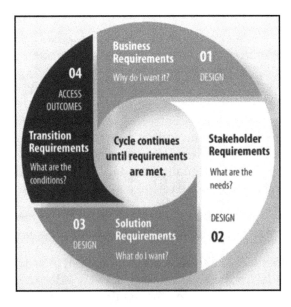

Figure 5.2: Requirements classification schema summary

Business requirements

A business requirement is a statement of a business goal, objective, or desired outcome that describes why a change has been initiated.

An example of a business requirement is as follows: the payroll department must upgrade existing payroll procedures to cater for the growth in employee numbers.

It is important to realize that the business requirements describe and justify the high-level business functionality that is needed in the resulting solution. In order to define a solution, the business requirements will be progressively elaborated and decomposed to the next level of detail, which brings us to the stakeholder requirements."

Stakeholder requirements

The stakeholder requirements describe the needs of the stakeholders that must be met in order to achieve the business requirements.

These requirements define the needs of stakeholders and how they will interact with a solution. Stakeholder requirements act as a bridge between the business requirements and the solution requirements. The stakeholder requirements identify what is needed from the user's perspective and define "big picture" capabilities that the resulting solution must possess.

An example of a stakeholder requirement is as follows: the Payroll team must be able to set up new employee accounts.

Note that the stakeholder requirement is written and expressed from the perspective of a particular stakeholder or stakeholder group. The stakeholder requirements might be common or different between different stakeholder groups and should be considered as such.

Solution requirements

The solution requirements describe the specific solution characteristics that the solution will need to possess to be able to meet the stakeholder requirements. These are the requirements that contain enough detail that a solution can be developed and implemented.

Solution requirements are divided into two categories:

- **Functional requirements:** These requirements describe the specific functionality that is required by the new solution – in other words, the functional requirements describe the capabilities that a solution must provide to its users.

    Although there are many acceptable functional requirement formulation approaches, an example of a functional requirement could be as follows:

    "The teller scans barcodes to calculate the total grocery bill for the customer upon checkout."

    You could phrase the same requirement as follows:

    "As a teller, I scan barcodes to calculate the total grocery bill for a customer."

    In this example, the functionality that is being described is about the ability to calculate the total grocery bill. In another example, you might have similar functional requirements for searching for products, printing receipts, or processing payments. It is about the functions the system provides to the end-user.

- **Non-functional requirements or quality of service requirements:** These types of requirements describe the characteristics that are expected of the solution. This is best described with a few different types of non-functional requirement categories.

    Examples of non-functional requirements include requirements describing the performance requirements for a system, the transaction volume capability of a system, the security requirements of a system, and the usability of a system. There are many other non-functional requirements categories that can be used to describe the required characteristics of a solution.

Remember those non-functional requirements are also referred to as quality of service requirements or quality attributes.

Transition requirements

Last but not least are the transition requirements. These types of requirements define what is needed to transition from a project or a pre-production solution to an operational solution or to transition from the current state to the future state.

An example of a transition requirement is as follows: to migrate all existing employee payroll information from the current manual systems to the new payroll calculator database.

The reason this example is a transition requirement is that once all the data has been migrated successfully to the new system, the requirement is complete and will not be required beyond the temporary tasks of migrating data.

Requirements and designs

It has been an ongoing debate or area of confusion that requirements and designs are being used and elaborated upon interchangeably. In the past, we have said that you must first establish the requirements and then another role, such as a solution architect, will typically be responsible for elaborating on the design aspects of the initiative or planned solution. However, through our years of experience, we have realized that this is not always practical and not always appropriate. In some situations, requirements will be defined and elaborated initially, and, in some cases, the design will initiate further definition of more requirements.

People are solution-driven, which means that, occasionally, design or solution sometimes drives the analysis of requirements rather than requirements being the first step in the life cycle. Regardless of whether requirements are defined up front and then designs are considered, it is important for the business analyst to understand that, in some situations, they will be responsible for doing designs (or at least part of it), as well as the requirements for a solution. It remains really important for the business analyst to always ask "why" design or a requirement is being considered and how it aligns with the business goals and objectives.

The following are some comparison examples of requirements and designs:

- **Example 1**:
  The requirement: View 6 months of order information across all departments in a summary report.
  The design equivalent of the requirement: A sketch of a dashboard-style user interface or screen layout.

- **Example 2**:
  The requirement: To capture employee personal information in a central database.
  The design equivalent: A wireframe or screen mockup showing all the required fields and general design of the screen layout.

In conclusion, the business analyst will be responsible for defining the requirements throughout the life cycle of the development of the solution. The business analyst will also be responsible for being closely involved during the design steps of the process to ensure that designs are aligning with the requirements and that they ultimately meet the business objectives of the organization.

Summary

In this chapter, you have learned about the core concepts that are used in business analysis practices.

In all, we learned about business analysis and business analysts, the Business Analysis Core Concept Model, the key terms, the various stakeholders involved, and the requirements classification schema.

Make sure you revise these key learnings before completing the knowledge quiz at the end of this chapter.

Business analysis and Business Analyst

Business analysis is the practice of understanding business needs and enabling change, including the recommendation of solutions. The business analysis can deliver value before, during, or after a project or business initiative.

Any person in the organization who performs the tasks described within the BABOK® Guide is considered to be a business analyst.

Business Analysis Core Concept Model

During this chapter, you learned about the newly introduced Business Analysis Core Concept Model™, which is used to describe what business analysis is without giving any regard to which perspective, industry, methodology, or level in the organization it is being performed from. You are now able to relate to the six dimensions addressed as part of the Business Analysis Core Concept Model.

Key terms

You are able to recognize, interpret, and use the key terms used in the business analysis profession, including business analysis, business analysis information, design, enterprise, organization, plan, requirement, and risk.

Stakeholders

Another takeaway from this chapter is your understanding and ability to contextualize the different stakeholder roles when working within the business analysis domain. These roles primarily include the business analyst, customer, domain subject matter expert, end user, implementation subject matter expert, operational support, project manager, regulator, sponsor, supplier, and tester. You also understand the variations of role titles used in practice for each of the aforementioned roles.

Requirements classification schema

There are four main types of requirements. These are fundamental to business analysis and require you to fully understand each classification entirely. They include business requirements, stakeholder requirements, solution requirements, and transition requirements. Solution requirements is also further defined into two subtypes: functional requirements and non-functional requirements, or quality of service requirements. You are now able to articulate the different types of requirements classifications and recognize each type when reviewing real-world examples.

Knowledge quiz

Consider the following real-world scenario and complete the micro mock exam based on this chapter that follows:

REAL-WORLD SCENARIO:

You have been working as a business analyst on a project for 6 months. The project aims to implement a new human resource management solution that can manage employee records and performance management processes more effectively than the current manual processes. Jane, the HR executive, is the sponsor for the project and has asked you to provide an overview for the new business analyst who has just joined the project and to also introduce her to all the other stakeholders involved with the project. Katie, the new business analyst, is very interested to meet people and you promised to introduce her to everyone during the team meeting. The first person to attend the meeting is Chris, the guy who is responsible for making sure all deliverables are delivered on time and within budget! Then, Susie walks in with her usual coffee in hand and a general sigh about being so busy trying to explain to the vendor team that the human resources policies and procedures in this company are simply more complex than other companies.... The software vendor manager, Bruce, is quite a stubborn guy and is only concerned with delivering what they have available today in their solution; he is not very interested in understanding the nuances of the company's policies and special procedures. This means that Cassandra, the change manager, will have her hands full when implementing the solution in the human resources team. You haven't had the opportunity to introduce Katie to the HR operational manager or the test lead yet, but promise to do so after the meeting. You have to run off after the meeting to continue a workshop, which is all about defining the capabilities and qualities of the requirements to ensure that all stakeholder requirements are being met. You provided Katie with information regarding the goals and expected outcomes for the initiative that she needs to become familiar with before you introduce her to more people.

Question 1

Using the provided case study, which one of the following stakeholder types best describes the role that Chris plays?

    A. Project manager

    B. Project analyst

    C. Quality assurance analyst

    D. Project sponsor

Question 2

Using the provided case study, which one of the following stakeholder types best describes the role of Cassandra as the change manager?

A. Domain subject matter expert

B. Implementation subject matter expert

C. Supplier

D. End user

Question 3

Which one of the following stakeholder types listed here is not mentioned at all in the case study?

A. Tester

B. Supplier

C. Sponsor

D. Operational support

Question 4

Using the provided case study and your knowledge of the requirements classification schema described in BABOK® v3 Guide, which two options best describe the types of requirements that you are currently defining as an outcome to a workshop you are part of currently?

A. Business requirements

B. Functional requirements

C. Quality of service requirements

D. Detailed stakeholder requirements

Question 5

Using the provided case study, who controls the budget and scope of the project?

    A. Chris

    B. Jane

    C. Bruce

    D. Katie

Question 6

Using the provided case study, which of the following best describes the type of information you gave Katie to read?

    A. Project scope

    B. Stakeholder requirements

    C. Business opportunities

    D. Business requirements

Question 7

"Once you have finished defining the solution requirements, it might be a good idea to start working on the transition requirements of the project. Knowing that there are lots of manual procedures that will change and hence lots of training to do before go live, you realize that there might be quite a few requirements that need to be captured to ensure a successful transition from the current state to the future state of this project."

Choose whether you believe this is a reasonable or unreasonable summary of the next steps you could take on in the project.

    A. Reasonable

    B. Unreasonable

Question 8

As an extension to the provided case study, Katie has asked you whether you have any design artifacts that you might be able to share with her to help her understand the requirements and scope. Which of the following can be considered a design artifact in the context of business analysis?

    A. A recorded conversation with a stakeholder

    B. Textual workshop notes

    C. Requirements transcript

    D. Process model

Question 9

Using the provided case study, do you think that you should raise a risk that the vendor may not be paying enough attention to the company-specific policies and procedures and that this could potentially cause operational issues once the solution is being implemented?

Choose whether it is your responsibility in this scenario to raise a risk (Yes) or to not raise a risk (No):

    A. Yes

    B. No

Question 10

Match the items on the left with the items on the right:

A. Design	1. … A proposal for doing or achieving something
B. Plan	2. … Interact directly with the solution
C. Customer	3. … Uses products or services produced by the enterprise
D. End user	4. … A usable representation of a solution

Question 11

What project role focuses on understanding business problems and opportunities?

    A. Project sponsor

    B. Project manager

    C. Business architect

    D. Business analyst

Question 12

Which one of the following options does NOT describe a knowledge area, as defined in BABOK® Guide Version 3.0?

    A. Requirements life cycle management

    B. Requirements analysis and design definition

    C. Enterprise analysis

    D. Solution evaluation

Question 13

According to BABOK® Guide Version 3.0, a _____ is a discrete piece of work that may be performed formally or informally.

    A. Task

    B. Job

    C. Activity

    D. Process

Question 14

Select the best option that describes what reflects knowledge, skills, behaviors, characteristics, and personal qualities to help someone successfully perform the role of the business analyst.

    A. Problem-solving competencies

    B. Underlying competencies

    C. Communication capabilities

    D. Business acumen

Question 15

The perspectives described in BABOK® Guide Version 3.0 are the only perspectives that business analysis can be performed on.

Choose whether the statement is true or false:

    A. True

    B. False

Question 16

The conceptual framework that has been included in BABOK® 0Guide Version 3.0 to define the business analysis profession is referred to as what?

    A. Business Analyst Core Concept Model

    B. Business Analysis Core Concept Model

    C. Business Analyst Core Competency Model

    D. Business Analyst Competency Concept Model

Question 17

Which of the following options describe the core concepts of the BACCM as described in BABOK® Guide Version 3.0?

    A. Change, opportunity, solution, stakeholder, value, context

    B. Change, need, solution, stakeholder, value, context

C. Change, opportunity, solution, stakeholder, value, capability

D. Change, need, solution, stakeholder, value, capability

Question 18

"It is appropriate for a business analyst to be involved with the design aspects of a solution. The design aspects of a solution can be used to trigger further requirements."

Choose whether this statement is true or false:

A. True

B. False

Question 19

This type of expert is an individual with in-depth knowledge of a topic relevant to the business need or solution scope.

A. Topic subject matter expert

B. Project subject matter expert

C. Implementation subject matter expert

D. Domain subject matter expert

Question 20

BABOK® Guide Version 3.0 defines a requirements classification schema that should be understood and applied by business analysts in practice. Which two of the following options describe the defined subtypes of solution requirements?

A. Detailed requirements

B. Transition requirements

C. Functional requirements

D. Quality of service requirements

Answers

Questions	Answers
1	A - Project manager
2	B - Implementation subject matter expert
3	D - Operational support
4	B - Functional requirements and C - Quality of service requirements
5	B - Jane
6	D - Business requirements
7	A - Reasonable
8	D - Process model
9	A - Yes
10	A and 4 B and 1 C and 3 D and 2
11	D - Business analyst
12	C - Enterprise analysis
13	A - Task
14	B - Underlying Competencies
15	B - False
16	B - Business Analysis Core Concept Model
17	B - Change, need, solution, stakeholder, value, context
18	A - True
19	D - Domain subject matter expert
20	C - Functional requirements D - Quality of service requirements

6
Business Analysis Planning and Monitoring

This chapter covers the tasks that are used to organize and coordinate the efforts of a business analyst. This chapter dives into BABOK® tasks: planning a business analysis approach, planning stakeholder engagement, planning business analysis governance, planning business analysis information management, and identifying business analysis performance improvements and bringing them to life with practical real-world scenarios.

The purpose and context of these knowledge areas are as follows:

- The Business Analysis Planning and Monitoring knowledge area
- The Plan Business Analysis Approach task
- The Plan Stakeholder Engagement task
- The Plan Business Analysis Governance task
- The Plan Business Analysis Information Management task
- The Identify Business Analysis Performance Improvements task
- Real-world case studies
- Test your knowledge

The concepts you will learn about are as follows:

- Understanding the context of the BABOK® knowledge areas with real-world scenarios
- Understanding and applying the planning business analysis approach task to real-world scenarios
- Understanding and applying the planning stakeholder engagement task to real-world scenarios
- Understanding and applying the planning business analysis governance task to real-world scenarios

- Understanding and applying the planning business analysis information management task to real-world scenarios
- Understanding and applying the identifying business analysis performance improvements task to real-world scenarios
- Interpreting a real-world scenario and applying the knowledge learned in this chapter
- Doing a micro exam-style assessment

Understanding Business Analysis Planning and Monitoring

Business Analysis Planning and Monitoring focuses on laying the foundation for successfully defining, planning, and completing the business analysis work that is used as a key guideline for other tasks throughout the project life cycle as it is performed by the business analyst:

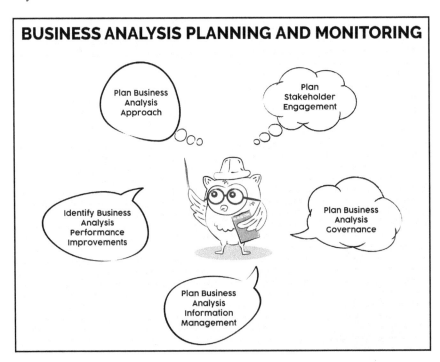

Figure 6:1: The Business Analysis Planning and Monitoring knowledge area and tasks

The Business Analysis Planning and Monitoring knowledge area includes the following tasks:

- Planning a business analysis approach
- Planning stakeholder engagement
- Planning business analysis governance
- Planning business analysis information management
- Identifying business analysis performance improvements

These tasks focus on planning how the business analysis team approaches a specific effort.

The Business Analysis Core Concept Model™

Here, we will how the **Business Analysis Core Concept Model™ (BACCM™)** applies to Business Analysis Planning and Monitoring as a knowledge area using an example.

The six core concepts, which are described as BACCM™, are as follows:

- Change
- Need
- Solution
- Stakeholder
- Value
- Context

Let's discuss each of these concepts in the following sections.

Change

This core concept really refers to how change is managed in response to when a need is identified. Specifically, in the knowledge area of Business Analysis Planning and Monitoring, the concept of "change" is applied in terms of how the changes that arise from business analysis results will be requested and approved within a specific project or initiative's context and environment.

Let's look at an example to bring this concept around change to life:

Let's say you have just finished completing requirements documentation for a new sales solution and all the stakeholders have signed off your requirements documents. The project is now ready for the design and implementation of the solution. You then receive a phone call from one of the stakeholders, who is asking you to please change the requirements for deleting old customer records. Now, you already have signed off the requirements that state that old customer records must be deleted after two years of accounts being closed. However, the stakeholder wants you to make a change that allows these old customer records to be archived and stored for 10 years. In a real-life business analysis scenario, you will have defined a procedure or approach around how a stakeholder can request changes to requirements and what authorization steps would be involved as part of the Business Analysis Planning and Monitoring activities. So, you can now simply refer to the stakeholder, who is waiting for you to respond on the phone, to the agreed procedure or change request form. Or even better, you can offer to complete the change request for the stakeholder to review and then submit it for approval!

This example illustrates how the core concept of "change" is implemented within the Business Analysis Planning and Monitoring knowledge area.

Need

This core concept really refers to how a need is defined and addressed within a given context. Specifically in the knowledge area of Business Analysis Planning and Monitoring, the concept of "need" is applied in terms of what would be the most appropriate business analysis approach to addressing the need sufficiently.

Let's look at an example to bring this concept of need into the real world:

- **Scenario 1**: *Consider being placed in a business analysis team that is responsible for implementing a brand new payment product that utilizes new token technology. All the team really knows about this new technology is that there will be an impact on the way people pay for goods and the way payments are processed between the merchant, the processing service, and the bank. This technology is so new that it has not been implemented by anybody anywhere in the retail market.*

- **Scenario 2**: *Now consider being placed in a business analysis team that is responsible for upgrading a well-understood customer records system with a web-based version of the system. Your role is to work closely with the vendor to identify any procedural and functional differences between the current system and the future system. The expectation is that there will be very minor changes required.*

Based on these two real-world scenarios, you can see that during Business Analysis Planning and Monitoring activities, the approach chosen to manage the business "need" will be different between these scenarios.

Scenario 1 will need an approach that analyzes the current end-to-end payment processes and existing systems in depth in order to redesign and define a future state payment process that can accommodate the brand new technology.

In scenario 2, the analysis approach will be less detailed and more focused on unknown and understood areas where there might be differences that need to be planned accordingly.

This example illustrates how the core concept of "need" is implemented within the Business Analysis Planning and Monitoring knowledge area by considering the context it is raised in.

Solution

This core concept really refers to how a solution satisfies one or more needs within a given context. Specifically, in the knowledge area of Business Analysis Planning and Monitoring, the concept of "solution" is applied in terms of how you evaluate whether the business analysis performance was a key contributor to the successful implementation of a solution.

Let's look at an example to bring this concept of solution into the real world. This could be reflected in tangible cost-saving results due to business analysis performance by uncovering inefficiencies within existing processes or systems. Alternatively, it could be reflected in a less-tangible success result, such as customer satisfaction, with a well-understood user experience requirement due to careful business analysis planning of an appropriate elicitation approach.

This example illustrates how the core concept of "solution" is implemented during the Business Analysis Planning and Monitoring knowledge area with a focus on monitoring the performance of business analysis as it contributes to the initiative's success.

Stakeholder

This core concept really refers to how the stakeholder has a relationship with need, the change, and the solution. Specifically, in the knowledge area of Business Analysis Planning and Monitoring, the concept of "stakeholder" is applied in terms of how the stakeholder's needs and characteristics are understood within a given context.

Let's look at an example to bring this concept of the stakeholder into the real world:

In this example, you will appreciate that these stakeholders are geographically dispersed and not necessarily used to providing stakeholder or solution requirements for systems. As part of the Business Analysis Planning and Monitoring activities, you need to incorporate their unique characteristics and needs and therefore make sure that whichever requirements elicitation plan and approach are defined will work well with these types of stakeholders and their environment.

Value

This core concept refers to how the value, worth, or importance of something within a specific context is perceived by the stakeholder. When we look at the knowledge area of Business Analysis Planning and Monitoring, the concept of "value" is applied in terms of ensuring that the business analysis activities performed are of adequate value to the stakeholders involved.

Let's look at an example to bring this concept of "value" into the real world:

Let's say you are working on a project where you are documenting the operational processes for the current state in a retail environment using notation that is not well understood by the stakeholders. You will be perceived as doing something that is of limited value to your stakeholders. However, if you did the same activity using notation or a format that is well understood by your stakeholders, the value of what you are contributing to your business analysis activities would immediately increase. To you, the value might be the same but it is important to always consider the value of your activities through the eyes of your stakeholders.

Context

This core concept refers to how the context or circumstances of a change has a direct impact on how we approach business analysis activities. It is therefore very important to completely understand the context that the analysis will be applied to.

Let's look at an example to bring this concept of "context" into the real world:

In all the examples we have looked at so far, it was clear that the context of each scenario was different and that from a Business Analysis Planning and Monitoring perspective, this should be considered closely when planning a business analysis approach.

The scenario of a payment system with new technology is clearly set within a context of high uncertainty, significant risk, and high demand for detailed analysis, whereas the scenario of upgrading a well-understood customer records system was within the context of low risk, low uncertainty, and high confidence among stakeholders.

Due to the differences in contexts for these two example scenarios, the Business Analysis Planning and Monitoring activities will result in different analysis approaches for each.

Task: Plan Business Analysis Approach

According to the BABOK® v3 Guide, the purpose of the task Plan Business Analysis Approach is "to define an appropriate method to conduct Business Analysis activities."

This task is about assessing the initiative from a stakeholder, scope, organizational environment, and expected outcomes perspective. The business analyst may not know everything about the new environment or initiative during the early planning and approach formulation and so it is important to remember that the business analyst can change and update their approach and planning as they learn more during the initiative. However, in the earlier stages of the initiative, it is important to consider which techniques it may be most appropriate to apply based on the knowledge available to the business analyst.

It is also important for the business analyst to understand any existing methodologies that are followed by the organization or any previously defined and repeatable standard business analysis practices that might be expected by stakeholders. This isn't to say that if there is such a standardized process that the business analyst shouldn't tailor this to suit the needs of a particular initiative.

The key considerations for the business analysis approach is as follows:

- It should be in alignment with the objectives of the change or initiative.
- It should also be aligned and be coordinated to work in harmony with the overall changes and deliverables planned for the initiative.
- It should consider how the approach will cater to tasks to support any risks that may emerge during the initiative. An important aspect of this effort is for the business analyst to repeat processes, techniques, and tools that have proven to work well for the organization.

The elements of Plan Business Analysis Approach

These are the three key elements when you plan the business analysis approach:

- Planning the approach.
- Should you plan for a lot of detail and formality or not?
- Planning your business analysis activities.

We will now cover the key elements of the Plan Business Analysis Approach task by considering it a description and explaining each element with an example.

Element 1: Planning the approach

There are many ways to approach business analysis work and various planning methods are used across different perspectives, industries, and enterprises. Many of the planning methods are a variant of an interpretation of either a predictive or an adaptive approach.

A predictive approach

A predictive approach (in some places referred to as a plan-driven approach) is an approach that plans upfront with maximum control what the expected implementation would be. The waterfall project methodology supports a predictive approach to planning.

A real-world example of when a predictive approach might be the most suitable planning approach would be in a project or initiative where a lot of certainties exists, such as an infrastructure project or a system upgrade initiative.

Both of these examples include a high degree of certainty in terms of what exactly is involved to make the change (do the upgrade) and it is clear what the expected outcome would be. This can, therefore, be planned upfront with a high degree of certainty of what is to come and what it would take to complete.

Another good example of when a predictive approach is a relevant approach is when an "off-the-shelf" solution (such as a new timesheet solution) is being implemented with a minimal or no option of customization.

This example also has a very clearly defined set of steps that must be executed in order for the solution to be implemented successfully. Therefore, a predictive approach can work very effectively in this case. It is important to understand with this example that the scope doesn't allow for any special changes or customization of the software, or if it does, this will be minimal. If this is not the case and the stakeholders have the freedom to introduce a lot of change, then an adaptive approach may be more suitable.

An adaptive approach

An adaptive approach (in some places referred to as a change-driven approach) is an approach that is more incremental or exploratory in nature and focuses on the rapid delivery of business value in short iterations. The agile project methodology applied in software development projects supports adaptive planning approaches.

A real-world example of when an adaptive approach might be most suitable would be where there is a lot of uncertainty about what exactly the scope and/or the end result would be. This scenario applies to almost every software development project where the scope and requirements are not known in any detail and the understanding is that stakeholders will participate in the initiative to assist with formulating the requirements and specific design artifacts.

In today's world, new web development projects, e-commerce storefronts, and mobile applications are perfect candidates for an adaptive or change-driven planning approach to be applied.

It is important to realize that both predictive and adaptive approaches can be applied within the same initiative. When deciding which approach to apply during business analysis planning, it is key to always consider which of the approaches will deliver the most value within your context.

 Remember the alternative terminology of the adaptive (change-driven) and predictive (plan-driven) approaches.

Element 2: Formality and the level of detail of business analysis deliverables

All business analysis deliverables or results should be defined in the business analysis approach. Predictive planning approaches are typically quite formal and produce very detailed document sets requiring formal approval, whereas adaptive planning approaches can be quite informal and often limit the documentation to the minimum until more detail is required. When an adaptive approach is used, business analysis work is typically approved informally through team interaction and feedback.

An example could be when a business analyst is working on a large enterprise-wide system implementation in the public sector using a waterfall methodology (hence, using a predictive approach). Typically, there would be a lot of detailed documentation required to facilitate the progression of the project through its phases.

Often in these scenarios, detailed documentation is the vehicle used to obtain approvals from the steering committee for budget release at pre-defined intervals or phases of the initiative. In this scenario, a lot of the analysis and documentation efforts are done in the early part of the initiative.

Another example where less formality and detail might be required would be in a change-driven or adaptive environment. This might be a web development project where documentation is developed on an as-needed basis and only to the level of detail that is required to achieve a functioning piece of software. This scenario is often misunderstood as minimal documentation whenever an adaptive approach is followed because people make a blanket assumption that there is very little documentation required. This is incorrect. The difference between predictive and adaptive documentation detail needs is simply that predictive approaches will document every aspect of the solution to the lowest-agreed level of detail whereas, in an adaptive environment, the specific story (or requirement) being developed will dictate the required level of documentation. This can still be a low level of detailed documentation if the story or the feature being developed warrants that. Every story in an adaptive approach still needs enough detail to be successfully tested, even if the development aspect doesn't need that must detail to be developed.

Element 3: Business analysis activities

The business analyst must decide on the process to follow for planning a project's business analysis activities. The business analysis work plan is often a sub-set of the overall project plan and should, therefore, be done in coordination with the project manager. To ensure the business analysis part of the work plan fits in well with the overall project plan, make sure that you know what the estimation standards are and what the level of the task's detail should be. Aim to always have open communication with the project manager in terms of what business analysis activities are being planned for and agree on what the overall planning approach will be.

Element 4: The timing of business analysis work

It is important to plan for when the business analysis work will be performed for a specific initiative. If it is a predominantly predictive approach that is being taken on the initiative, you will know that most of the business analysis work will be performed in the earlier phases of the project. However, the business analysis work will be evenly spread for the duration of the initiative or project if a predominantly adaptive approach is followed. So, make sure that you align and plan for the correct number of resources to be available for your project to ensure the timely execution of the business analysis work plan.

Element 5: Complexity and risk

As you can probably imagine, when you are faced with a large project that is attempting a complex subject matter or high-risk context, you will need to consider complexity and risk when planning the business analysis approach, as well as the specific activities.

For example, if you are planning the business analysis work activities for an airline flight control system, there will be a lot of very detailed and accurate analysis required upfront and potentially on an ongoing basis, too. However, if you were planning business analysis activities for a mobile application development project that is focused on customer experience, you will probably be more interested in planning with an adaptive approach in mind.

Other factors that can affect the complexity of the business analysis effort could include geography and cultural considerations, technology complexities, the number of systems involved, and the sheer size of the change. A change affecting everyone in an organization is likely to be more complex than if only a small isolated team in an organization is affected.

Element 6: The acceptance of the business analysis approach and plan

It is important for the business analyst to socialize the business analysis approach and plan with the stakeholders who will be affected by the work that will be performed. If everyone understands the approach and feels comfortable that the plan is achievable, then the business analyst has a strong position to start executing the business analysis activities for the initiative from. Often, when the stakeholders, project manager, or board doesn't have a clear view of how the requirements will be managed on a project, it creates a lot of resistance, confusion, and unengaged stakeholders.

The inputs and outputs of this task

With the Business Analysis Planning and Monitoring task Plan Business Analysis Approach, there are the following key inputs and outputs:

Inputs: Needs

Outputs: Business analysis approach

When you understand the scope and purpose of a task, it is a great idea to imagine what you would need as an input to perform a task as well as imagine what you deliver an output. If you contextualize this, it is much easier to remember this for the exam.

Now that you have a good understanding of what elements are considered during the Plan Business Analysis Approach task, we will discuss the task describing what you should consider when you plan your stakeholder engagement activities in the next section.

Task: Plan Stakeholder Engagement

According to the BABOK® v3 Guide, the purpose of Plan Stakeholder Engagement is as follows:

> *"to plan an approach for establishing and maintaining effective working relationships with the stakeholders."*

Here is a football analogy: a good way to think about this task is to consider the stakeholders as members of a football team. Every team member has a different role to play, directly or indirectly, but ultimately, everyone has the same goal. Some play positions that are only required for part of the game and other team members stay for the whole duration of the game. There are stakeholders who don't actively play in the game but they contribute by bringing water to the players or by putting the score on the board. The business analysis team needs to understand who all the different stakeholders are and understand what type of role they play within the initiative's context.

The number of stakeholders

Something that the business analyst should also keep in mind when planning the stakeholder engagement is the number of stakeholders that would need to be engaged with. This will enable the business analyst to consider the engagement complexities that could arise when the number of stakeholders grows and so the format and engagement models might need to change.

The elements of Plan Stakeholder Engagement

These are the three key elements when you plan stakeholder engagement:

1. Perform stakeholder analysis
2. Define stakeholder collaboration
3. Define the stakeholder communication needs

We will now cover the key elements of Plan Stakeholder Engagement by considering it as a description and understanding each element with an example.

Element 1: Performing stakeholder analysis

The ultimate goal when planning the stakeholder engagement for your business analysis activities is to make sure that you are engaging with all the relevant and impacted stakeholders or groups. This will ensure that you have comprehensive requirements or needs a definition for the future planned solution.

This means that you should identify the stakeholders who are affected by the planned solution in both a direct and indirect way. It is important to continuously develop your stakeholder list as the project progresses so that you or the team don't overlook anyone who may have valid and valuable requirements to contribute.

How you build your initial stakeholder list will differ between different organizations, projects, and methodologies. However, it is important to compile this list earlier rather than later in the project.

Roles matter

It is very useful for a business analyst to know which roles a particular stakeholder or group of stakeholders plays within the organization. This will help the business analyst to determine their influence later on and will help in planning the engagement type required for that stakeholder or group.

For example, in a project where the solution will mean a different process for customers when using Automatic Teller Machines (ATMs) to get cash out, it is important to not only identify the customers as key stakeholders to engage with but also the customer support personnel who would need to support those customers during the change and transition period. If the project doesn't identify the customer support team as a key stakeholder group due to the role that they play in the overall proposed changes, the risk of failure increases dramatically for the project.

Attitudes of stakeholders

A critical aspect of stakeholder analysis is to gauge the stakeholder's attitude in terms of the proposed change or solution. If you have a positive stakeholder or group who understands the purpose of the project and can see the benefits to them as well as the overall company, then you should ensure they remain positive with the appropriate engagement and attention from the project.

A negative stakeholder can often be quite destructive towards the project or initiative and should be engaged with in a way that helps them see the value of what is being delivered. Very often, stakeholders are only negative towards an initiative because they feel like the project team has not engaged them appropriately. Often in these cases, if you engage those seemingly negative stakeholders carefully and with great attention, they will become positive and even champions of your initiative.

The decision-making authority

It is essential for a business analyst to understand how much influence and authority a particular stakeholder has over the business analysis output and results for the project. This puts the business analyst in a better position when seeking approval from stakeholders who influence for their deliverables.

Understanding who your stakeholders are in terms of their overall influence to support the proposed changes will provide a way to gauge whether the project has enough influential stakeholder support to ensure a successful outcome.

Element 2: Defining stakeholder collaboration

In some contexts, the stakeholder collaboration activities will be formally planned and executed whereas in other environments the collaboration activities may be much less structured and quite spontaneous. Regardless of the nature of the collaboration, it is important for the business analyst to consider the following aspects when planning a formal or informal collaboration with stakeholders:

- The timing and frequency of the collaboration
- The location
- The available tools to be used for collaborations
- Will the collaboration be virtual or in person?
- What type of collaboration do the stakeholders themselves prefer?

You can also document the collaboration plan for your project in the format of a stakeholder collaboration plan.

Element 3: Stakeholder communication needs

The last element of this task is about considering the communication plan for this engagement. Specifically, considering aspects such as what messages need to be communicated and what the delivery methods will be—email, verbal meetings, or presentations, for example. You also need to determine who to communicate with, when to communicate, and how frequently to communicate. The geographic location, level of detail, and level of formality are all considerations when putting together a communication plan.

It is vital to realize that every stakeholder on your list will not require the same communications and so you should categorize your stakeholders and determine in your stakeholder communication plan who will receive which communications when.

The inputs and outputs of this task

With the Plan Stakeholder Engagement Business Analysis Planning and Monitoring task, there are the following key inputs and outputs:

Inputs: The needs and business analysis approach

Outputs: The stakeholder engagement approach

In the next task, we will discuss what forms an integral part of the Business Analysis Planning and Monitoring knowledge area, which is the Plan Business Analysis Governance task.

Task: Plan Business Analysis Governance

According to the BABOK® v3 Guide, the purpose of Plan Business Analysis Governance is as follows:

> "*to define how decisions are made about requirements and designs, including reviews, change control, approvals and prioritization.*"

Planning what the processes are, who the decision-makers will be, and what information is required for effective decision-making around the requirement and design changes are very important in ensuring the governance business analysis activities run smoothly during the project.

Often in the real world, the planning of governance activities falls by the wayside and causes significant confusion and delay when it is time to approve requirements and designs. Change procedures are essential to facilitate the ever-changing nature of business needs, requirements, and ultimately, designs.

When planning the governance approach, the business analyst must give consideration of the following aspects and make sure to include them in their plans:

- What is the business analysis approach and how will work be prioritized?
- What is the change procedure? This entails consideration around who can ask for changes, who is involved in discussions and analysis of these changes, and ultimately, who is responsible for approving the changes?
- What type of documentation will be required for the changes?

So as you can see, most of the governance planning activities revolve around managing changes to business analysis information as it happens during the project.

The elements of Plan Business Analysis Governance

These are the four key elements to understand and include when you plan the business analysis governance. These elements are as follows:

- Decision-making
- Changing the control process
- Planning a prioritization approach
- Planning for approvals

We will cover each of the key elements of the Plan Business Analysis Governance task by considering its description and understanding each element with an example.

Element 1: Decision-making

Without effective decision-making practices in the project, there will be a lot of uncertainty created, which in turn causes stress and introduces unwelcome risks. Therefore, it is important to take the time to explicitly decide what the decision-making process is for the team, including understanding the escalation paths when a stakeholder collaboration cannot resolve or make a decision. It is also crucial that the roles and responsibilities of stakeholders are well understood in the context of decision-making processes.

Some example ways of facilitating effective decision-making could include the following:

- *A weekly decision-making project meeting where outstanding decisions are discussed and finalized. It is suggested to also document these decisions in a central decision register.*
- *Alternatively, a daily stand-up meeting could provide a time-slot or opportunity to clarify any new decisions that were made or highlight decisions that need to be made prior to being able to proceed. This provides the team with the opportunity to frequently mention the need for decision-making as well as the ability to confirm any decisions that have been made.*

Element 2: Changing the control process

Earlier, we mentioned that planning business analysis governance is predominantly carried out to ensure the effective management of changes to business analysis information during the project.

There are seven main things you must include when designing your change request processes. They are as follows:

1. Determine what steps must be followed by stakeholders to request a change.
2. What are the elements of the change request you want to analyze; for example, the change cost and time estimates, the benefits of implementing the change, the risks of not implementing the change, its priority, and what should be the next steps in relation to the specific change?
3. Determine how the changes you receive will be prioritized.
4. How will you document each change request?
5. Determine the communication method for updating stakeholders on new changes received and changes currently being considered, finalized, and included or excluded.
6. Determine who in the team will be performing the impact analysis for each change request.
7. Finally, the business analyst should define who can authorize any decisions made relating to the change requests received.

An example of a real-world change request process could be that as a business analyst, you will provide or help a stakeholder who wants to change the attributes used to capture a customer record to define what exactly the change is that they need. This could be done using a change request template. Once you understand what their change request is and you have it fully documented, you will involve other stakeholders to assist with impact analysis, cost and time estimates for the implementation of the change, risk analysis in terms of what it means if those attributes are not included, and so on. All of these change considerations will be included in a change control board meeting held on a weekly or fortnightly basis to discuss changes like this one. The change control board will typically then agree to prioritize the change request based on factors such as the benefits, risks, and effort to implement. The change request will then be approved and scheduled or it will be declined. As a business analyst, you will provide the necessary updates to the stakeholders who have raised the request in terms of the decisions that were made. You will typically communicate information including but not limited to the impact analysis, identified risks, cost and time to make the change, and any other specific determinations you may have learned about during the change request analysis.

The example change request process described here may not necessarily be complete and appropriate for all project types. However, something similar should always be in place for a project.

You will now also see that without having a change control process, it will become very difficult to manage the project's scope, requirements, and ultimately, you will not have much control over which requirements have been implemented, changed, or discarded.

Element 3: Planning a prioritization approach

In an ideal world, as business analysts, we would like to implement all the requirements so that we can delight all our stakeholders. However, this is not feasible and doesn't always make sense financially or operationally. It is therefore important to plan what the approach around prioritizing requirements on the project will be.

Common aspects to consider when planning a prioritization approach are the cost, risk, and value to the business. As part of the activity of planning the prioritization approach, you should also consider the stakeholders who will be part of the prioritization as well as decide on which techniques you will use during the prioritization activities.

Element 4: Planning for approvals

A good way to ensure efficient and effective requirements and to design artifact approvals is to plan for the approvals, the method, and the format that will be used and the people who will be required to approve them. It is important to consider the type of project you are involved in—for example, is the project very structured and governed by the organization or is the project being run very flexibly and quite informally? This will help you to determine what format and structure your approval processes should take.

In a very controlled or complex environment, it will most likely make sense to have a formal and well-defined approval process for the requirements and designs. However, in a more informal environment, a structured walkthrough showing example prototypes might be all you require in the form of approvals. It is, however, very important to confirm early in the project, while you are carrying out your business analysis planning and monitoring activities, what the most appropriate approval processes should be in your specific situation.

The inputs and outputs of this task

With the Plan Business Analysis Governance Business Analysis Planning and Monitoring task, there are the following key inputs and outputs:

Inputs: The business analysis approach and the stakeholder engagement approach

Outputs: The governance approach

The next task we will discuss that forms an integral part of the Business Analysis Planning and Monitoring knowledge area is Plan Business Analysis Information Management.

Task: Plan Business Analysis Information Management

According to the BABOK® v3 Guide, the purpose of Plan Business Analysis Information Management is as follows:

> *"to develop an approach for how business analysis information will be stored and accessed."*

Business analysis information includes all the different artifacts that are generated during the different business analysis activities in a project. Examples include everything from scope statements, models, and elicitation meeting notes to requirements documentation and designed prototypes! If you start listing all the different types of business analysis information types that could be generated by a team, it is easy to realize that a plan should be agreed early on in the project for managing, linking, and tracking all the different business analysis information types.

Ideally, as a business analyst, you should plan for aspects such as the level of detail of information and how the information should be organized, accessed, and stored. A business analyst should also plan for any relationships that might exist between information types and agree on any specific characteristics that you might want to maintain throughout the project for the business analysis information.

The elements of Plan Business Analysis Information Management

There are six key elements to understand and include when you perform the Plan Business Analysis Information Management task. These elements are as follows:

- The organization of business analysis information
- A level of abstraction
- Planning a traceability approach
- Planning for requirements reusability
- Storage and access
- Requirements attributes

We will now cover each of the key elements of the Plan Business Analysis Information Management task by considering its description and understanding each element with an example.

Element 1: The organization of business analysis information

Now that we had a look at some of the different types of business analysis information that exist, it would be easy to agree that the organization of all these types of business analysis information is important.

The earlier in the project you are able to start planning how you want to organize the information the better, simply because this means you will limit the chances of misplacing information, everyone on the team will know where to find information, and you will avoid unnecessary duplication of information.

It is, however, not always practical or realistic to know the best structure and process for organizing information from a very early stage in the project and so it is a good idea to start with a simple but robust enough organizational system to enhance and improve during those early stages of the project. You will then be in a good position to have an efficient and effective way of managing all the business analysis information when the project starts to mature and develop.

An example of a common approach when organizing business analysis information could be something like the following:

Create a document management repository with a file storage area (or folder) for the documentation for each main phase (or iteration) of the project. Then, have a sub-folder area for each main type of document. For example, there might be an area for all the analysis stage documents, which is sub-organized into "Elicitation Output," "Requirements," and "Project Meetings."

Element 2: The level of abstraction

This element is about considering the level of detail that is required when you describe the requirements to stakeholders. In some types of projects, the requirements may well be understood conceptually and the business analyst doesn't need to delve into a high level of detail when describing the requirements. However, it may also be that the stakeholder group really needs to review the requirements in a high level of detail to have comfort and confidence that the necessary complexities of the requirements have been documented and understood. Therefore, when planning the level of abstraction, the business analyst should consider the stakeholders' needs and plan for them accordingly.

An example of planning for a level of abstraction could be when you as the business analyst are working on a high profile, high risk, and complex area of the business and the stakeholders are concerned that they must demonstrate in-depth analysis and an understanding of the specific subject area prior to proceeding to the next stage of the project. In this type of project or environment, the business analyst should plan to manage the business analysis information in a way that allows for detailed analysis and design activities to take place.

Element 3: Planning a traceability approach

The traceability of requirements is all about being able to trace requirements in different ways and for different purposes. One of the most common reasons for tracing requirements is to be able to keep track of the requirement's status or progress during the life cycle of the project. This is because it is important to be able to validate at the end of a project whether a particular requirement was implemented or not by referring back to the requirement's life cycle during the project.

It can, however, in some environments or projects, happen that the value of knowing the exact life cycle of each and every detailed requirement is not high enough to justify the time and effort spent to keep track of it.

Let's look at an example. Let's say you are working on a project to implement a new train ticket booking system for a train that runs every hour between the beach and the main town. It is a council-based project, so the budget is tight and the project already knows which solution they will choose to implement because they have confidence that the neighboring town's trains are using their chosen booking system with great success. It is, therefore, fair to say that although you need to capture the requirements for the new train booking system, you probably don't need to spend too much time tracing every detailed requirement through to completion. You may only need to keep track of a few requirements that have been identified as being unique for this town's trains. However, if you are the business analyst working on a project to implement a new mortgage calculation solution for a bank, you would not only choose to define requirements to a high level of detail but due to the high profile and high risk of missing a requirement during the design and build phases, you would also be tracing every requirement through the project's life cycle to avoid missing any critical requirements and as a result, you increase the chances of a successful implementation.

So, you need to weigh up the risks, complexities, and expectations of your stakeholders when deciding what your traceability approach will be.

Element 4: Planning for requirements' reuse

Some types of requirements lend to being reused in future business analysis projects and other requirements are too specific to the current project to be considered for reuse. The most common types of requirements that can in some cases be reused include requirements such as the following:

- Regulatory requirements
- Contractual requirements
- Quality standards
- Service-level agreements
- Some types of business rules and business processes
- Requirements describing a cross-functional product or service that applies to many different areas within the business

So, it is a good idea to try and plan ahead in terms of which of your requirements can be reused by other projects and by doing so, ensure that the requirements are stored and accessible by people needing it in the future.

Element 5: Storage and access

When the business analyst considers the elements of storage and access, they should consider the business analysis approach, the tools and storage facilities available within the organization, and any specific notations or artifacts planned that may have special access requirements. Ideally, the storage that is planned for should allow users to edit and change business analysis information and be accessible over a period of time.

An example storage tool could be a SharePoint site or a similar document management tool. This is a common storage place for business analysis information on projects in many organizations. It is, however, recommended that the business analysis team have access rights that will enable them to plan and organize how they would prefer to store and access the information during the project.

Element 6: Requirements attributes

Requirements attributes provide information about the requirements and help in the ongoing management of the requirements throughout the change.

The most commonly used requirements attributes are as follows:

- An absolute reference: This is the unique identifier. This identifier is completely unique to this requirement and never changed or reused, even if the original requirement is deleted.
- The author of the requirement is the person who formulated the requirement and also the person who should be contacted regarding ambiguity, something being unclear, or if there is a conflict relating to the requirement.
- The complexity indicates how difficult it will be to implement the requirement.
- The ownership refers to the stakeholder or stakeholder group that will be the business owner of the requirement once the solution is implemented.
- The priority refers to the relative importance of the requirement. This can indicate the value or sequence of implementation.
- Risks identify uncertain events that may impact the requirement.
- The source indicates where the requirement comes from. This could be from a specific stakeholder or group of stakeholders or it can be from an existing system.
- The stability shows how mature the requirement is. In other words, how likely the requirement is to change.
- The status shows whether the requirement is proposed, accepted, verified, postponed, canceled, or implemented.
- The urgency is the attribute that shows how soon the requirement is needed.

The inputs and outputs of this task

With the Plan Business Analysis Information Management Business Analysis Planning and Monitoring task, there are the following key inputs and outputs:

Inputs: The business analysis approach, the governance approach, and the stakeholder engagement approach

Outputs: The information management approach

Task: Identify Business Analysis Performance Improvements

According to the BABOK® v3 Guide, the purpose of Identify Business Analysis Performance Improvements is as follows:

"to assess business analysis work and to plan to improve processes where required."

As we gain more experience in our roles as business analysts, we will naturally also learn how to perform better in the same situations we may have been unsure about in a previous role. However, by formally identifying ways to monitor and improve performance on a project, it is necessary to identify, more specifically, performance measures and perform analysis using those measures in order to be able to then report on the business analysis performance results. Ultimately, as a business analyst or a business analysis team, it should always be our goal to identify actions we can take to correct, prevent, or improve upon our work.

The elements of Identify Business Analysis Performance Improvements

There are four key elements to understand and include when you perform the Identify Business Analysis Performance Improvements task These elements are as follows:

- Performance analysis
- Assessment measures
- Analyzing results
- Recommending actions for improvement

Let's now consider each element in more detail and learn about them with a practical example.

Element 1: Performance analysis

Every project or environment has its own expectations of what constitutes good quality business analysis work or performance. This could range from formal reviews and reports generated to informal verbal feedback to individuals or the team.

An example of performance analysis could be that every business analyst on the team provides peer-level review feedback on the business analysis artifacts. This simple procedure will increase the overall performance of each individual and thereby the overall team, simply because you introduced informal accountability measures in the form of peer reviews.

Element 2: Assessment measures

Different types of assessment measures can be applied to determine the quality of the performance of business analysis within a project or environment. Just as with any measure, there are tangible and intangible ways that performance can be measured. It is not always very easy to identify true quantitative measures in terms of business analysis work outputs, but some ideas could include adhering to project time frames or the number of reviews required before being able to finalize specific artifacts. Some qualitative measures could include stakeholder feedback and general task efficiency levels on the project. Accuracy, completeness, knowledge as a business analyst, and effectiveness are some of the other intangible or qualitative measures that a team can implement to measure business analysis performance.

Element 3: Analyzing results

Once the assessment measures have been set and agreed for the business analysis function or team, they are then analyzed by involving the different stakeholders that can provide input to analyze each measure.

An example could simply be that the project manager provides feedback by assessing the business analysis team's performance in terms of delivery of artifacts against the agreed timelines set in the project plan. This is assuming that one of the assessment measures was agreed to be the timely delivery of business analysis artifacts.

Element 4: Recommended actions for improvement

Once all the assessment measures have been analyzed and the results have been gathered and understood, it is time to recommend some actions for improvement in the future. This could take the form of recommendations for the overall team and/or for the individual business analyst to which the feedback applies.

It is important to remember that measuring and assessing the performance of business analysis is generally very qualitative and it should, therefore, be carefully considered whether the results could possibly be subjective or biased in any way before providing the feedback to a team or an individual.

The recommended actions will typically be preventative, corrective, or improvement-focused in nature.

The inputs and outputs of this task

With the Identify Business Analysis Performance Improvements Business Analysis Planning and Monitoring task, there are the following key inputs and outputs:

Inputs: The business analysis approach and performance objectives (external)

Outputs: The business analysis performance assessment

We have now discussed each task in the Business Analysis Planning and Monitoring knowledge area. In the next section, we will cover a summary of the key things we have learned.

Summary

In this chapter, you learned about the Business Analysis Planning and Monitoring knowledge area.

The following are the key concepts and tasks we covered in this chapter:

- The Business Analysis Planning and Monitoring knowledge area
- The Plan Business Analysis Approach task
- The Plan Stakeholder Engagement task
- The Plan Business Analysis Governance task
- The Plan Business Analysis Information Management task
- The Identify Business Analysis Performance Improvements task

Make sure you revise these key areas before completing the knowledge quiz at the end of this chapter.

The Business Analysis Planning and Monitoring knowledge area

You now have a holistic understanding of the importance and purpose of the Business Analysis Planning and Monitoring knowledge area in terms of the role it plays in defining, planning, and completing the business analysis work you do. You are able to describe this knowledge area in the context of the BACCM using real-world practical situations. You are also able to visualize the key inputs and outputs to perform this task effectively.

The Plan Business Analysis Approach task

In this chapter, you learned about the task of planning a business analysis approach and you are now able to describe the purpose of this task and describe the key elements that need to be considered when performing this task, using real-world scenarios and concepts. You are also able to visualize the key inputs and outputs to perform this task effectively.

The Plan Stakeholder Engagement task

In this chapter, you learned about the task of planning stakeholder engagement and you are now able to describe the purpose of this task and describe the key elements that need to be considered when doing this task, using real-world scenarios and concepts. You are also able to visualize the key inputs and outputs to perform this task effectively.

The Plan Business Analysis Governance task

Another key learning from this chapter is your understanding and ability to describe the task of planning business analysis governance in terms of its purpose and you are able to describe the key elements that need to be considered when performing this task, using real-world scenarios and concepts. You are also able to visualize the key inputs and outputs to perform this task effectively.

The Plan Business Analysis Information Management task

In this chapter, you learned about the task of planning business analysis information management and you are now able to describe the purpose of this task and describe the key elements that need to be considered when carrying out this task, using real-world scenarios and concepts. You are also able to visualize the key inputs and outputs to perform this task effectively.

The Identify Business Analysis Performance Improvements task

In this chapter, you learned about the task of identifying business analysis performance improvements and you are now able to describe the purpose of this task and describe the key elements that need to be considered when doing this task using real-world scenarios and concepts. You are also able to visualize the key inputs and outputs to perform this task effectively.

Knowledge quiz

Consider the following real-world scenario and complete the micro mock exam based on this chapter.

Case study: The GO technology payment program

You have been assigned as the lead business analyst on a new program of work with the European Bank Corporation in London. It is very exciting to be part of this program because it is a very high profile and the senior stakeholders in the bank are closely involved. The objective of the program is to implement a mobile technology payment solution to enable customers to use their mobile devices to pay for goods and services in retail outlets. It is a brand new technology that has not been implemented anywhere in the world in quite the way that is planned with this program. Your role is to work on the business analysis approach for the program, including a comprehensive stakeholder analysis, work activities, and estimates around business analysis resourcing.

It promises to be a complex piece of work for you and your team overall and you should plan the team's business analysis activities accordingly. The project manager has set up a meeting with you to discuss the business analysis work activities and your thoughts about how best to manage team performance. He also wants to understand your views on whether this project should be a predictive or adaptive approach and how this will impact your business analysis approach. You have learned that the stakeholders you have to involve are geographically dispersed but they are used to convening in virtual meeting setups. Because this project is of such high importance to the bank, it is expected that you follow the correct procedures and approval processes throughout the project. You are also expected to manage any changes very efficiently and so there may be situations where you would need to be flexible in your approach.

Question 1

Using the provided case study, and considering the need for you as the lead business analyst to plan the business analysis approach for the project, which one of the following should you include as a key input in your planning activities?

    A. A stakeholder list

    B. The systems used

    C. The needs

    D. Performance measures

Question 2

Using the provided case study and the following additional information you obtained from the project manager, choose which approach you believe he is in favor of.

They said to you "In all my years at the bank, the project methodology has always been a waterfall methodology and I think it will be too risky to change the methodology for this high profile project."

    A. A reactive approach

    B. A proactive approach

    C. A change-driven approach

    D. A plan-driven approach

Question 3

Considering the nature of the project described in the case study, what level of detail in the business analysis documentation would you suggest is the most appropriate, considering the complexity, uncertainty, and risk associated with this project?

A. A high level of detail will likely be appropriate.

B. A minimum level of detail will likely be appropriate.

C. A conceptual level of detail will likely be appropriate.

D. A low level of detail will likely be appropriate.

Question 4

Using the provided case study, is the following statement a reasonable assessment of the stakeholder engagement level that should be implemented as part of the business analysis approach?

"The primary stakeholders are not physically available at our geographical location and they are very busy at this time of year, so due to these reasons, we will only send them an email every month to let them know how we are progressing with this project."

Choose whether this is an acceptable or unacceptable approach to stakeholder engagement:

A. Unacceptable for a project of this nature

B. Acceptable for a project of this nature

Question 5

Using the provided case study and planning the change control process to document as part of the business analysis planning activities, which of the following would be relevant factors for you to consider?

Choose the correct option:

A. The willingness of team members to help write up change requests

B. The level of change fatigue in the group

C. The process for requesting changes

D. The technology solution the project chooses to implement

Question 6

Using the provided case study, would you say that the stakeholders mentioned as part of your program would be able to influence and steer decision-making and change facilitation for the program?

Choose whether you believe there are stakeholders of influence assigned to the program:

1. A
2. B

Question 7

When you define the business analysis information management for the project, which of the following are some of the attributes you should include when planning what information to capture for each requirement?

A. The absolute reference, author, complexity, ownership, priority, and risks

B. The absolute reference, author, category, ownership, priority, and risks

C. The absolute reference, author, category, ownership, priority, and role

D. The absolute reference, author, complexity, trace code, priority, and risks

Question 8

Using the provided case study and after having another conversation with the project manager about the business analysis activities for the project, you discovered that the project manager is very serious about adhering to the timeline for this project. He made it very clear that the business analysis team will have to perform well against the project's planned timelines due to the high profile nature of the project. Considering this conversation, which one of the following assessment measures would be most important to include when you define the content for the business analysis performance assessment?

Select the correct answer from these options:

A. Adherence to the change control procedures

B. The number of revisions needed to finalize a deliverable

C. Adherence to project timelines

D. Meeting stakeholder expectations for delivery

Question 9

Using the provided case study, when you are starting to plan the most appropriate stakeholder collaboration approach, which one of the following options would be the most important consideration to include in your plans?

Select the correct answer from the choices:

A. The content of collaboration

B. The location and available collaboration tools

C. The preferences of stakeholders

D. The influence of stakeholders

Question 10

Using the provided case study, would you say that the nature of this project will have any impact on the business analysis approach for the project?

A. Yes, the nature of the project environment will impact the business analysis approach taken.

B. No, every business analysis approach is the same regardless of the project environment.

Question 11

The BABOK® v3 Guide defines some specific inputs for the Business Analysis Planning and Monitoring tasks. Which of the following options are inputs for the knowledge area's tasks?

Select the correct answer from the choices:

A. Performance objectives (external)

B. Performance objectives (internal)

C. A stakeholder list

D. A governance approach

Question 12

When the business analyst performs this task, they need to consider the overall goals of the initiative or change because it will affect their ability to align business analysis activities with the initiative.

Which BABOK® v3 Guide task are we referring to?

A. Plan Business Analysis Activities

B. Plan Business Analysis Resources

C. Plan Business Analysis Approach

D. Plan Business Analysis Goals

Question 13

What is meant by when it is said that the level of detail and formality of documentation is somewhat less of a focus when an adaptive approach is followed than when a predictive approach is followed?

A. The detail and documentation are less important when an adaptive approach is followed.

B. The detail and documentation are developed when needed and no earlier.

C. The detail and documentation are not required when an adaptive approach is followed because everything is agreed upon verbally.

D. Formal documentation is only required when a predictive approach is followed.

Question 14

Which of the following factors should be considered when assessing the risk level associated with the business analysis effort on a project?

Select all the correct options:

A. The experience of the business analysis team

B. The domain knowledge of the business analysis team

C. Stakeholder attitudes towards the business analysis effort

D. The cultural norms of the organization

Question 15

Which of the following techniques should be considered appropriate when trying to determine how long it will take to perform business analysis activities?

Select the most relevant technique from the following choices:

A. Scheduling

B. Workshops

C. Estimation

D. Brainstorming

Question 16

Which of the following techniques should be considered appropriate when reviewing existing organizational assets that might assist in planning the approach?

Select the most relevant technique from the following choices:

A. Document analysis

B. Reviews

C. Business cases

D. Interviews

Question 17

Which of the following techniques should be considered appropriate when assessing the level of power or influence a particular stakeholder or stakeholder group may have on the initiative?

Select the most relevant technique from the following choices:

A. The stakeholder list

B. The stakeholder matrix

C. The persona

D. Prioritization

Question 18

When the business analyst develops a change control process, which of the following attributes should be considered for inclusion as part of the definition of the change request?

Select all the correct choices:

    A. Benefits

    B. Risks

    C. Stakeholder influence

    D. Resource availability

Question 19

When a requirement is being described in terms of its stability, what exactly are we referring to in relation to that requirement?

Select the correct choice:

    A. Indicates the state of the requirement

    B. Indicates the completeness of the requirement

    C. Indicates the level of maturity of the requirement

    D. Indicates the likelihood for implementation of that requirement.

Question 20

Which task is described as the task to assess business analysis work and to plan to improve processes where required?

Select the correct choice:

    A. Identify Business Analysis Performance Improvements

    B. Manage Business Analysis Performance Indicators

    C. Identify Business Analysis Performance Measures

    D. Manage Business Analysis Performance Improvements

Answers

Questions	Answers
1	C
2	D
3	D
4	A
5	C
6	A
7	A
8	C
9	B
10	A
11	A
12	C
13	B
14	A, B, C, D
15	C
16	A
17	B
18	A, B
19	C
20	A

Elicitation and Collaboration 7

Elicitation and collaboration is a Knowledge Area that focuses on engaging with stakeholders at different levels and stages of the journey toward defining the business needs and requirements for any initiative.

By the end of this chapter, you will have learned about the tasks involved during the process of obtaining information from stakeholders and confirming the results of that information. This chapter also discusses the type of communication that must be performed as part of the elicitation activities. We'll dive into the detail of the BABOK® v3 guide tasks: Prepare for Elicitation, Conduct Elicitation, Confirm Elicitation Results, Communicate Business Analysis Information, and Manage Stakeholder Collaboration, and will bring them to life with practical real-world scenarios and examples. The following shows the workflow of this chapter:

- Purpose and context of this Knowledge Area
- Task: Prepare for Elicitation
- Task: Conduct Elicitation
- Task: Confirm Elicitation Results
- Task: Communicate Business Analysis Information
- Task: Manage Stakeholder Collaboration
- Real-world case study
- Test your knowledge

Topics and learning objectives for this chapter include the following:

- Understand the context of this BABOK® v3 guide Knowledge Area within a real-world scenario.
- Understand and apply the Prepare for Elicitation task to real-world scenarios.
- Understand and apply the Conduct Elicitation task to real-world scenarios.
- Understand and apply the Confirm Elicitation Results task to real-world scenarios.

- Understand and apply the Communicate Business Analysis Information task to real-world scenarios.
- Understand and apply the Manage Stakeholder Collaboration task to real-world scenarios.

Understanding elicitation and collaboration

The focus in elicitation and collaboration is on the preparation, conducting, and confirming the requirements elicited from business stakeholders and other information sources. This Knowledge Area also describes the best practices and considerations for communicating business analysis information and collaboration activities with stakeholders as shown in the following image:

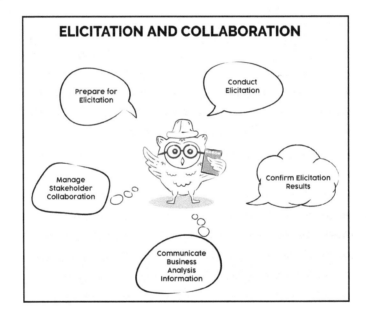

The Elicitation and Collaboration knowledge area and tasks

The Elicitation and Collaboration Knowledge Area includes the following tasks:

1. Prepare for elicitation.
2. Conduct elicitation.
3. Confirm elicitation.
4. Communication business analysis information.
5. Measure stakeholder collaboration.

These tasks focus on what is involved when the business analyst performs elicitation to uncover requirements and collaborates with stakeholders throughout the initiative they are assigned to.

 It is important to note that elicitation and collaboration is *not a phase* in the project or initiative, but rather an **ongoing and recurring** part of your role as a business analyst. Elicitation and collaboration is a **collaborative activity** and it may lead to further analysis and elicitation activities.

The objective of all elicitation and collaboration activities is to formulate a complete, relevant, and accurate set of defined business needs and requirements to use during the next stages of the initiative. The outputs of this Knowledge Area will become the basis for all other business analysis activities that you'll perform.

The Business Analysis Core Concept Model™

Here we consider how Elicitation and Collaboration as a Knowledge Area apply to the Business Analysis Core Concept Model ™ with an example.

The six core concepts that describe the Business Analysis Core Concept Model ™ are as follows:

- Change
- Need
- Solution
- Stakeholder
- Value
- Context

Let's take a look at these sections in more detail and explore how it can be related to the Elicitation and Collaboration Knowledge Area.

Change

This core concept refers to how change is explored with business stakeholders by utilizing elicitation techniques to identify change characteristics and any concerns that a stakeholder may have about the change.

Let's look at an example to bring this concept around change to life:

Let's say you have been assigned as a business analyst on a project where the goal is to merge two different general ledger software systems utilized by the company you are currently working for. The project is the result of a merger that happened two years ago, and since then the company has been running two general ledger systems with two different finance teams. This is causing a lot of duplication of effort and finance-related reporting errors.

In a real-life business analysis scenario, your role is to elicit the requirements for a single general ledger solution by running requirements elicitation workshops with the key stakeholders from both finance teams. You capture not only the main requirements, which must be met by the new general ledger solution but also the host of concerns raised by these stakeholders as a result of this change.

This example illustrates how the core concept of change is implemented in the Elicitation and Collaboration Knowledge Area.

Need

This core concept refers to how the business need evolves through the continuous elicitation, confirmation, and communication that happens as a result of business analysis elicitation activities.

Let's look at an example to bring this concept of need into the real world:

If we continue with the example of the merging of the two financial teams' different general ledger software, you will clearly relate to the elicitation of requirements during those workshops as a way of elaborating and clarifying the needs of the finance team stakeholders. Your main role during the elicitation activities is to understand the business needs.

This example clearly illustrates how the core concept of need is implemented during the Elicitation and Collaboration Knowledge Area by actively exploring the changes required through elicitation in order to meet the business need for a single general ledger solution.

Solution

This core concept refers to the characteristics that you identify for the new solution through elicitation, collaboration, and communication activities.

Let's look at an example to bring this concept of solution into the real world:

During all the elicitation and collaboration activities you perform with the finance teams, you are developing a clearer view of the characteristics required of a new solution for the company.

This example illustrates how the core concept of the solution is implemented during the Elicitation and Collaboration Knowledge Area with a focus on eliciting solution requirements, which will meet the business need.

Stakeholder

This core concept refers to how the stakeholder has a relationship with the need, the change, and the solution. Specifically, in the Knowledge Area of Elicitation and Collaboration, the concept of stakeholder is applied in terms of the collaboration with the stakeholders during the elicitation process.

Let's look at an example to bring this concept of the stakeholder into the real world:

If we continue with our previous example of the single general ledger software solution requirement, then it will be clear that without continuous stakeholder involvement and collaboration it will be hard to elicit requirements for the project.

Therefore, it is clear that stakeholders play a vital part in requirement elicitation and collaboration activities with a clear relationship to the solution, the need, and the change.

Value

This core concept refers to how the value, worth, or importance of something within a specific context is perceived by the stakeholder. When we look at the Knowledge Area of Elicitation and Collaboration, the concept of value is applied in terms of ensuring that the relative importance of the information provided during elicitation is confirmed and communicated using a variety of techniques.

Let's look at an example to bring this concept of value into the real world:

Let's say you have just completed a requirements elicitation interview with a key stakeholder. When you review and synthesize the information you received from the stakeholder you will be able to assess the relative value of that elicitation activity by either using that information to validate existing requirements you may already have or to use the information to inform any future requirements and elicitation meetings you might be scheduling.

Context

The final core concept refers to how the context or circumstances of a change has a direct impact on how we approach elicitation and collaboration-related business analysis activities. It is therefore very important to have an understanding and awareness of the context you are eliciting requirements from.

Let's look at an example to bring this concept of context into the real world:

The context described in the previous example of the two finance teams coming together suggests that there will be a lot of general ledger-related information and procedures already in existence within each team. This suggests that you may be able to approach the requirements elicitation and collaboration activities from a requirements validation perspective (using the pre-existing information) rather than running elicitation workshops based on there being no existing information to reference.

In this example, the context provides some direction to you as a business analyst in terms of how to plan and execute the elicitation and collaboration activities.

Task: Prepare for Elicitation

Elicitation and collaboration can be planned, unplanned, or both. Planned activities such as workshops, experiments, and/or surveys can be structured and organized in advance. Unplanned activities happen at the moment without notice, such as last-minute or just-in-time collaborations or conversations.

In this section, we'll look at the planned elicitation and collaboration activities and discuss all the key considerations for when you prepare to conduct elicitation sessions or engagements. Elicitation and collaboration is a fundamental business analysis activity and should be treated with care and thorough preparation and planning. We will discuss aspects such as the most appropriate elicitation approach, what to consider when choosing techniques, logistical aspects, and stakeholder engagement.

Purpose

According to the BABOK® v3 guide, the purpose of the task: Prepare for Elicitation is as follows:

> *"to understand the scope of the elicitation activity, select appropriate techniques, and plan for (or procure) appropriate supporting materials and resources."*

When business analysts start the activity of preparing for an elicitation session, they will consider what the key outcomes of the session or sessions should be, who should be involved in all the elicitation activities, and what the overall goals of the initiative are.

The definition of the goals of the elicitation includes defining the deliverables that should be produced as a result of the elicitation as well as considering and preparing any logistical aspects and materials needed for each session, and gaining a good understanding and interpretation of the circumstances surrounding the elicitation activities.

Example of preparing for elicitation

Consider the example of being a business analyst responsible for preparing for the elicitation of requirements for a new Offender Management System. Your goal with the elicitation meeting is to understand the main problems faced by prison wardens who are responsible for capturing offender progress details during their term of imprisonment. Because the prison wardens work in shifts, it is not practical to have them all attend a requirements workshop, so you decide to combine the techniques of sending a survey to them with a scheduled follow-up in a one-on-one elicitation interview to suit their shift timetable. You also want to demonstrate to these stakeholders that you understand the fundamentals of the main challenges they face within their roles and therefore you decide to prepare some models to show the prisoner journey pictorially.

So with this example, you can already identify different aspects, such as the goal of the elicitation, availability of stakeholders, preparation materials needed, and appropriate elicitation techniques as some of the considerations when starting to prepare for elicitation activities on your project.

Elements

When you prepare for Elicitation and Collaboration as a business analyst, there are certain activities and considerations to incorporate to ensure a successful elicitation result. These are referred to as the key elements for this task.

These are the five key elements when you prepare for elicitation:

- Understand the scope of elicitation.
- Select elicitation technique.
- Set up logistics.
- Secure supporting material.
- Prepare stakeholders.

Element 1: Understand the scope of elicitation

There are a number of different aspects that the business analyst should consider when preparing for the elicitation session. Considering these aspects will assist the business analyst in understanding what type of business analysis information will be discovered during the elicitation and will also assist in the process of deciding which elicitation techniques to apply.

The most important aspects to consider include the following:

- The business domain
- Overall culture and environment
- Stakeholder locations
- Stakeholders who are involved and their group dynamics
- Expected outputs the elicitation activities will contribute to
- Skills of the business analysis practitioner
- Other elicitation activities planned to complement this one
- A strategy or solution approach
- Scope of future solution
- Possible sources of business analysis information that might contribute to the current elicitation activity

The larger the number of stakeholders involved in the stakeholder elicitation activities, the more time should be spent to prepare for the session following a formal and structured approach. This includes pre-session materials/information emails, agendas, and elicitation techniques that can be effectively executed with larger groups.

Example of understanding the scope of elicitation

An example of these aspects you need to consider could be in the insurance domain, where the culture is formal and procedural. Most insurance brokers you have to elicit requirements from are based in the head office in Sydney. They know each other and work together closely on a daily basis. As the business analyst, you are well versed in running elicitation workshops and because you have been working for some time on this insurance project you have a lot of existing business analysis process models that you can utilize during the detailed elicitation activities you are preparing for.

In this example, you can clearly identify considerations around the scope of the elicitation activity.

Element 2: Select elicitation techniques

It is important to realize that with any elicitation activity, it is very likely that the business analyst will apply multiple elicitation techniques. It often depends on factors such as the constraints that might exist around cost and time, what information is available to the business analyst, the culture of the organization, and of course the planned ideal outcomes of the elicitation sessions themselves. It is also key for the business analyst to consider factors such as the needs of the stakeholders who are involved, their availability, and their geographical location.

Another aspect of being effective in preparation for the elicitation activities is to research and understand which elicitation techniques have been used successfully by the organization in the past, and if possible, to re-use those techniques again, providing they are suitable for the current situation and elicitation goals.

Another key reason why it is a good idea to conform to a known elicitation method or technique is simply that stakeholders would already understand the format and what is expected of them, and would be able to hit the ground running.

Example of selecting an elicitation technique

Let's consider an example of these considerations by looking back at our insurance project mentioned earlier. You know that the stakeholders you need to elicit requirements from are all used to participating in requirements workshops and that this technique is often utilized on projects in this environment. Because of this, you choose to plan for a series of requirements workshops instead of surveys or one-on-one requirements interviews. People are busy too, which makes it much more suitable to have a couple of short workshops during the quieter times of the insurance monthly processing cycles. You have done a lot of elicitation workshops before and therefore are personally also very familiar with the preparation you need to do as well as how to facilitate the workshop to get the best elicitation results.

In this example, you are considering the culture, what people are used to, your own professional skills and abilities, and people's location and availability.

Element 3: Set up logistics

A key step in preparing for elicitation is to ensure that the logistics of the session or series of sessions are well planned for by considering the following key aspects:

- The goals of the session.
- Who are the participants and what are their roles?
- Scheduled resources including people, rooms, and tools such as flip charts.
- Locations and communication channels.
- Techniques that will be used.
- Languages used by the stakeholders specifically being prepared to understand subject matter terminology and key abbreviations.

 Remember that for a formal elicitation activity, the business analyst should prepare and share an agenda with all the elicitation participants well in advance of the session.

When you prepare for the elicitation session and you have considered all these key aspects about logistics, it is always good to ensure you have confirmed and agreed with your approach and decisions with the rest of the business analysis and project team. This way you have everyone on board with the logistical arrangements and this often yields some new ideas that you might not have thought about.

Element 4: Secure supporting material

As part of the preparation activities for the elicitation session, the business analyst needs to make sure to collate, prepare, and understand the information that exists prior to the session. The information can come from people, systems, historical data, materials, and other documents. Documents can include any type of relevant documentation that can help support the goals of the elicitation activities.

For example, the business analyst may produce end-to-end draft business process models to take to the workshop for validation by stakeholders.

Element 5: Prepare stakeholders

There may be a need for the business analyst to explain to the business stakeholders how an elicitation activity works prior to conducting the session. It may also be required by the business analyst that stakeholders prepare specific information for the elicitation session itself.

A good practice is to ensure that the stakeholders clearly understand the purpose of the planned elicitation session and what the benefits are. This will help ensure that all stakeholders attend and come with a motivated attitude to participate actively. When stakeholders understand the goals and expectations well before the elicitation session, the session will have a much better chance of yielding high-quality requirements, so it is well worth the effort to engage stakeholders in this way before the elicitation session is conducted.

Continuing the previous example:

If you are unsure whether your insurance project's stakeholders are prepared and comfortable with what you are planning in terms of the elicitation workshops, it would be a good idea to send out a detailed agenda and make personal contact with individuals to discuss and share information of the planned elicitation activity. This way people will be more prepared and feel included, if not also positive about what you are planning.

Inputs and outputs

With the Elicitation and Collaboration task: Prepare for elicitation, there are the following key inputs and outputs:

- **Inputs**: Needs and stakeholder engagement approach
- **Output**: Elicitation activity plan

Now that you have learned about the preparation activities, elements, and the key inputs and outputs, you are ready to learn about what is involved in the task of conducting the elicitation session.

Task: Conduct Elicitation

The second task of the Elicitation and Collaboration Knowledge Area is: Conduct Elicitation. This task describes the execution of elicitation sessions as it was planned and is now performed by the business analyst.

There are a number of different ways of conducting elicitation with stakeholders and in most cases, the business analyst will use a combination of different approaches, techniques, and styles to obtain and complete the elicitation activities. In this section, we discuss the primary categories of how elicitation can be conducted and we discuss the role of the business analyst during the elicitation session itself.

Let's start by considering the purpose of the task of conducting elicitation and the types of elicitation the business analyst can perform.

Purpose

According to the BABOK® v3 guide, the purpose of the task: Conduct Elicitation, is as follows:

"to draw out, explore, and identify information relevant to the change."

Types of elicitation

The BABOK® v3 guide has identified three common types of elicitation:

- Collaborative
- Research
- Experiments

Let's see what they mean in the following sections.

Collaborative

Collaborative is when the elicitation involves direct interaction with stakeholders, and the elicitation activity relies on the stakeholders' experiences, skills, and general judgment within their subject area.

Research

This involves systematically analyzing and reviewing information that was obtained from materials or sources other than the direct conversations with stakeholders involved in the change. This type of elicitation can still involve stakeholders and can also include data analysis of historical data to identify trends.

Experiments

Experiments are a way for business analysts to discover new information that can only be obtained by performing a controlled test or study. Experiments help discover information that is required and not readily available from stakeholder engagement or document analysis.

Examples of different elicitation types

To bring these different types of elicitation into real-life practical scenarios, consider these examples:

Scenario 1: When you run a requirements workshop with a number of stakeholders you invited to elaborate on requirements for a new customer records system, you are utilizing the collaborative elicitation type.

Scenario 2: When you review the policy or legislative documentation to understand the new payment laws as part of defining requirements for a payment gateway solution, you are utilizing the research elicitation type.

Scenario 3: When you prepare multiple prototypes for a new screen layout and ask a random number of people to vote for their favorite screen layout, you are performing an experimental elicitation type.

Elements

These are the two key elements to consider when performing the task: Conduct Elicitation:

- Guide elicitation activity.
- Capture elicitation outcomes.

Let's take a look at these elements in the following sections and explore what the business analyst should do, include, and consider when applying the task of conducting an elicitation session.

Element 1: Guide elicitation activity

During the elicitation session, it is important for the business analyst to understand the proposed representations of business analysis information (prepared during the preparation task) so that the elicitation session can be guided toward the anticipated results for the session at the relevant level of detail.

To help guide and facilitate these planned outcomes/results, business analysts consider the following:

- The elicitation activity goals and agenda.
- The scope of the change (and of the session).
- What forms of output the activity will generate.
- What other representations, the activity results will support.
- How the output fits into what is already known.
- Who provides the information?
- Who will use the information?
- How will the information be used?

It is the role of the business analyst to ensure that the elicitation session is executed in a way that is goal-oriented and produces the desired results as was planned for during the preparation task.

Although it is recommended that the business analyst keeps a close eye on the goals and planned results for the session, it is worth remembering that the stakeholder engagement and relationships are also very important and hence the business analyst should remain flexible in their approach and means of achieving the elicitation goals and results.

Example of guiding the elicitation activity

An example could be when you are conducting your elicitation workshop with a clear agenda of validating the end-to-end business process for making an insurance claim. During the workshop some of the stakeholders start to discuss the non-functional aspects of a potential software package they are hoping will be chosen as the new solution. This line of conversation is not only hypothetical at this stage of the project but also completely out of scope for what was planned for your elicitation workshop. Although you would always like to encourage communication and ideas generated during your elicitation workshops, it would be your role to steer the conversation back to the agreed agenda to ensure you achieve the elicitation activity goals.

Element 2 – Capture elicitation outcomes

Although the conducting of elicitation is frequently iterative and takes place in a series of sessions, it is imperative to capture the elicitation outcomes in a well-organized and succinct fashion. If the elicitation activity happens in an ad hoc or unplanned way, the conversations and decisions or outcomes must also be documented and integrated into the planned outcomes.

When a business analyst consistently captures all elicitation outcomes in a formal and comprehensive manner, it builds confidence in the business stakeholders' view of how the information they have provided the business analyst is being valued and used.

Inputs and outputs

With the Elicitation and Collaboration task: Conduct Elicitation, there are the following key inputs and outputs:

Inputs: Elicitation activity plan

Outputs: Elicitation results (unconfirmed)

 The output here is unconfirmed elicitation results because the business analyst has not reviewed and confirmed that what they captured during the elicitation session is, in fact, correct and complete.

Now that we have conducted an elicitation session, there is the task of confirming that the elicitation results the business analysis team has captured are in fact accurate and complete. The next task we discuss is confirming the elicitation results.

Task: Confirm Elicitation Results

The third task of the Elicitation and Collaboration Knowledge Area is Confirm Elicitation Results. This describes the tasks of checking that the information gathered during an elicitation session is accurate, complete, and consistent with any other or previously documented elicitation results.

During this section, we will discuss the purpose and scope of this task at this stage of the requirements definition process. It is important to note that during this stage you have prepared and conducted the elicitation session and you are now ready to confirm with stakeholders, peers, and any existing sources of information that the results you obtained during the elicitation session(s) are accurate, complete and consistent with other sources of elicitation results and information.

Purpose

According to the BABOK® v3 guide, the purpose of Confirm Elicitation Results is as follows:

"to check the information gathered during an elicitation session for accuracy and consistency with other information."

The primary reason the business analyst should always check the information that was obtained during an elicitation session is to uncover any errors, conflicting information, any missing information, and potential ambiguities that might need to be clarified with stakeholders.

The business analyst should compare the elicitation results against any existing information and/or the results of similar sessions to ensure the information is consistent. It might be required for the business analyst to engage stakeholders to clarify or confirm that their information was correctly captured during the elicitation session. Depending on how accurate the information is, it might be required to plan additional elicitation sessions to elaborate or clarify any misinformation or discrepancies with stakeholders. It is however recommended to try to avoid unnecessary repeats of similar conversations or elicitation sessions to prevent stakeholders from losing confidence in the business analysis team's capabilities during elicitation itself.

It is worth noting that this task of confirming the elicitation results is much less rigorous and more of an informal review than what occurs during the analysis stages of business analysis work.

Example of confirming elicitation results

In a practical example, you might simply compile all the elicitation results into a formatted document, which is then circulated back to the stakeholder group who participated during the elicitation workshop you facilitated. You then invite everyone to review the provided information with a view to ensure it is accurate and captures the scope of what was agreed during the elicitation activity itself. As a business analyst, you should make sure to follow up with any stakeholder who requires changes or corrections to ensure you maintain a strong and trusted relationship for future elicitation activities.

Elements

These are the two key elements when you carry out the Confirm Elicitation Results task:

- Compare elicitation results against source information.
- Compare elicitation results against other elicitation results.

We will describe the key elements of the task: Confirm Elicitation Results and understand each one with an example.

Element 1: Compare elicitation results against source information

This element describes how the business analyst performs follow-up meetings or reviews and compares elicitation results against what stakeholders provided during the elicitation sessions to correct or update any elicitation results that may not be fully accurate or complete. It may also happen that the stakeholders confirm elicitation results independently from the business analyst's follow-ups.

Example of comparing elicitation results against source information

An example could be when, as the business analyst who conducted the elicitation workshop recently, you decide the most time-efficient way to confirm elicitation results would be to organize a short follow-up workshop. During this session you present the updated end-to-end business process models originally presented during the elicitation session, to confirm accuracy and completeness.

Element 2: Compare elicitation results against other elicitation results

This element describes the further activity of comparing the elicitation results from elicitation sessions against any source information or alternative elicitation results that may exist. Where variations in results are identified, it is the business analyst's role to resolve these variations by working in collaboration with stakeholders. If historical data or other reliable information exists, the business analyst can also use that to remove any variations identified.

 It is a good idea to collaborate during an elicitation session with stakeholders to help build these models to help avoid variations or omissions early on in the elicitation activities.

In many cases, inconsistencies in elicitation results are uncovered when business analysts develop specifications and/or models.

Inputs and outputs

With the Elicitation and Collaboration task: Confirm Elicitation Results, there are the following key inputs and outputs:

Inputs: Elicitation results (unconfirmed)

Outputs: Elicitation results (confirmed)

Note: Now that you performed the task of confirming the elicitation results, a key output of this task is elicitation results with a status of being confirmed.

As a result of this task, you are now in a position to communicate the business analysis information, specifically relating to the elicitation results you have defined with your business and other stakeholder groups. During the next section, we discuss the task of communicating business analysis information with stakeholders.

Task: Communicate Business Analysis Information

The fourth task of the Elicitation and Collaboration Knowledge Area is to Communicate Business Analysis Information. This task describes the activities a business analyst performs when communicating the business analysis information gathered during elicitation sessions to business and technology stakeholders.

During this section, we discuss the key considerations when the business analyst formulates the business analysis information into a package that is suitable, relevant, and effective for presenting to stakeholders. We also discuss the importance of understanding your stakeholder audience and their preferences as well as the need to have clear objectives when preparing the business analysis information for stakeholders.

Purpose

According to the BABOK® v3 guide, the purpose of the task: Communicate Business Analysis Information is as follows:

"to ensure stakeholders have a shared understanding of business analysis information."

A key success factor in effectively managing business analysis information is that the information is communicated at the right time and in formats digestible and relevant to the intended stakeholder audience. It is therefore also important that the business analyst pays attention to the tone, style, and language used when deciding to communicate business analysis information to a particular stakeholder audience.

 Always consider the perspective of the audience that you are communicating business analysis information to. For example: If you are communicating business analysis information to a senior or executive audience, include visual representations and key summaries that highlight the main points that need to be conveyed.

When the business analyst communicates information to stakeholders, it is important to understand that this process is iterative and interactive, meaning the information and feedback flows between the business analysts and the stakeholders in a two-way communication format. The business analyst should, therefore, be clear about the audience that business analysis information is being shared with, and be equally clear on the content, purpose, context, and what the business analyst is expecting to receive as a result of the business analysis information sharing.

It is important to remember that it might be required for the business analyst to distill information in multiple ways to cater to different audience communication styles. It is also important that the business analyst works with stakeholders to ensure that they provide their agreement that the information is accurate and relevant to the purpose of what the delivery is working toward.

Example of communicating business analysis information

In a practical example, you will have a set of draft requirements that you elicited from a group of stakeholders during your recent requirements workshop. As a first step of communicating your findings, you may send out an email with the draft requirements available for review. You know that some of your stakeholders don't really respond to or read detailed emails and therefore decide to follow up the message with an invitation for a short meeting to walk them through the details of the requirements.

By providing the stakeholders with these two different opportunities to review and understand your requirements, you are optimizing communication with your stakeholder audience.

Elements

These are the two key elements when you move to the Communicate Business Analysis Information task:

- Determine objectives and the format of communication.
- Communicate the business analysis package.

We will describe the key elements of the Communicate Business Analysis Information task and understand each with an example.

Element 1: Determine objectives and format of communication

Business analysis information is often developed and shared as a business analysis package. The business analysis package is used as a communication vehicle for requirements and other business analysis information. The information package may be prepared for a variety of different reasons, including the following:

- Communication of requirements and designs to stakeholders
- Early assessment of quality and planning

- Evaluation of possible alternatives
- Formal reviews and approvals
- Inputs to solution design
- Conformance to contractual and regulatory obligations
- Maintenance for reuse

As we mentioned before, it is important to pay attention to different aspects of the audience, purpose, content, context and expected outcomes in order to deliver an effective business analysis package. The following types of questions should be answered during the preparation of the business analysis package:

- Who is the audience of the package?
- What will each type of stakeholder understand and need from the communication?
- What is each stakeholder's preferred style of communication or learning?
- What information is important to communicate?
- Are the presentation and format of the package, and the information contained in the package, appropriate for the type of audience?
- How does the package support other activities?
- Are there any regulatory or contractual constraints to conform to?

Formats of packages

- **Formal documentation**

  The most common format for business analysis information packages is when an organization follows a predefined template that contains text, matrices, and/or diagrams and visual models. Formal documentation provides the organization with a referenceable, long-term record of the business analysis information.

- **Informal documentation**

  The other format that business analysis information can sometimes take is the less formal documentation consisting of text, diagrams, or matrices developed during the initiative or change, but which doesn't form part of the formal documentation process or templates used by the organization.

- **Presentations**

  These deliver high-level overviews are appropriate for understanding the goals of a change, the functions of a solution, or information to support decision-making.

  The final format that is often used to convey business analysis information at a more summarized level to describe the key points of concepts of a change, functions that are in scope, or information pertaining to decision-making efforts is a presentation.

  The business analyst should consider what is the best combination to present materials so that an effective and well-considered message is communicated. Packages can be stored in different online or offline repositories, including documents or tools.

Element 2: Communicate the business analysis package

The main aim of communicating the business analysis package of information is to provide stakeholders with the relevant information pertaining to the change or initiative at a level that enables them to have a good understanding of what is being described. Often the stakeholders will get the opportunity to review and ask questions about the business analysis information package and raise any issues or concerns that they may identify.

There are different options available to the business analyst when it comes to choosing the appropriate communication method or platform. Some of the more common communication platforms have been identified as follows:

- Group collaboration
- Individual collaboration
- Email or other non-verbal methods

Example of communicating business analysis packages:

*You are assigned to a **Human Resources** (**HR**) project, which has the goal of implementing a cloud-based system to manage all employees' performance and personal record data. As the business analyst, you have done your first round of requirements interviews and have compiled the first version of the stakeholder requirements for this initiative. You now need to make sure that the first draft is complete, accurate, and a true reflection of the requirements raised by all of the HR stakeholders.*

You decide that, because stakeholders are geographically dispersed, you will communicate these requirements using the following three methods:

- *You will invite all stakeholders to attend a presentation-format virtual webcast to receive a summary of all the requirements you have compiled.*
- *You will also send all of the detailed requirements in the format of a formal template document for stakeholders to do a detailed review.*
- *Thirdly, you decide to invite stakeholders to communicate any feedback they may have back to you via email or by simply having an informal conversation.*

By using multiple formats to communicate your requirements in this environment, as the business analyst, you make sure that different types of stakeholders with different needs and information requirements are catered for.

Inputs and outputs

With the Elicitation and Collaboration Task: Communicate Business Analysis Information, there are the following key inputs and outputs:

Inputs: Business analysis information and stakeholder engagement approach

Outputs: Business analysis information (communicated)

 The business analysis information is being shown as a key output with the status of 'communicated' because at the end of this task you would have communicated the findings in the format of the business analysis information package.

In the next section, we'll look at the last task of this Knowledge Area, namely: Manage Stakeholder Collaboration. This is a key task that is performed not just under the Elicitation and Collaboration Knowledge Area, but throughout all stakeholder interactions during the life of any initiative.

Task: Manage Stakeholder Collaboration

The fifth task of the Elicitation and Collaboration Knowledge Area is Manage Stakeholder Collaboration. This task describes the activities a business analyst performs when working with stakeholders to collaborate effectively toward a common goal.

In this section, you will learn about the importance of monitoring the stakeholders' collaboration activities and attitudes, as well as covering the business analyst's role to obtain stakeholder participation commitments early on and especially during the elicitation and collaboration stages of any initiative.

Let's start this discussion by referring to the purpose of this task.

Purpose

According to the BABOK® v3 guide, the purpose of Manage Stakeholder Collaboration is the following:

> *"to encourage stakeholders to work toward a common goal."*

The business analyst works with many different stakeholders across the breadth of the business analysis work activities. These stakeholders hold different levels of influence and power in terms of the approvals and buy-in of the work products or deliverables of the business analysis function. The stakeholders are also in many cases the primary source of information about needs and requirements and hence it is important for the business analyst to confirm the stakeholder's roles in a way that ensures the right stakeholders are involved at the right level and at the best possible times during the initiative.

The business analyst will be responsible for working with the stakeholders in a collaborative way as an ongoing task. It is important to remember that new stakeholders are often identified as the initiative progresses and they should be incorporated into the business analysis activities in terms of their role, influence, responsibilities, cultural attitude, and any authority they may have over the initiative and work products delivered by the business analysis team.

 A strong relationship with your stakeholders will support you in your business analysis activities and hence it is worth making an effort to build sound, trusted relationships with your stakeholders throughout the initiative.

Example of managing stakeholder collaboration:

You are currently engaging with a number of different stakeholder groups across the organization about the final solution requirements for a new timesheet system due to be implemented in the next 3 months. One of these stakeholder groups is the payroll department. The payroll department manager and his staff have been extremely supportive and happy to contribute a lot of their time to help finalize the solution requirements from a payroll perspective because they believe this new system will make their role much easier. Unfortunately, the CEO has announced a restructuring of the payroll and HR departments this week, which means that the company will no longer manage payroll internally but have made the decision to outsource this function. This means that the current payroll department will no longer exist and all staff in this department will be made redundant. You must still deliver the timesheet system solution requirements but are now faced with a stakeholder group that may have very different attitudes and roles in relation to your project's objectives.

It is therefore important for you as the business analyst to know your stakeholders' perspectives and motivations in order to manage the relationship and ultimately influence, where possible, their attitude toward the project.

Elements

These are the three key elements in the Manage Stakeholder Collaboration task:

- Gain agreement on commitments.
- Monitor stakeholder engagement.
- Collaboration.

We will now describe the key elements of the Manage Stakeholder Collaboration task and understand each with an example.

Element 1: Gain agreement on commitments

A key challenge that business analysts often face is the availability and focused commitment of the relevant stakeholders to participate and contribute to the business analysis efforts. It is therefore recommended that the business analyst determines what level of commitment of time and resources would be required as early as possible so that this could be planned for and agreed on early in the initiative. This agreement can be made formally or informally as long as the expectations are clear from the perspectives of both the business analysis team and the business stakeholders.

Example of gaining an agreement on commitments:

For example, a subject-matter expert from the payroll department maybe promised you one day per week for the next four weeks to help with defining solution requirements. It would be a good idea for you as the business analyst to set up some requirement definition meetings in advance by sending calendar invitations to this individual. This will then informally commit the subject-matter expert to spend time on the project.

Element 2: Monitor stakeholder engagement

Business analysts stay informed of the level of the participation and performance from stakeholders to make sure of the following:

- The right subject-matter experts and other stakeholders are participating effectively.
- Stakeholder attitudes and interest levels are staying constant or improving.
- Elicitation results are confirmed in a timely manner.
- Agreements and commitments are maintained.

Another responsibility of the business analyst is to keep abreast of any risks of stakeholders being diverted away from the agreed business analysis work effort and raise these risks or issues with the relevant parties to avoid any delays in the delivery of the business analysis artifacts and approvals.

Example of monitoring stakeholder engagement:

In the real world, these types of risks are very common and in most cases become issues on a project. It happens because people are often expected to contribute time and effort to a project whilst also performing their daily jobs. It is therefore important for the business analyst to try their best to be prepared prior to engaging stakeholders who might be under other work pressures and minimize the time and effort you require from these types of stakeholders. Another key aspect is to plan ahead and communicate clearly to the stakeholders when you would expect to use their time for elicitation activities so that they can plan their diaries accordingly.

Some mitigation strategies could be to identify these risks as early as possible and to address them by engaging the appropriate people to release the stakeholders from daily duties for a short period of time or where there are delayed approvals to ensure the approval processes are designed to be as easy and seamless as possible during the business analysis approach planning.

Element 3: Collaboration

The key to successful stakeholder collaboration is for the business analyst to work closely with the stakeholder in a way that makes them feel important, valued, and involved in a worthwhile endeavor. It is important for the business analyst to encourage two-way communication in an environment that is open to new ideas, suggestions for improvements, or any innovations. The business analyst needs to create a routine of frequent and easy-flowing communication channels between the stakeholders and the business analysis team.

Inputs and outputs

With the Elicitation and Collaboration Task: Manage Stakeholder Collaboration, there are the following key inputs and outputs:

Inputs: Business analysis performance assessment and stakeholder engagement approach

Outputs: Stakeholder engagement

Summary

During this chapter, you have learned about the Knowledge Area of Elicitation and Collaboration.

The following are the key concepts and tasks we covered during this chapter:

- The Elicitation and Collaboration Knowledge Area
- Task: Prepare for Elicitation
- Task: Conduct Elicitation
- Task: Confirm Elicitation Results
- Task: Communicate Business Analysis Information
- Task: Manage Stakeholder Collaboration

Make sure you revise these key learnings before completing the knowledge quiz at the end of this chapter.

You now have an understanding of the importance and purpose of the business analysis Elicitation and Collaboration Knowledge Area in terms of what is involved when eliciting requirements and business needs from stakeholders as well as what to consider when communicating this information to the relevant stakeholders and groups effectively.

During the next chapter of this study guide, we discuss the Knowledge Area of Requirements Life Cycle Management, which is about learning the different processes and tasks surrounding the management of the requirements through the different stages of their evolution in an initiative.

Task: Prepare for elicitation

During this chapter, you learned about the task of preparing for elicitation and you are now able to describe the purpose of this task and the key elements to consider when performing this task using real-world scenarios and concepts. You are also able to visualize the key inputs and outputs to perform this task effectively.

Task: Conduct elicitation

You learned what the task of conducting elicitation consists of. You are now able to describe the purpose of this task and you know what the key elements are to consider when you perform this task in a real-world scenario. You can relate this task to your own practical experience and you can explain this concept to others. You are also able to describe the key inputs and outputs to perform this task effectively.

Task: Confirm elicitation results

You learned what the task of confirming elicitation results is used for and you know the purpose of this task, as well as having an understanding of the key elements to consider when you confirm elicitation results in a real-world scenario. You can relate this task to your own practical experience and you can explain this concept to others. You are also able to describe the key inputs and outputs of this task in a way that makes sense in a practical and logical way.

Task: Communicate business analysis information

During this chapter, you learned about the task of communicating business analysis information and you are able to relate the purpose of this task to the real world as well as describe the key elements to consider when performing this task. You have considered real-world practical scenarios where this task is performed and can also convey what the key inputs and outputs are of this task.

Task: Manage stakeholder collaboration

You learned about the task of managing stakeholder collaboration during this chapter and why it is important. You have an understanding of the key elements to consider when you manage stakeholder collaboration as well as what is important to be successful in a real-world scenario. You can convey the key inputs and outputs of the task to others as well as relate it to your own practical work experience.

Knowledge quiz

Consider the following real-world scenario and complete the micro mock exam based on this chapter that follows.

Real-world case study – cardholder portal project

You are the business analyst responsible for the elicitation activities on a cardholder portal project. You have prepared some initial scope-based project materials to take with you when having one-on-one requirements elicitation interviews. Your first interview was today with the head of the department, Mr. Martin. This is how it went...

> *You*: *"Good day Mr. Martin. Thank you for meeting with me today, I know you have a very busy schedule."*

> *Mr. Martin*: *"That's no problem, I am actually very excited to get this project off the ground!"*

> *You*: *"That's wonderful. Now we spoke a few weeks ago about the general scope of this project so I will not cover that again! Let's jump right into your key requirements. Is that alright?"*

> *Mr. Martin*: *"Yes – I have a few great ideas for this system..."*

> *You*: *"What would the most important things be that you would like this system to be able to do?"*

Mr. Martin: *"So glad you asked... here are some of the things that spring to mind: I want the system to be able to register any new cardholder online so that they can activate their cards that way. I don't want an admin person to have to activate cards because it will make the maintenance costs astronomical and we won't sell any cards. I also want them to manage their own personal details on the new portal but they mustn't be allowed to update key details such as addresses or names! Fraud is such a problem with these cards so we must also have some fraud rules built in to prevent criminals from misusing the cards. Oh and another very important thing, we must make sure only approved users can use the system..."*

You: *"Wow, you know what you want! Thank you..."*

Mr. Martin: *"I have a lot more where that came from, but unfortunately I have to run. Come back any time to discuss my other requirements!"*

You: *"Thank you, I believe we still have a lot of detail to cover. I will go and compile all this information we have discussed so far in a requirements document and send it back to you for confirmation. How would you prefer to receive this information?"*

Mr. Martin: *"You can send an email if you like but I wouldn't mind also having another follow-up meeting. As you know, I hardly ever get to my emails. The rest of my team also has some ideas for requirements; so make sure to include them for our next session. "*

You: *"Thanks again Mr. Martin, your input has been extremely valuable and I really look forward to working with you on the detailed solution requirements for this project. I will organize another session and include the wider team."*

Question 1

Using the provided case study, as the business analyst you should monitor your stakeholders' attitudes toward the project.

Which of the following options describes Mr. Martin's attitude toward this initiative best?

    A. Mr. Martin comes across as very supportive of the project

    B. Mr. Martin comes across as neutral and impartial toward the project

Question 2

Which of the Elicitation and Collaboration tasks does the majority of the case study describe an example of?

Choose the correct answer:

    A. Prepare for elicitation

    B. Run an elicitation session

    C. Conduct elicitation

    D. Confirm the elicitation results

Question 3

Using the provided case study, which of the following elements should be part of your preparation activities for the follow-up elicitation session suggested that will include the rest of Mr. Martin's team?

Choose the correct answer:

    A. Select elicitation techniques, and set up logistics

    B. Capture elicitation outcomes, and set up logistics

    C. Select elicitation techniques, and guide elicitation activity

    D. Capture elicitation outcomes, and guide elicitation activity

Question 4

To answer this question, use the provided case study and consider the following additional information: you are required to also engage an entirely new team to also understand their requirements for the cardholder portal solution. Since they have not been involved or worked with you before, would it be appropriate to educate them on how you use elicitation techniques?

Choose the correct answer:

    A. No, it should be assumed they know how it works and it would be an inappropriate use of their time

    B. Yes, but only if they confirm that they have not used the techniques before

Question 5

Using the provided case study, which of the following methods of communication do you believe will be the most effective to use when communicating to Mr. Martin the business analysis information captured so far?

Choose the correct answer:

A. Print a copy of the requirements and leave it on his desk

B. A combination of email and face-to-face meetings

C. Only communication via email is needed

D. Mr. Martin doesn't need to be informed at this stage

Question 6

To answer this question, use the provided case study and consider the following additional information: you have finished the follow-up with the wider team as suggested by Mr. Martin. Mr. Martin now wants you to present him and his team with an overview of the requirements you have elicited so far.

Select the best approach for this task considering that the stakeholders have limited availability and are all located in the same building:

A. A group meeting presenting the requirements packages in a presentation format

B. A group meeting presenting the requirements packages in a detailed formal document.

C. A group meeting presenting the requirements packages in an informal format open for discussion

D. Individual meetings to ensure every stakeholder understands each requirement

Question 7

To answer this question, use the provided case study and consider the following situation that has occurred with one of Mr. Martin's team members: you have been promised that one of Mr. Martin's team members, Jennifer, can spend at least 1 day per week with you to define the detailed solution requirements. She has not attended any of the prearranged meetings, as she claims to have higher priorities to attend to. Your project deadlines are fast approaching.

What is the best way to resolve this situation?

A. This is normal – don't do anything

B. Just try and find another stakeholder that is not as busy as Jennifer

C. Tell Jennifer to drop everything and help you as promised

D. Raise the situation as a risk to the project, as you are not getting the stakeholder time that was agreed upon

Question 8

Using the provided case study and considering that you have now finished the follow-up elicitation session with the wider team, do you think it is necessary to confirm the elicitation results from the last session or can you assume it is all OK?

A. It is safe to assume it is OK and not waste more time with the further confirmation

B. You should always confirm that elicitation results are accurate and complete

C. You should in some cases confirm that elicitation results are accurate and complete

D. You should only confirm that elicitation results are accurate and complete if you have low confidence in your results

Question 9

Using the provided case study, while you are preparing for the follow-up session with Mr. Martin and his team, your colleague tells you that he has some additional elicitation results from sessions he recently conducted that could help you prepare and define the requirements.

What should you do with these additional elicitation results?

A. Keep the elicitation results for review and analysis after the next session you are preparing for now

B. Include any relevant information from this new information in your preparation for the next elicitation session

C. Disregard the additional elicitation results because it is likely to be out of date and incomplete

D. Thank your colleague and say you will look at it later when you have time

Question 10

To answer this question, use the provided case study and consider the following additional information: you have conducted your final elicitation session with Mr. Martin's team and everyone has agreed that your elicited requirements are correct and relevant.

Which of the following options best describes the output of this task?

A. Elicitation results (communicated)

B. Elicitation results (confirmed)

C. Requirements (communicated)

D. Requirements (confirmed)

Question 11

The Elicitation and Collaboration Knowledge Area consists of five different tasks.

Which of the following tasks are not tasks described as part of this Knowledge Area?

A. Prepare stakeholders for elicitation

B. Conduct elicitation

C. Manage stakeholder collaboration

D. Communicate elicitation results

Question 12

The Elicitation and Collaboration Knowledge Area is a series of activities that are not performed in isolation. What else is true about the nature of activities in the Elicitation and Collaboration Knowledge Area?

Choose the correct answer:

A. Any stakeholder engagement is valid elicitation input

B. Tasks are always performed in a sequential way

C. It is always a planned activity

D. It can be performed as a planned or unplanned activity

Question 13

Which of the following options describe the output(s) of the Elicitation and Collaboration task: Conduct Elicitation?

Choose the correct answer:

A. Elicitation results (communicated)

B. Elicitation results (clarified)

C. Elicitation results (unconfirmed)

D. Elicitation results (confirmed)

Question 14

Which of the following options describe the output(s) of the Elicitation and Collaboration task: confirm elicitation results?

Choose the correct answer:

A. Elicitation results (communicated)

B. Elicitation results (clarified)

C. Elicitation results (unconfirmed)

D. Elicitation results (confirmed)

Question 15

Which of the Elicitation and Collaboration Knowledge Area tasks has the purpose of checking that the information gathered during an elicitation session is accurate and consistent with other information?

Choose the correct answer:

A. Conduct Elicitation

B. Confirm Elicitation results

C. Check Elicitation results

D. Validate Elicitation results

Question 16

When you prepare a requirements package, you can choose from a variety of different forms.

Select all the forms you can choose to use when developing your requirements package:

A. Presentations

B. Formal documentation

C. Meetings

D. Informal documentation

Question 17

It is part of a business analyst's role to monitor the participation and performance of stakeholders to ensure that stakeholder interests and attitudes toward the initiative and work that they are participating in stay constant or improve.

Is this true or false?

A. True

B. False

Question 18

Which of the following options describe the input(s) of the Elicitation and Collaboration task: Manage Stakeholder Collaboration?

Choose the correct answer:

    A. Business analysis information

    B. Communication plan

    C. Stakeholder matrix

    D. Business analysis performance assessment

Question 19

The primary goal of developing the business analysis information package is to convey information clearly and in a useable format for continuing change activities. To help decide how to present requirements, business analysts ask the following types of questions.

Choose all the correct options:

    A. What information is important to communicate?

    B. Are the requirements we include approved and verified?

    C. Who is the audience of the package?

    D. Are there any regulatory or contractual constraints to conform to?

Question 20

There are three common types of elicitation. When information cannot be drawn from people or documents, it often means the information is unknown. Which elicitation type is employed to help uncover this type of information?

Choose the correct answer:

    A. Creative games

    B. Experiments

    C. Workshops

    D. Collaboration

Answers

1	A – Mr. Martin comes across as very supportive of the project
2	C – Prepare for elicitation
3	A – Select elicitation techniques, and set up logistics
4	B – Yes, but only if they confirm that they have not used the techniques before
5	B – A combination of email and face-to-face meetings
6	A – A group meeting presenting the requirements packages in a presentation format
7	D– Raise the situation as a risk to the project, as you are not getting the stakeholder time that was agreed upon
8	B – You should always confirm that elicitation results are accurate and complete
9	B – Include any relevant information from this new information in your preparation for the next elicitation session
10	B – Elicitation results (confirmed)
11	A – Prepare stakeholders for elicitation D – Communicate elicitation results
12	D – Any stakeholder engagement is valid elicitation input
13	C – Elicitation results (unconfirmed)
14	D – Elicitation results (confirmed)
15	B – Confirm Elicitation results
16	A – Presentations B – Formal documentation D – Informal documentation
17	A – True
18	D – Business analysis performance assessment
19	A – What information is important to communicate? C – Who is the audience of the package? D – Are there any regulatory or contractual constraints to conform to?
20	B– Experiments

8
Requirements Life Cycle Management

Requirements Life Cycle Management is the knowledge area that describes the tasks that a business analyst performs to manage and maintain requirements from initiation right through to final implementation.

During this chapter, we discuss the detail of the following BABOK® v3 guide tasks: Trace Requirements, Maintain Requirements, Prioritize Requirements Assess Requirements Changes, and Approve Requirements. We'll be bringing them to life with practical real-world scenarios and examples. By the end of this chapter, you will have learned about the tasks that are involved during the process of managing and maintaining requirements through the life cycle of an initiative. The following topics will be covered in this chapter:

- Purpose and context of this knowledge area
- Task: Trace Requirements
- Task: Maintain Requirements
- Task: Prioritize Requirements
- Task: Assess Requirements Changes
- Task: Approve Requirements
- Real-world case study
- Test your knowledge

Here is what you will be able to do by the end of this chapter:

- Understand the context of this BABOK® v3 guide knowledge area within a real-world scenario
- Understand and apply the Trace Requirements task to real-world scenarios
- Understand and apply the Maintain Requirements task to real-world scenarios
- Understand and apply the Prioritize Requirements task to real-world scenarios

- Understand and apply the Assess Requirements Changes task to real-world scenarios
- Understand and apply the Approve Requirements task to real-world scenarios

What is Requirements Life Cycle Management?

Requirements Life Cycle Management refers to the tasks and activities that a business analyst performs as part of their role to manage requirements throughout the duration of any initiative, from the start to the very end. These activities also include maintaining requirements during this process.

Ultimately, the goal of Requirements Life Cycle Management is to make sure that all the different types of requirements and designs are not only aligned and consistent with each other but also that these requirements are maintained and implemented in the initiative's solution. This means that the business analyst has control over the requirements as well as input into how these requirements will be implemented and delivered as part of the solution:

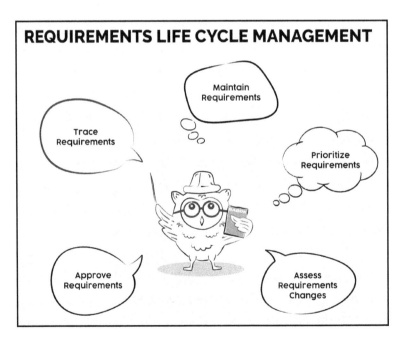

Requirements Life Cycle Management knowledge area and tasks

The Requirements Life Cycle Management knowledge area includes the following tasks:

- Trace Requirements
- Maintain Requirements
- Prioritize Requirements
- Assess Requirements Changes
- Approve Requirements

The Business Analysis Core Concept Model™

Here we consider how Requirements Life Cycle Management as a knowledge area applies to the Business Analysis Core Concept Model with an example.

The six core concepts of the Business Analysis Core Concept Model™ are listed here:

- Change
- Need
- Solution
- Stakeholder
- Value
- Context

We will see how these core concepts are related to Requirements Life Cycle Management in the following sections.

Change

This core concept refers to how change is managed when proposed changes to requirements and designs are evaluated during an initiative.

Let's look at an example to bring this concept of change to life:

One of the stakeholders in the Customer Services area approaches you as the business analyst to mention to you that he has changed what he wants in terms of the way that customers request a review of their electricity supply charges. He now wants the customer to be able to complete the full request online via the Customer Portal instead of only initiating the request online as per the documented requirements. In response to this, you tell the stakeholder that there is a formal process for requesting changes to approved requirements such as this one and that you will guide him through what this change request process entails. You then help this stakeholder to formulate the exact required change to the existing requirements using the change request template. Once the change request is submitted, you inform the stakeholder that the Change Control Board will review the request. You also promise to keep the stakeholder informed regarding the progress of his change request.

This example illustrates how the core concept of change is implemented in the Requirements Life Cycle Management knowledge area.

Need

This core concept refers to how requirements are traced, prioritized, and maintained to ensure that a need is met.

Let's look at an example to bring this concept of need into the real world:

If we continue with the example of the change request for the electricity supply charges review process, you will also capture the details of this change request as part of your requirements traceability activities. You will, therefore, know in future why the approved requirement was changed and what the new requirement entails. This change request may also have an impact on the priorities associated with the affected requirements.

This example illustrates how the core concept of need is implemented during Requirements Life Cycle Management by tracing changes to requirements, carefully maintaining the requirements, and considering a potential change in priority to deliver the requirements that meet the business needs.

Solution

This core concept refers to how requirements are traced to solution components to ensure that the solution satisfies the need.

Let's look at an example to bring this concept into the real world:

You have created a traceability matrix that contains all the approved requirements as well as any changes that have been made to the requirements. As the project progresses into the implementation stage, you are now in a position to trace each requirement to the specific solution component that is being implemented to meet the need.

In the example of the requirement for a customer to request the electricity supply charge review using the online portal, you can trace the relevant requirements directly to the solution artifacts that describe the online web pages' design and build components that solve for the electricity supply charge review process.

This example illustrates how the core concept of the solution is implemented during Requirements Life Cycle Management with the focus on maintaining, tracing, and prioritizing requirements to meet the business need.

Stakeholder

This core concept refers to how the stakeholder engages with the project team to maintain understanding, agreement, and approval of requirements and designs.

Let's look at an example to bring this concept into the real world:

Let's continue with our previous example of the requirement to create a solution, which allows the customer to submit a request for an electricity supply charge review via an online portal. The stakeholder who asked for this change is closely involved with the requirement and has a very good understanding of the requirements. He also agrees with the requirements in general and is willing to approve requirements supporting this change.

Therefore, it is clear that stakeholders play a vital part in Requirements Life Cycle Management activities with a clear relationship to the solution, the need, and the change.

Value

This core concept refers to how the value, worth, or importance of something within a specific context is perceived by the stakeholder. When we look at the knowledge area of Requirements Life Cycle Management, the concept of value is applied in terms of ensuring that the requirements are maintained as far as possible for potential reuse beyond the current initiative.

Let's look at an example to bring this concept of value into the real world:

Let's say you have completed all the requirements analysis work and identified that all the usability requirements relating to the user interface of the online portal will also apply to any other online initiative that is undertaken by the company. Other teams can, therefore, reuse these requirements in the future and therefore it will be of great value in terms of saving time and effort as well as promoting consistency in user interface requirements.

Looking at this example, it is clear to see how Requirements Life Cycle Management can add a lot of value in terms of future reuse of requirements.

Context

The final core concept refers to how the context or circumstances of a change plays a part in how requirements tracing and prioritization is supported.

Let's look at an example to bring this concept of context into the real world:

In the previous example, we described a formal change control process being in place for the project that was used to manage changes to electricity supply review project requirements. Due to the high importance of uninterrupted electricity supply to customers and the highly regulated environment this electricity company has to operate in, it is fair to assume the context is very structured and formal and requires rigorous governance processes.

So, in this particular context, the tracing and prioritization of requirements will be a supported and closely managed process.

Task: Trace Requirements

The first task described as part of the Requirements Life Cycle Management knowledge area is that of tracing requirements during the life of the initiative. In this section, we will gain an understanding of why requirements are traced and learn about the key elements of traceability that a business analyst should consider.

Purpose

According to the BABOK® v3 guide, the purpose of Trace Requirements is to do the following:

> "*...ensure that requirements and designs at different levels are aligned to one another, and to manage the effects of change to one level on related requirements.*"

So, ultimately, the purpose of requirements traceability is to trace where each requirement or design comes from or originated from and what its life cycle is throughout the project.

If it is known why a requirement exists, or where it originated from, it will ensure that once the solution has been delivered, it does in actual fact solve the original requirement.

By knowing where a requirement came from, or what the need that should be addressed is, the business analyst will know who to communicate to as well as be able to manage the risk, scope, and any changes associated with that requirement.

Why trace requirements?

There are a number of reasons why you should want to trace a requirement:

- It will enable quick identification of gaps within the supplied solution, as well as the supplied requirements.
- It will aid in the understanding of the size of the change.
- By tracing a requirement through development, testing, and implementation, you keep track of the requirement's status throughout the life cycle of the project.
- Traceability also supports requirements allocation and release planning.

Requirements traceability provides a clear view of requirements in a way that allows the team to plan and allocate which requirements to include into which releases. In this way, when looking at requirements within the same subject matter area, they can potentially be allocated to the same resource group for implementation as well as the same release period. This, in turn, will speed up solution delivery.

Elements

There are three elements to consider when you trace requirements:

- Level of formality
- Relationships
- Traceability repository

Let's now consider each of these elements to understand the scope of the task in more detail.

Element 1: Level of formality

Is a high level of formality and detail required?

Always remember that the more the level of formality increases, the more difficult it becomes to effectively trace a requirement.

There might be a few reasons why a certain level of detail is being documented for a specific requirement.

Let's consider the following example to explain this further:

The requirement is to implement a new product within a bank's credit card division.

A high level of formality and detail will likely be chosen, as there will be many aspects, business rules, and other business area impacts to consider relating to this requirement.

For example, some of the complexities with this example can include product-specific business rules, product features, customer application rules, and customer verification processes. Even physical card designs and delivery processes will possibly need to be considered for this requirement. In this case, the detailed requirements will be traced formally and at a low level of detail.

Here's a second example:

The same credit card division has a requirement to be able to send their customers a text message once a new card has been issued for their account. Due to the simpler nature and size of this requirement as well as the smaller overall business impact, the level of formality and hence level of detail to trace the requirement to will be a lot lower than in the first example.

Element 2: Relationships

What are the relationships between requirements?

There are several types of relationships between requirements; it helps to know and understand these relationships in order to determine the most appropriate traceability approach for your specific project situation and traceability needs.

Let's consider the following example to explain these relationships further:

A bank is required to build an online loan application solution.

These relationships are as follows:

- **Derive** – *An applicant would need to log in to the bank's online system to use the online loan application solution. The information required to validate whether the user is a valid and registered user of this system is derived from the login process.*
- **Depends** – *For an applicant to be able to complete a loan application form, the applicant would need to be logged in and validated on the bank's online system. Thus, the completion of the form requirement is dependent on the login and validation requirements process.*

    There are two further types of dependency relationships to consider in this example:

    - **Necessity** – *It is required to now also add new database fields to the bank's existing database to hold user online registration details. Without this data, it will be impossible for the validation process to function and is thus a necessity.*
    - **Effort** – *It will most likely be easier to implement all file changes at the same time, seeing that some changes to a specific file or table are currently required, but because future fields on the same tables are envisaged, it will be less effort to implement all file changes at the same time.*

- **Satisfy** – *Has the implemented solution satisfied the need to allow an applicant to complete an online application securely, according to the company standards, for example?*
- **Validate** – *Has the requirement successfully been validated against the test case?*

For the exam, you must ensure that you understand the different relationship types that exist when tracing requirements in a practical way. Relate each of these relationships back to your own practical experience on an initiative to make sure you fully understand the concepts that underpin each.

As a business analyst, you should, therefore, consider the purpose of each of these types of traceability relationships prior to finalizing the traceability approach that you will be implementing for your project.

Element 3: Traceability Repository

Requirements traceability is documented and maintained in line with the methods and tools identified by the business analysis approach. Many organizations today will manage traceability with elaborate spreadsheet templates, but it should be noted that there are sophisticated requirements management software tools, such as Jira, that are available to facilitate effective traceability on projects.

In this section, we have learned about the purpose of tracing requirements as well as understanding what the different types of relationships are that could be used as a base for tracing requirements. In this section, we also covered some of the tools used to trace requirements, as well as gain an understanding of the level of formality required when it comes to tracing requirements on an initiative.

In the following section, we will take a look at the importance of maintaining requirements throughout the life of the initiative.

Inputs and outputs

With the Requirements Life Cycle Management task Trace Requirements, there are the following key input and outputs:

- **Inputs**: Requirements and designs
- **Outputs**: Requirements (traced) and designs (traced)

You will notice that the output status of the requirements and designs changed to being traced when you complete the task of tracing requirements.

Task: Maintain Requirements

You will know that when working with requirements on an initiative, there are many factors that can influence the requirements on a regular basis. The task of maintaining requirements is all about working to keep requirements as accurate and consistent as possible throughout the entire initiative.

In this section, we will learn about the underlying purpose of maintaining requirements in their entirety and explore which types of requirements are suitable for reuse on multiple initiatives.

Purpose

According to the BABOK® v3 guide, the purpose of the Maintain Requirements task is to do the following:

> " ... *retain requirement accuracy and consistency throughout and beyond the change during the entire requirements life cycle, and to support reuse of requirements in other solutions.*"

To understand the purpose of this task better, consider the following example:

Consider building a vehicle that is designed to perform at the peak of its group and level, such as a race car.

There are certain specific requirements, for example, rules and regulations around vehicle weight, engine size, and capacity. These are prescribed by the racing industry and must be followed in order for a new car to be eligible to compete.

Thus, in the future, when someone builds a vehicle designed for racing, or they repair an existing vehicle, the rules, regulations, and requirements have been documented and maintained for future use.

A requirement that continues to remain valid or continue, to exist after a project has been completed must be maintained.

In order to maximize the benefits of maintaining and reusing requirements, the requirements should be as follows:

- Consistently represented
- Reviewed and approved for maintenance using a standardized process that defines proper access rights and ensures quality
- Easily accessible and understandable

Elements

There are three key elements to consider when you maintain requirements:

- Maintain requirements
- Maintain attributes
- Reusing requirements

Let's now consider each of these elements to understand the scope of the task in more detail.

Element 1: Maintain requirements

It is required that a business analyst continuously conducts maintenance to ensure that the requirement is correctly and accurately documented and readily available. If anything with regards to the requirement changes, it should be analyzed and updated in a timely way. The business analyst must also aim to maintain the relationships between requirements and any associated information describing the context in order to ensure that the requirements remain in line with the original intent of each requirement.

Element 2: Maintain attributes

The attributes of a requirement can continuously change throughout a project and need to be maintained at all times. The documentation thereof is referred to as Maintain Attributes.

Requirements attributes refer to things such as a requirement's source, priority, and complexity. This might change even if the requirement itself remains the same. For the exam, be clear about the term requirements attributes. This is an example of where the BABOK® v3 Guide terminology is important for exam purposes.

Let us consider this element in the context of a practical example:

A requirement was logged by the Head of Credit at a financial institution to rework the interest calculation on home loans.

Due to the fact that not all detail around this requirement has been finalized and the stakeholders continuously change the detail of what is required, this has always been identified as a lower-priority requirement.

During the course of a routine audit, however, it was found that the interest calculation on home loans was in actual fact incorrect and could cause major implications for the financial institution; this needs to be corrected as a matter of urgency.

Thus, the attributes of this requirement have now changed, from low priority to high priority, with a specific time deadline, and need to be updated.

Element 3: Reusing requirements

It will drastically decrease the time spent on future analysis of requirements if certain requirements can be reused and are documented.

During the course of an initiative, you will often find that there are some requirements that can be reused, either in different areas of the business or within other current projects.

 Generally speaking, requirements that are described at an abstract level or have a somewhat general nature lend themselves to being candidates for reuse. These types of requirements are often stable and don't have specific reference to a particular solution or situation.

Some example requirements categories that often contain requirements that are suitable for reuse include the following: non-functional requirements such as performance, availability, and usability standards; and security requirements. Examples of business-focused requirements categories that often contain reusable requirements are data privacy requirements, regulatory and compliance requirements, and fraud-related business rules that must be met. Different industries may have different categories of reusable requirements.

It is recommended to document these types of requirements without any links to a specific project.

In this section, we covered the key elements for maintaining requirements on an initiative and specifically outlined the considerations for maintaining and reusing requirements throughout the life cycle of the project.

Inputs and outputs

With the Requirements Life Cycle Management task Maintain Requirements, there are the following key inputs and outputs:

- **Inputs**: Requirements and designs
- **Outputs**: Requirements (maintained) and designs (maintained)

Once the business analyst has performed the task of maintaining the requirements, the status of the requirements as an output to this task changes to being maintained.

In the next section, we will learn about the role of the task Prioritising Requirements during the initiative life cycle.

Task: Prioritize Requirements

The task of prioritizing requirements is important to the overall life cycle of requirements because it reflects the level of importance that stakeholders place on a specific requirement relative to all other requirements.

During this section, we will delve into the reasons why prioritizing requirements on an initiative is important. We will discuss the key elements that the business analyst should know and apply during prioritization activities. We cover the elements describing the basis of prioritization, the challenges that arise during prioritization activities, and the continuous nature of prioritization during the life cycle of requirements.

Purpose

According to the BABOK® v3 guide, the purpose of the task Prioritize Requirements is to do the following:

"... rank requirements in the order of relative importance."

Let's look at a practical example to understand this task further:

A company has decided that they require a new website, and the following high-level requirements have been documented:

- *The technical director wants the website to be fast and responsive.*
- *The sales director requires the website to increase the number of new customers visiting the website.*

- *The creative director says the website must be aesthetically pleasing with lots of images as they have a big portfolio to display.*
- *The technical website design company requires the website to be mobile-friendly.*

However, when enquiring about the priorities of these requirements, you find that each stakeholder has their own opinion of the relative importance of each. It is your role as the business analyst to facilitate a session with all the stakeholders involved to prioritize the requirements according to an agreed prioritization method.

Let's consider the detail of the prioritization activities.

Why do we need to prioritize requirements?

Requirements are prioritized in order to document their relative importance to stakeholders. This is a very important step in the Requirements Life Cycle Management knowledge area because when the requirements of a project have been prioritized, you can determine the order in which they will need to be delivered. It will also aid in understanding the value that the stakeholders attach to each of the requirements.

Dependencies between requirements can also often assist in the prioritization of requirements.

The prioritization of requirements is not a one-off activity but rather an ongoing activity that needs to be closely monitored and actively managed by the business analyst in close collaboration with all other stakeholders.

Elements

There are three elements to consider when you prioritize requirements:

- Basis of prioritization
- Challenges of prioritization
- Continual prioritization

We will describe the elements of the task of prioritizing requirements and understand each with an example.

Element 1: Basis of prioritization

There are many factors that influence the priority of a requirement. It is important to consider each of these factors and do so in collaboration with stakeholders to determine which of these factors will carry the most weight when requirements are being prioritized within the team.

Factors that influence prioritization include the following:

- Benefit
- Penalty
- Cost
- Risk
- Dependencies
- Time sensitivity
- Stability
- Regulatory or policy compliance

 Remember that more than one of these factors will likely play a role in prioritization activities. It is important to get some level of agreement between stakeholders about what the relative importance of each factor is before you start facilitating prioritization sessions for the requirements as a whole.

Let's consider each of these prioritization factors in more detail and with practical examples.

Benefit

Generally, the requirements with the greatest business benefits or value associated with it will be implemented first.

For example, if you needed to choose between a requirement that would increase sales or one that would decrease fraud, each group of stakeholders would have a different view on priority. Conflict resolution skills might beneficial here to assist in the stakeholders' agreement. The requirement with the greatest benefit would need to be identified and prioritized as such.

Penalty

The penalty factor refers to the consequences of not implementing a given requirement.

If, for example, a financial fine or other penalties will be incurred by the organization if a specific requirement is not met, that requirement will have a higher priority associated with it.

Cost

This factor refers to the costs associated with the effort and the resources necessary to implement the requirement.

Often a requirement is documented and requested initially, but when the stakeholder or team realizes the cost to fulfill the requirement might be much higher than the perceived benefits to the organization, it might be reconsidered as a lower priority.

Risk

The risk describes the likelihood that the requirement cannot deliver the potential value, or cannot be met at all.

For example, requirements with a high operational risk associated with them, such as fraud prevention-related requirements, will likely be prioritized to the top of the list.

Dependencies

If certain requirements cannot be completed without others being done first (or at all), all dependent requirements should be prioritized together.

For example, let's say increasing sales is seen as a priority; however, to be able to increase sales effectiveness, new products must be created. For these new products, there are new fields required within certain database tables. These new fields were not seen as a priority when considered on their own. But from a strategic point of view, the increase in sales is the highest priority and can only be achieved by adding new products. The new database fields immediately also get a higher priority.

Time sensitivity

This factor describes the "best-before date" of the requirement. Once this date passes, the implementation of the requirement loses significant value to the organization. This includes time-to-market scenarios, in which the benefit derived will be exponentially greater if the functionality is delivered ahead of the competition. It can also refer to seasonal functionality that only has a value at a specific time of year.

For example, delivering a new electronic gift card solution after the Christmas season has passed will have a much lower financial benefit to the organization than delivering it in the appropriate timeframe before the Christmas season.

Stability

If the stakeholder has not agreed on the final details of a requirement, it might be changed to a lower priority due to the immaturity, or what we refer to here as the stability level, of the requirement. This is because it is assumed that the requirement will still change as and when new information becomes available. From an initiative delivery point of view, it doesn't make sense to spend time and resources on requirements that are not finalized or considered somewhat unstable, due to the fact that any work and effort might have to be reworked once the stakeholders come to an agreement on the intent and content of a particular requirement.

Regulatory or policy compliance

A specific requirement might have a specific deadline due to industry bodies' rules and regulations.

For example, auditors and other government bodies might set rules and deadlines that the project needs to adhere to in order to ensure company compliance.

Element 2: Challenges of prioritization

What are the challenges when it comes to requirements prioritization?

We have already determined that prioritization is really an assessment of the relative value of requirements. Each stakeholder may value a different aspect of the requirements set and have different motivations for supporting certain requirements to have a high priority for implementation. This can cause conflict among stakeholders. It is the role of the business analyst to notice these conflicts and to work with stakeholders to determine the appropriate priories for requirements, even if this includes making some trade-offs. It is important to help stakeholders avoid the temptation to indicate certain requirements at levels of priority that will affect other requirements' priorities.

Element 3: Continual prioritization

Priorities may continuously change. For example, stakeholders may initially prioritize based on benefits. The implementation team may then re-prioritize the requirements based on the sequence in which requirements must be implemented due to technical constraints. Once the implementation team has provided the cost of each requirement, the stakeholders may choose to re-prioritize again.

Inputs and outputs

With the Requirements Life Cycle Management task Prioritize Requirements, there are the following key inputs and outputs:

- **Inputs**: Requirements and designs
- **Outputs**: Requirements (prioritized) and designs (prioritized)

Once the business analyst has performed the task of prioritization of the requirements, the status of the requirements as an output to this task changes to being prioritized.

In the next section, we will discuss the activities that are part of performing the task of assessing changes to requirements. The introduction of changes to requirements would impact the prioritization, maintenance, and traceability aspects of managing the requirements throughout the life cycle of requirements.

Task: Assess Requirements Changes

Every business analyst knows that change is a constant factor that must be managed during any initiative. The task of assessing requirements changes outlines the purpose of these tasks as well as the key elements to consider when change occurs with the requirements. These key elements include assessing the formality required for a particular initiative in terms of the nature of the initiative, which factors may have an impact on the initiative and need to be considered during this task, and the final outcome of whether a change is to be accepted or rejected.

Let's now start this section with a clear understanding of the purpose of assessing requirements changes as a core business analysis task.

Purpose

According to the BABOK® v3 guide, the purpose of the Assess Requirements Changes task is this:

> *"to evaluate the implications of proposed changes to requirements and designs".*

Ultimately the business analyst must determine whether a change that is being proposed to a requirement will increase the value of the overall solution. If it will increase the value, it is important to then determine what action should be taken to make this happen.

Let's consider a practical example to understand this task further:

A company that owns an online store has a requirement to be able to do deliveries to customers. It was initially decided that full integration into another specialized delivery company would be the best solution. However, it was later decided by the stakeholders that the same delivery company would still be used but full electronic integration will no longer be required and that the orders need to be reworked in-house before being manually submitted to the delivery company for execution.

In this example scenario, the Assess Requirements Changes task needs to be performed in order to determine whether the proposed change to the solution will increase the value of the solution and if so, what action should be taken to ensure this is implemented.

When the business analyst assesses changes to a requirement or set of requirements, the following must be considered:

- Does the proposed change align with the overall strategy?
- Will the proposed change affect the value delivered to the business or stakeholder groups?
- Will the proposed change have an impact on the time to deliver or the resources required to deliver the value?
- Will implementing the proposed change make a difference to any of the risks, opportunities, or constraints associated with the overall initiative?

Elements

There are three key elements to consider when the business analyst assesses requirements changes:

- Assessment formality
- Impact analysis
- Impact resolution

Let's now consider each of these elements to understand the scope of the task in more detail.

Element 1: Assessment formality

Is a high level of formality and detail required when assessing a proposed change to a requirement?

The amount of information available may determine the level of formality required in the assessment process. The other two factors that may impact the level of formality that is required during the assessment of the change to a requirement include the perceived importance of the proposed change as well as the organization's governance process.

Predictive and adaptive approaches

As you know, there are two main types of approaches that exist: predictive and adaptive. The predictive approach to delivery is a more formal approach and hence can cause a rework of tasks and activities already completed when a change is implemented as well as of the activities required to assess the proposed change on the whole.

A lot of requirements elicitation and analysis done in the early phases of a project follow the predictive approach. This means when a change is required during later phases of this type of project, there is often a higher impact on the time, cost, and effort required.

An adaptive approach will try and minimize the impact of changes with iterative implementations from an early stage of the project. This approach typically lends itself to a less formal and more adaptable approach to manage the impact of change that is introduced during the life cycle of the project. Within the adaptive approach to delivery, the idea of an evolutionary delivery may also reduce the need for a formal impact assessment to be performed when a change is proposed to a requirement.

Element 2: Impact analysis

What are the effects of a change to a requirement?

An impact analysis determines the effect of a change by considering certain factors relating to the requirement and the proposed change of that requirement.

 For the exam, take special care to understand the considerations when assessing the impact of a proposed change. It is important to note that "scope" is not listed explicitly as an impact consideration. The scope is being defined as a cost consideration in this context.

Let's consider the following example to illustrate these factors:

A bank has decided to add a credit card product to its portfolio. The new magnetic strip credit cards have been designed and manufactured for the bank; however, the Banking Regulatory Body has determined that all credit cards issued after a certain date must have a microchip installed and specific data must be carried on this microchip.

Here are some key factors to consider when assessing this change to the requirements:

Benefit: What is the benefit that will be gained by adding this change to the requirement? Compliance with the Banking Regulatory Body and improved security for customers and the bank.

Cost: What is the cost associated with the original requirement, and the cost impact to add this change? In this case, the cost of the original credit cards already exists and due to the regulation, these will need to be destroyed, thus the cost of this change in requirement is the sum of the original cards plus the new and more expensive compliant cards.

Impact: The number of customers or business processes affected if the change is accepted. By approving this change, the customers that have already been issued with the existing credit card might be impacted, as they could potentially need to replace their current cards. A new business process must also be designed and implemented to facilitate this recall of cards.

Schedule: What is the impact on existing delivery timelines if this change is approved?

Urgency: How urgent is this change? For example, what is the timeframe to become compliant with this microchip requirement?

Element 3: Impact resolution

Document impacts and resolutions to help stakeholders make a decision.

The business analyst is required to document and communicate all impacts and resolutions resulting from the change analysis to share information with all stakeholders. The stakeholders will be responsible for approving or rejecting the proposed change based on the impact analysis and results presented by the business analyst.

 The decision, as well as the details of the proposed change, must be traced to the requirement being assessed for a potential change. In the exam, you must be able to relate this task to the other tasks in this knowledge area by applying it to a practical scenario.

Once the decision to proceed or not has been made by the change control decision-makers, the business analyst should document and keep this information available and up to date for any further reference that may be required during the initiative's life cycle.

Inputs and outputs

With the Requirements Life Cycle Management Assess Requirements Changes task, there are the following key inputs and outputs:

- **Inputs**: Change (proposed), requirements, and designs
- **Outputs**: Requirements change assessment and designs change assessment

As an output to this task, the proposed change has been assessed both to a requirement or a design. The status of this means that the change assessment is completed.

Task: Approve Requirements

The business analyst will reach the stage in the requirements life cycle when the requirements and designs must be approved in order for the life cycle to progress to the next stage of an initiative.

In this section, we will gain a deeper understanding of why the task of approving requirements is an important step during the requirements life cycle, and we also discuss what to consider when addressing conflicts and issues during this task. We will discuss aspects to include when gaining consensus among stakeholders regarding the requirements under discussion and we cover the final stage of getting the final approvals from the appropriate stakeholders.

Purpose

According to the BABOK® v3 guide, the purpose of the Approve Requirements task is to do the following:

> *"… obtain agreement on and approval of requirements and designs for business analysis work to continue and/or solution construction to proceed."*

A key responsibility of business analysts is to ensure clear communication of requirements, designs, and other business analysis information to the stakeholders who are responsible for approving the business analysis information.

The level of formality associated with the approval processes often depends on the type of delivery approach that is being followed, be it predictive or adaptive. During an initiative that follows the predictive approach, the approvals are often performed during end-of-phase meetings or during change control meetings. With initiatives where an adaptive approach is applied, the requirements are often approved on a just-in-time basis prior to building and implementation activities. This is an ongoing process that happens as part of a typical iteration or release cycle.

The communication of a required approval of a proposed change can be illustrated with a practical example:

Let's consider that a change is proposed in the loan application process within a banking environment; all stakeholders need to be aware of and approve the proposed changes.

Communication in connection with this change needs to include stakeholder groups such as the following:

The Credit Department: To ensure that they have all the information required to do correct credit scoring and all this information is still valid and included in the proposed solution.

The Call Centre: To ensure they have all the information at hand to perform all current and future required customer service tasks within the call center environment.

The Collections Department: To ensure that they agree that the proposed change will not affect their processes in an adverse way and that they agree with the proposed change.

All impacted stakeholder groups should be involved during the assessment of the proposed change but most crucially receive the relevant communication about providing their responsibility to also approve the change apply the required format or forum for the initiative.

Elements

There are four key elements to consider when a business analyst performs the Approve Requirements task:

- Understand stakeholder roles
- Conflict and issue management
- Gain consensus
- Track and communicate approval

Let's now consider each of these elements to understand the scope of the task in more detail.

Element 1: Understand stakeholder roles

It is the responsibility of the business analyst to understand who holds the decision-making power to approve a change. The business analyst should also be aware of whom to inform or consult with regard to a requirement. It is important for the business analyst to consider that there may only be a small number of stakeholders who have the authority to approve or reject requirements or changes to requirements, but many stakeholders will have some level of influence and input into these approval decisions.

Let us consider the following example to elaborate on stakeholder roles:

A vehicle dealership is required to implement a time clocking system for their workshop staff members.

The following stakeholders could potentially be involved in this decision:

- *The service manager who is responsible for managing the workshop staff will have certain requirements for such a system. For example, they would like to be able to see how many hours each workshop staff member works per day or per week.*
- *The financial manager has a list of requirements on what they would prefer to see in such a system, for example, the rate per staff member per hour.*
- *The workshop staff, who will be the main users of the system, want it to be user-friendly.*

However, it remains the board of directors for that dealership that will ultimately give the final approval for a specific time clocking solution to be selected for implementation.

In this example, it is important for the business analyst to understand that the service manager and financial manager can only support the requirements and suitability of a specific solution, but cannot approve the implementation thereof. They may, however, have some strong influence on the board of directors, who are likely to rely on their input and confirmation of which solution would fulfill their requirements best.

Element 2: Conflict and issue management

As a business analyst, you are responsible for gaining consensus on requirements well in advance of asking stakeholders to formally approve any requirements. Stakeholders and stakeholder groups may have different opinions, priorities, and perspectives with regard to the requirements and hence conflicts may need to be identified and resolved prior to seeking formal approval from stakeholders or key decision-makers. It is the role of the business analyst to continuously monitor and work with stakeholders to resolve any issues or points where there may be conflicts.

Let's consider the following practical example to understand this concept further:

Choosing a new family vehicle might cause a lot of issues and conflict, as mom might place high value on a vehicle that has enough space for groceries and kids' sports equipment, and that comes at a very low price. Dad, on the other hand, might be looking at a vehicle that is safe for his family and fuel-efficient as a priority. This type of vehicle might be a bit smaller and more expensive.

The requirement remains the same for both stakeholders here: a new family vehicle is required; however, the design and detail requirements of that vehicle might be very different for each stakeholder, and conflict may arise as mom might have a very different interpretation of why dad requires a more expensive vehicle.

In this example, it will be the task of the business analyst to facilitate communication between stakeholders in the areas where conflict exists.

Element 3: Gain consensus

It is the responsibility of the business analyst to ensure that the stakeholder with approval authority is comfortable and in agreement with the requirements and the business value they will generate. The business analyst can gain consensus by facilitating effective communication with accountable individuals and ensuring that all decision-makers are in agreement and accepting the requirements of the solution being delivered.

Ideally, all stakeholders will be in agreement about the requirements, but where this is not the case and it is decided to proceed with some stakeholders, not in full agreement, it is important to assess the risks this poses to the initiative's successful delivery.

If we refer to our previous example, it will be the responsibility of the business analyst to ensure that both stakeholders agree on which family vehicle with which features would be most suitable for their needs.

Element 4: Track and communicate approval

The business analyst is required to keep a record of all approval decisions and of current approval statuses. Stakeholders must be able to determine what requirements and designs are currently approved and ready to progress to the next phase of the project.

Inputs and outputs

With the Requirements Life Cycle Management Approve Requirements task, there are the following key inputs and outputs:

- **Inputs**: Requirements (verified) and designs
- **Outputs**: Requirements (approved) and designs (approved)

As an output to this task, the requirements or designs have been approved.

In a nutshell, as a business analyst, it is important to plan and execute the activities required to achieve the output of approved requirements and designs.

Now that we have covered all the core tasks involved in Requirements Life Cycle Management, you will be in a better position to appreciate that this task is ultimately what the business analyst is working toward during all the other core tasks described during previous chapters.

Summary

During this chapter, you have learned about the Requirements Life Cycle Management knowledge area.

The following are the key concepts and tasks that we covered during this chapter:

- The Requirements Life Cycle Management knowledge area
- Task: Trace Requirements
- Task: Maintain Requirements
- Task: Prioritize Requirements
- Task: Assess Requirements Changes
- Task: Approve Requirements

Make sure you revise these key topics before completing the knowledge quiz at the end of this chapter.

You now have an understanding of the importance and purpose of the Requirements Life Cycle Management knowledge area and know what the scope is of managing a requirement or design throughout the entire life cycle of an initiative.

Task: Trace Requirements

During this chapter, you learned about the task of tracing requirements and you are now able to describe the purpose of this task and describe the key elements to consider when performing this task using real-world scenarios and concepts. You are also able to visualize the key inputs and outputs to perform this task effectively.

Task: Maintain Requirements

You learned what the task of maintaining requirements consists of and you are now able to describe the purpose of this task. You know what the key elements to consider are when you perform this task in a real-world scenario. You can relate this task to your own practical experience and you can explain this concept to others. You are also able to describe the key inputs and outputs to perform this task effectively.

Task: Prioritize Requirements

You learned what the task of prioritizing requirements consists of. You are able to formulate the purpose of this task in your own words and you know what the key elements are, including their key attributes and considerations. You can relate this task in its entirety to your own practical project experience and you can explain this concept with examples to others. You are also able to describe the key inputs and outputs to perform this task effectively.

Task: Assess Requirements Changes

You learned about the task of assessing requirements changes. You are able to define the purpose of this task in your own words and you know what the key elements are, including their key attributes and considerations such as impact assessment factors. You can relate this task in its entirety to your own practical project experience and you can explain this concept with examples to others. You are also able to describe the key inputs and outputs to perform this task effectively.

Task: Approve Requirements

You learned what the task of approving requirements consists of. You are able to describe the purpose of this task in your own words and you know what the key elements are with detailed considerations for gaining approvals from stakeholders. You can relate this task in its entirety to your own practical project experience and you can explain this concept with examples to others. You are also able to describe the key inputs and outputs to perform this task effectively.

During the next chapter of this study guide, we discuss the Strategy Analysis knowledge area, which is about learning the different processes and tasks when identifying and managing business needs of strategic or tactical importance. Overall, the Strategy Analysis knowledge area provides a context for the next stages of the requirements analysis and design tasks.

Knowledge quiz

Consider the following real-world scenario and complete the micro mock exam based on this chapter that follows.

Real-world case study: Car booking system project

You are the business analyst on a project that is in the process of defining, building, and implementing a car booking system for the car rental company that you currently work for. You have been working on this project for the last 6 months and have documented approximately 150 different requirements from all the project's stakeholder groups. It is now time to get your baseline of requirements agreed and then to start planning the next stages of the project. Before you are able to get the final approvals from the key stakeholders, they have requested that you organize a prioritization meeting. They left it up to you to suggest a prioritization technique but you know that they wouldn't want to spend much time on this. They are very focused on getting the solution implemented as soon as possible and they don't really care that much about how expensive it might be, as long as they get their solution in time. They also want to ensure they have the requirements, which will maximize business value identified as a high priority. The project manager also recently employed a change manager for the project, Jane. Jane has a lot of change management experience but wanted your help with the stakeholder identification and the definition of the change request process. She is also very keen to set up the change control board for the project. One thing Jane doesn't have much familiarity with (which is somewhat surprising) is the use of traceability matrices. She asked you to please assist her with understanding how this works and why it is important. You said to Jane that because the project has only 150 requirements listed, you decided the traceability matrix (spreadsheet) is the easiest way to manage the requirements life cycle for the duration of the project. She said this doesn't make much sense to her yet but she will ask you more specific questions later to clarify. Now you are off to go organize the requirements prioritization meeting.

Question 1

Refer to the case study provided. Jane came to you about a requirement that relates to the online credit check that is performed when someone books a car. She wanted to know which stakeholder group originally requested this requirement. Which one of the following Requirements Life Cycle Management tasks that you have performed will help you to answer Jane's question?

    A. Elicit Requirements

    B. Trace Requirements

    C. Reuse Requirements

    D. Approve Requirements

Question 2

Refer to the provided case study. You finally found some time to sit down to explain to Jane what the Trace Requirements task is all about. Which of the following are inputs to this task?

Select one or more correct options:

    A. Requirements

    B. Needs

    C. Designs

    D. Stakeholders

Question 3

Refer to the provided case study. You are in the process of defining the approach that you will take with the traceability of the requirements. You would like to include relationships that indicate when two requirements have to be implemented together because of a dependency that exists between them. Which of the following terms describes this relationship type best?

    A. Derive

    B. Validate

C. Ratify

D. Necessity

Question 4

Refer to the provided case study. Which two aspects will be most important for stakeholders to consider when prioritizing requirements during the upcoming prioritization session?

A. Timeliness and business risk

B. Timeliness and complexity

C. Timeliness and cost

D. Timeliness and business value

Question 5

Refer to the provided case study. During the prioritization session, one of the stakeholders said that the team must remember that new legislation for capturing personal driver details is coming into effect before the project will be completed and that the project must adhere to this legislation. The team agrees that this must now be another aspect to consider when prioritizing requirements. Which element of the Prioritize Requirements task describes this type of consideration factor?

A. Continual prioritization

B. Risks of prioritization

C. Challenges of prioritization

D. Basis for prioritization

Question 6

Refer to the provided case study. When you and Jane start discussing the change request process of the project, you mention to her that this project is using a predominantly predictive approach. What does this mean for the level of formality around the assessment of proposed changes?

A. A formal assessment of change is not required but you would prefer it to remain formal.

B. The formality level of change assessments is not affected by the project approach.

C. A more formal assessment of change is likely to be required.

D. A less formal assessment of change is likely to be required.

Question 7

Refer to the provided case study and choose the individual or group of stakeholders who are most likely the approvers of change requests.

A. Change manager

B. Project team

C. Project stakeholders

D. Change control board

Question 8

Refer to the provided case study. You have been asked to perform an impact analysis on a proposed change that was received. The most obvious impact you can see is that the size of the change will impact the schedule. Which are some of the other considerations you should analysis?

Select one or more correct answers from the choices given here:

A. Priority

B. Source

C. Benefit

D. Cost

Question 9

Refer to the provided case study. You are about to submit your requirements for final approval. Which of the following inputs describes your requirements best?

A. Requirements (verified)

B. Requirements (maintained)

C. Requirements (documented)

D. Requirements (ranked)

Question 10

Refer to the provided case study. A week after your prioritization session with the stakeholders, one of the primary stakeholders of the project comes to tell you that the budget for the project has been cut and they need to reprioritize the requirements to include cost as a consideration. Is this an acceptable request and should you organize another prioritization session, or should you decline to do another prioritization session and simply say that it is too late in the project?

> A. It is not good practice to run multiple prioritization sessions.
>
> B. It is acceptable to run several prioritization sessions if required.

Question 11

The Requirements Life Cycle Management knowledge area consists of five primary tasks. Which of the following tasks are *not* part of this knowledge area?

Select one or more correct options:

> A. Approve Requirements
>
> B. Approve and Review Requirements
>
> C. Trace Requirements
>
> D. Manage Stakeholder Collaboration

Question 12

Which of the following options describes a primary output of the Approve Requirements knowledge area task?

> A. Designs (assessed)
>
> B. Designs (approved)
>
> C. Requirements (validated)
>
> D. Requirements (acknowledged)

Question 13

Which of the following options describes a primary output of the Trace Requirements knowledge area task?

A. Requirements (maintained)

B. Requirements (reused)

C. Designs (traced)

D. Requirements (tracked)

Question 14

Considering the knowledge area tasks you learned about during this chapter, which one's purpose is to rank requirements in the order of relative importance?

A. Prioritize Requirements

B. Trace Requirements

C. Rank Requirements

D. Approve Requirements

Question 15

When you assess a proposed change, you should consider various aspects of this change. Select all the aspects you should consider from the provided options:

A. Benefit

B. Scope

C. Cost

D. Schedule

Question 16

"An adaptive approach may require more formality in the assessment of proposed changes."

Choose whether the statement is true or false:

    A. True

    B. False

Question 17

Which one of the following options describes an element of the Approve Requirements task?

    A. Conflict and issue management

    B. Issue identification and resolution

    C. Communication of requirements decisions

    D. Negotiation and risk mitigation

Question 18

Different types of relationships exist between requirements. Select all the relationships listed here that have a dependency related relationship.

Select one or more correct options:

    A. Interrelated

    B. Necessity

    C. Satisfy

    D. Effort

Question 19

When defining requirements with a view to reuse for future projects or initiatives, which of the following considerations should you keep in mind?

    A. Try and write all your requirements for reuse.

    B. Minimize references to the current project or solution.

C. Provide as much detail as possible to ensure clarity and understandability.

D. Ensure that these requirements reflect the future of the organization.

Question 20

Information such as a requirement's source, priority, and complexity aid in managing requirements throughout the life cycle. This type of information is referred to as requirements attributes. **Choose whether this statement is true or false**.

A. True

B. False

Answers

Questions	Answers
1	B
2	A, C
3	D
4	D
5	D
6	C
7	D
8	C, D
9	A
10	B
11	B, D
12	B
13	C
14	A
15	A, C, D
16	B
17	A
18	B, D
19	B
20	A

Strategy Analysis 9

An organizational strategy is a definition of how an organization applies its capabilities to reach desired outcomes in an effective and efficient way. Strategy analysis is about guiding and supporting the organization through analysis to remain successful at achieving those desired outcomes.

This chapter covers tasks that are used to define the most effective way for an organization to move toward a defined business goal or objective. It addresses the business analysis task of defining the current state by identifying business needs in collaboration with stakeholders, establishing a desired future state description, assessing risks, and defining a strategy to implement changes to the organization.

By the end of this chapter, you will have learned about the key activities a business analyst performs to support an organization, department, or initiative to achieve their desired future state.

This chapter dives into the Analyze Current State, Define Future State, Assess Risks, and Define Change Strategy BABOK® v3 guide tasks and brings each of them into the real world with scenarios and examples:

- The purpose and context of this knowledge area
- Task: Analyze Current State
- Task: Define Future State
- Task: Assess Risks
- Task: Define Change Strategy
- Real-world case study quiz
- Test your knowledge

Concepts you will learn:

- Understand the context of this BABOK® v3 guide knowledge area within a real-world scenario
- Understand and apply the Analyze Current State task to real-world scenarios
- Understand and apply the Define Future State task to real-world scenarios
- Understand and apply the Assess Risks task to real-world scenarios
- Understand and apply the Define Change Strategy task to real-world scenarios
- Interpret a real-world scenario and apply the knowledge learned in this chapter
- Do a micro exam-style assessment

What is Strategy Analysis?

Let's start this chapter by understanding the term strategy in the context of business and, more specifically, business analysis. **Strategy** refers to the concept of defining the most effective method or path to apply capabilities within the organization to achieve results for the desired set of goals or objectives.

In the specific context of business analysis, the Strategy Analysis knowledge area describes the work involved in defining a business need that is of strategic (or tactical) importance by working in collaboration with business stakeholders. This includes work that will enable the business to address the need as well as to align the change with other business strategies at higher and lower levels of the organization.

Strategy analysis is also about defining the future states that should be the result of addressing the identified business needs. This often also includes the identification of alternative solutions that would effectively address the business needs with the ultimate objective of delivering more value to business stakeholders and customers.

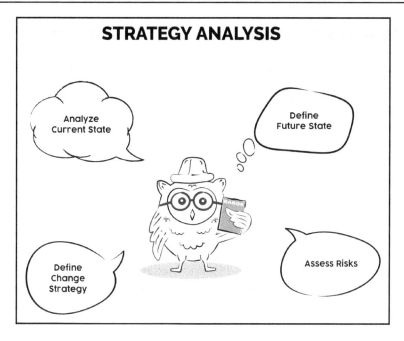

Strategy Analysis knowledge area and tasks

The Strategy Analysis knowledge area includes the following tasks:

- Analyze Current State
- Define Future State
- Assess Risks
- Define Change Strategy

With strategy analysis, there are a few different types of outputs or deliverables that typically get produced. These include artifacts such as a strategic plan, product vision, business case, product roadmap, and others.

Let's now explore how strategy analysis aligns with the Business Analysis Core Concept Model™.

The Business Analysis Core Concept Model™

First, let's refresh our memory of the six core concepts described in the Business Analysis Core Concept Model™:

- Change
- Need
- Solution
- Stakeholder
- Value
- Context

Here, we consider how strategy analysis as a knowledge area applies to the Business Analysis Core Concept Model™ through the use of a practical example.

Change

This core concept refers to how a change strategy is implemented to support the defined future state.

Let's look at an example to bring this concept of Change to life:

The New Orleans Electricity Company recently made the strategic decision to only issue electronic statements to their customers. A recent legislative change has allowed this to be implemented and, due to the high costs associated with paper-based statements and their distribution, the new legislation was a piece of very welcome news. A change strategy has to be defined to outline how customers will be transitioned from receiving paper-based statements in the mail to only receiving their statements electronically via email or via the electricity company's customer portal.

This example illustrates how the core concept of Change can be implemented when performing tasks defined in the Strategy Analysis knowledge area.

Need

This core concept refers to how needs within the current state are prioritized to determine the desired future state.

Let's look at an example to bring this concept of Need into the real world:

If we continue with the example of the electronic statements for the New Orleans Electricity Company, it is worth noting that the requirement or business need is to reduce operational costs associated with paper-based statements. Since this is the main business driver for this change, it forms the basis of defining the desired future state by ensuring a cost-effective solution is found.

This example illustrates how the core concept of Need is implemented during the strategy analysis by considering the needs in the current state and how this drives priorities for the change to be implemented in the desired future state.

Solution

This core concept refers to defining the scope of a solution as part of the change strategy.

Let's look at an example to bring this concept of Solution into the real world:

The change strategy that is developed for the New Orleans Electricity Company includes the transformation of paper-based statements into agreeable electronic statement templates. It doesn't include implementing a new customer portal to facilitate the retrieval or storage of those electronic statements. The scope of the solution in this scenario, therefore, excludes building a new customer portal. This, in turn, influences the change strategy that will be followed in terms of what solutions will be in scope to support the transition of customers from paper-based to electronic statements.

This example illustrates how the core concept of Solution can be implemented during strategy analysis with the focus on defining the scope and ensuring the change strategy aligns accordingly.

Stakeholder

This core concept refers to how stakeholders collaborate with the project team to understand the business need and define a change strategy and a desired future state that meets those needs.

Let's look at an example to bring this Stakeholder concept into the real world:

Let's continue with our example of the New Orleans Electricity Company. A key stakeholder for the paper-based to electronic statements project is the Customer Services department. It is important to understand the types of inquiries they receive today relating to statements, to ensure that when the new electronic statements are introduced, they understand the change fully and can continue to assist customers in the most effective way. Ideally, this stakeholder group could provide input into the future state in a way that will meet their specific business needs as well.

Therefore, it is clear that stakeholders play an important role in strategy analysis activities, having a clear relationship with the solution, the need, and the change.

Value

This core concept refers to examining the potential value of the solution to determine whether a change is justified.

Let's look at an example to bring this Value concept into the real world:

In the example of the New Orleans Electricity Company, the potential value of the paper-based to electronic statements project can clearly be illustrated with cost savings in the consumables and distribution areas. These cost savings should be assessed against new costs that may be introduced as a result of this initiative. This could include costs associated with additional customer service personnel that may need to be employed to support customers. Another cost could also be the potential introduction of a new software solution to generate and keep track of all electronic statements. Once this analysis has been completed, it will be easier to quantify and demonstrate the potential value of implementing this change.

Looking at this example, it is clear to see how strategy analysis plays a key part in determining the potential value of a planned change.

Context

The final core concept relates to how the context of the enterprise must be considered when developing a change strategy.

Let's look at an example to bring the Context concept into the real world:

In the utility industry, there are stringent rules around customer data privacy. The New Orleans Electricity Company needs to incorporate the rules that exist within the context in which this enterprise operates when they determine their change strategy for customers. For example, they may need to find a way to gain approval from customers to send them their personal statement information over the internet. It is, therefore, very important to consider the context in which this change is being planned when defining the change strategy.

So, in this particular context, the change strategy needs to adhere to any industry-related customer data privacy rules.

In this section, you have learned how the BACCM™ core concepts relate to the strategy analysis knowledge area of Business Analysis. These core concepts of Change, Need, Solution, Stakeholder, Value, and Context help business analysts to comprehend that business analysis is performed independently of perspective, industry, methodology, or even the level of the organization. It also helps you relate your daily work to each knowledge area using this conceptual framework.

Let's now have a closer look at the specific analysis tasks involved when working within the Strategy Analysis area.

Task: Analyze Current State

The first task described as part of the strategy analysis knowledge area is defined as analyzing the current state of the organization or business area under consideration. It is about understanding what is currently being done, performed, or executed to achieve particular goals or outcomes.

In this section, we cover the need to understand the current state of an organization and each element that should be considered when you perform a current state analysis. You will also learn that current state analysis is an essential analysis activity to help the organization understand the true nature of the business needs.

Purpose

According to the BABOK® v3 guide, the purpose of Analyze Current State is as follows:

> *"to understand the reasons why an enterprise needs to change some aspect of how it operates and what would be directly or indirectly affected by the change."*

The first step when assessing the current state is to gain a good understanding of why the change is needed. Most often, a potential change is needed when business problems or opportunities cannot be addressed without changing the current state.

Let's consider the following example:

A motor vehicle manufacturer has identified that there is a need to reduce the costs associated with the maintenance of its existing dealer management system. This system has been in use for 10 years and the vendor has almost doubled its licensing and maintenance fees in the last financial year. This, in turn, has caused increased dealership operational costs, which have an impact on dealership profitability ratios. The company has also received many more complaints in recent months from its end-user staff members. They are mostly complaining that the system is out of date and not meeting their expectations in terms of being able to serve customers well when using the system.

Based on the business need to reduce operational costs for the dealerships and manage ongoing system maintenance costs, a potential change in the way dealership management functions are managed and performed is being analyzed.

It is important to understand that the current state is analyzed and explored in just enough detail to validate and confirm the need for a change in a particular situation. As part of analyzing the current state, it is important to identify what changes would be needed and where in order to achieve the desired future state. Another important aspect is to identify a measure or method to use in order to assess whether the change that is implemented is effective.

The current state can be described at different levels, ranging from the entire organization to small parts of a solution.

It is also key to keep in mind that internal and external influencers, as well as other changes, can affect the current state in ways that force changes in the desired future state, change strategy, or requirements and designs.

Elements

There are eight elements to consider when you analyze the current state:

- Business needs
- Organizational structure and culture
- Capabilities and processes
- Technology and infrastructure
- Policies
- Business architecture
- Internal assets
- External influencers

We will now summarize each of these elements and describe them in the context of a practical example.

Element 1: Business needs

What is a business need and where does it come from?

Business needs are problems and opportunities of strategic importance experienced by the organization.

They can come from different levels within the organization. Here, we consider the different perspectives or directions these needs can come from within the organization:

From the top down: These are strategic goals that have been identified and need to be achieved.

In our motor vehicle manufacturer example, the board members of the motor vehicle manufacturer have identified a need to reduce operational costs within the dealerships.

From the bottom up: This is when a problem is identified with the current state of a process, function, or system.

Using our example, the current dealer management system vendor is not addressing the issues or problems identified and raised by staff members using the system. This is causing ongoing operational issues and increased inefficiencies.

From middle management: This is when a manager or a group of managers need further information to make sound decisions or have to perform additional functions to meet business goals and objectives.

Using our example to explore this further, the management at the dealership level is reviewing budgets for the future year. The expenses presented for the next year have brought to light that the dealer management system costs need to be addressed.

From external drivers: When we say a business need came from external drivers, we mean that the business need was identified as a result of a challenge that came from outside the organization. These types of external drivers could be described as things such as a change in customer demand or a change in business competition.

Using our example, the current dealer management system vendor is an external organization that has doubled its annual maintenance charges to the dealerships. This has a direct impact on the dealership's profitability ratios, which is driving the need for change.

Business needs are always expressed from the perspective of the organization, and not from the perspective of any individual stakeholder.

Business needs are often identified or expressed along with a suggested solution.

It is the business analyst's role to question the assumptions and constraints that might be disguised in the statement of the issue to make sure that the correct problem is being addressed and that the most optimal range of alternative solutions is being considered as part of the change.

Element 2: Organizational structure and culture

Do we need to carry out a cultural and structural assessment?

Firstly, the term organizational structure refers to the formal relationships between people working in the organization. The communication channels and relationships within the organization are not limited to the organizational structure, however, they are often driven by it. It is important, therefore, to analyze the structure thoroughly so that the impact (whether positive or negative) it can have on the planned change is well understood.

If for example, the senior stakeholders have a very strong and personal relationship with the current system vendor's management group, it might be difficult to change to another solution provider without affecting those relationships. It would be important to understand the impact those relationships will have on the decisions made regarding the necessary change.

If key stakeholders fail to agree that the current solution is unsatisfactory, a change will also be more difficult, and this needs to be addressed.

Element 3: Capabilities and processes

Identifying the activities performed within an organization.

Capabilities and processes are all the functions performed within the organization, including products, services, and decision-making methods.

The business analyst can use a capability-centric view or a process-centric view to assess the benefit of a change.

Let's now consider a practical example for each of these two different views when assessing the benefit of a change:

Capability-centric view: For example, an organization that provides short-term loans and home loan finance could simply add another product to be able to supply vehicle financing. This would be a change in capability. The benefit to the organization would be increased growth due to the new product (utilizing existing capabilities). This new capability is able to serve a new customer segment.

*Process-centric view: An organization that services and repairs vehicles have always ordered their vehicle parts stock on a weekly basis. When we change the business process to order and have these parts delivered by the warehouse on a daily basis, we can describe that as a **business process change** with a positive impact on the organization's ability to service clients.*

The outcome of this analysis would be to identify what new capabilities are possible by combining some of the existing capabilities within the organization and whether these could be developed as profitable solutions to the organization. Whereas, with the analysis of a process-centric view, it results in whether a change in process would be beneficial to address the current business needs within the organization.

Element 4: Technology and infrastructure

How can technology and infrastructure impact a solution?

Information systems used by the organization support people in using processes, making business decisions, and having interactions with vendors and customers.

The infrastructure describes the organizations in terms of their physical aspects and capabilities and most typically includes components such as computer hardware, physical plants, and logistics, as well as the operation and upkeep of those aspects.

Let's consider our current example in this context: *The business process was changed to deliver vehicle parts stock on a daily basis, however, for the business process change to be applied and be effective in all dealerships across the country, the organization's infrastructure needs to be assessed.*

It was determined that a few centralized stock warehouses need to be built or leased to ensure that enough stock is available in central business areas to meet the increased business need to deliver new parts on a daily basis to repair centers.

Element 5: Policies

How can policies impact a suggested solution?

Policies can be seen as a set of rules that provide guidance to staff on behavior and actions; they also address routine operations. The policies of an organization can impact the possibility of implementing a specific solution if the solution does not meet or is in conflict with the organization's policy requirements within a particular context.

Let's consider a practical example: *A company needs to employ a new accountant. Among the applicants for the position is a family member of one of the existing staff members. If there is a policy that exists that states family members of existing staff may not be employed, this application must be denied.*

Element 6: Business architecture

When analyzing the current state, the business analyst avoids considering only parts of the whole situation to avoid working on certain aspects in isolation from other parts. The business analyst must know how all the parts work and fit together in order to recommend changes that will be effective once implemented.

The existing business architecture typically meets a variety of current business and stakeholder needs and therefore must be carefully considered to ensure the desired future state also caters to those needs in order to prevent a loss of value to the organization and its stakeholders.

To better understand this, let's again consider the example of daily parts delivery in the car dealership scenario:

- *The business need for being able to service a customer within a day by having access to all required parts in a timely fashion has been established.*
- *An infrastructure need was identified and addressed by building warehouses closer to the central metropolitan areas, as well as the enhancement of the actual stock delivery process to and from this warehouse.*
- *The processes within the dealerships were enhanced in order to do real-time stock receipting and invoice reconciliation in order to streamline this process even further.*

If any of these needs were considered in isolation, the solutions and introduced changes would potentially have been much less effective or caused a loss of value in one or more of those business areas.

Element 7: Internal assets

As part of performing a current state analysis, business analysts will identify organizational assets. These assets can be tangible or intangible and can include assets such as financial resources, patents, reputation, know-how, and brand.

In our example, *the current good reputation of the vehicle repair centers across the country is an example of an intangible asset of this company*.

Element 8: External influences

There are external influences on the organization that could impact the change by introducing constraints, dependencies, or other drivers that affect the current state. Some of these sources of external influences come from the following areas:

- Industry structure
- Competitors
- Customers
- Suppliers
- The political and regulatory environment
- Technology
- Macroeconomic factors

Let's consider some of these factors in the context of the example of the vehicle repair company by asking some target questions:

- *What are the competitors doing to stay ahead in the industry?*
- *What other potential customer segments exist that we have not considered yet?*
- *What power or influence does the current supplier have over their customers, if any?*
- *Has technology innovation such as 3D printing been considered? This could affect the way the company obtains spare parts on an as-needed basis?*
- *Is the macroeconomy being considered when projecting the future sales revenue of spare parts? Macroeconomic factors to consider would be the effect of inflation on spare parts for vehicles that could affect the company's ability to deliver services at the same prices to customers.*

Inputs and outputs

With the Analyze Current State strategy analysis task, there are the following key inputs and outputs:

- **Inputs**: Elicitation results and needs
- **Outputs**: Current state description and business requirements

You have now covered the task of analyzing the current state, which results in a clear current state description. You also have a set of clear business requirements describing the key objectives for the planned change.

Let's now move on to the next strategy analysis task, Define Future State.

Task: Define Future State

The second task described as part of the strategy analysis knowledge area is to define the future state of the organization or business area under consideration. This task is an important business analysis activity to support the business on its journey to define the future vision for the solution to the business needs. This task is about understanding what the desired outcomes or results we are expecting are by making the change when addressing the business need.

In this section, we cover those business analysis elements that help you formulate and analyze all the aspects of establishing a desired future state. Each of those elements needs careful consideration as part of defining the future state.

Let's start this discussion by understanding the purpose of defining the future state.

Purpose

According to the BABOK® v3 guide, the purpose of Define Future State is as follows:

"*to determine the set of necessary conditions to meet the business need.*"

Ultimately defining the future state is about defining and expressing what you and your stakeholders are expecting in terms of the future outcomes once the change has been implemented. It is important to ensure that the future state is well defined and that it is achievable considering the resources that are available. Another key aspect when defining the future state is to ensure a common vision amongst stakeholders of what the expected desired outcome is.

A key reason you would perform a future state analysis is to gather enough information and details to make the best possible decisions when considering different potential solution options.

There is flexibility in defining a future state description because it can include any context or perspective of the desired future state. It can describe the new, removed, and modified components of the organization and can include aspects describing changes in terms of people, processes, and technology.

Let's revisit our previous example, *where the stakeholder requirement was to find an alternative solution to the current dealer management system, which was proven to be too expensive to maintain*.

The future state description will describe the changes in budget requirements for the implementation and maintenance of the new dealership management system. It will include the scope of the desired solution capabilities and any system integration aspects that will need to be built or changed. It will also include information about any business processes required changes, as well as any infrastructure changes. The future state description will also outline any people changes that may be needed to achieve the desired results.

Elements

There are eleven elements to consider when you define the future state:

- Business goals and objectives
- The scope of the solution space
- Constraints
- Organizational structure and culture
- Capabilities and processes
- Technology and infrastructure
- Policies
- Business architecture
- Internal assets
- Identify assumptions
- Potential value

We will now summarize each of these elements and describe each in the context of a practical example.

Element 1: Business goals and objectives

Very often, a future state is described in terms of business objectives or goals. These goals then act as a guideline to define and develop the change strategy and help define measures for the potential value to be had.

Goals tend to be long-term and ongoing statements. Goals are also more qualitative in nature and describe a state or condition that the organization wants to establish or maintain.

Some examples of business goals can include statements like the following:

- *Create a new capability or function*
- *Improve revenue by increasing sales or reducing costs*
- *Increase customer or employee satisfaction*
- *Reduce the time to deliver a product or service*

A goal will be broken down into objectives that are more granular and specific in nature. A key part of formulating objectives is to ensure they are measurable by nature. The organization will define specific measures as part of the objective statements, which can be used when planning key performance indicators for successful change implementation.

There is a well-known test for assessing objectives in terms of how well they have been defined, called **SMART**. The SMART test works as follows:

- **Specific**: Is your objective specific; does it describe a specific outcome or result?
- **Measurable**: Is the outcome or result measurable?
- **Achievable**: Is this objective feasible or achievable?
- **Relevant**: Is this objective aligned and relevant to the organization's vision and goals?
- **Time-bound**: What is the timeframe for this objective to be achieved?

An example of an objective for a vehicle manufacturing company could be *To increase vehicle sales by 20% by the end of the current financial year*.

Element 2: The scope of the solution space

This element is about describing which types of changes will be considered as in scope to achieve the desired future state. For example, would changes to the organizational structure, people, and processes be considered part of the solution? Or would the solution scope be limited to only updating technology solutions with minimal or no changes to the organizational structure or people?

We can also consider this practical example following on from the previous scenario of the dealership management system:

If there are multiple dealer management systems available to choose from to replace the existing solution, the scope of the solution should be documented for each alternative solution. This is because different solutions could cause changes in different aspects of the business. For example, solution A might require a complete change in computer hardware and printing devices, as well as a software implementation, whereas solution B may require a big change in business processes with minimal hardware changes.

By understanding the anticipated solution scope, it is possible to make critical business decisions about solution options using considerations deemed important within the current context.

Element 3: Constraints

Constraints are the boundaries that the current state and future state must be defined within.

For example, *a client requests a new website to be built for their company, however, it must be built using a specific framework, such as WordPress.*

It must be built in such a way that the clients can maintain it themselves after delivery, and the development of the new website cannot take longer than 7 days.

This is an example of a technology, time, and skills constraint, which needs to be considered when planning the future state.

Element 4: Organizational structure and culture

Often, when a large-scale change is introduced into an organization, the formal and informal working relationships that exist within the organization need to change to help achieve the desired future state.

An example when the organizational structure and cultural element should be considered in terms of the definition of the future state is a case where two teams will be merged and duplicate job functions will be created or changes will be made to the reporting lines of employees.

When these types of changes are included in the description of the future state description, it will assist in mitigating possible conflict that might arise during the realization of a future state.

Element 5: Capabilities and processes

When you define the future state, a key element to include is any changes to the current activities being performed in the organization. Any new processes or capabilities, or changes to existing ones, relating to any function being affected by the change should be included as the future state definition and description. For example, new or changed processes and capabilities could be in the areas of delivering new products or services, activities to comply with new regulations, or processes to improve the performance of the organization.

Let's consider a real-world example: *A new product is introduced within an existing business area. This new product will follow existing inventory processes, however, there is a handover point in the process where the new product is following a new labeling process. This new labeling process would need to be included as part of the future state description.*

Element 6: Technology and infrastructure

This element is about the business analyst assessing what the potential technology and infrastructure changes should include in order to achieve the desired future state.

Let's consider some real-world examples of where changes to technology and infrastructure may need to be identified and analyzed by the business analyst:

Example 1: *The current accounting software package at a financial institution runs on a Linux-based server. The solution identified for the future state requires a different operating system.*

A great way to learn the content of all the BABOK® v3.0 Guide tasks is to relate each and every task to a real-world scenario you have personal experience of. Do this by considering the task and the elements of the task, and then find your own real-world example based on previous experience. If you are unable to find a suitable memory of this, make up another real-world scenario that would be relevant and true.

Another consideration in this context may be that the existing technology in an organization may impose technical constraints on the design of the solution.

Example 2: *The existing technology within a financial institution may only accept file communication and integration if it is in a specific flat-file format. This constraint impacts the design of the solution for the file communication protocols needed for the desired future state.*

Element 7: Policies

Policies would need to be updated if the business analyst finds the current policies to be insufficient to cater to the desired future state.

Let's consider a real-world scenario where a policy can be impacted by a change. Consider a micro-lending organization that sets the maximum loan amount for small business loans to a new limit as part of the future state design. This change has an impact on current company policies and needs to be updated to incorporate the new limit for maximum loan amounts.

Element 8: Business architecture

All the components of any future state must support one another and work toward the business goals and objectives. The overall desired future state of the organization as a whole must be considered as part of the definition of the desired future state of any individual initiative or solution.

For example, *let's say that the desired future state of an organization is to have all staff members work remotely to reduce the need for maintaining a large physical office building. If this is the case, it would be a contradiction to the overall business objectives if a decision was made to implement a solution or business process that supports a central and co-located staff working model.*

It is therefore important to always consider the desired future state of the entire organization when working on a future state for a specific initiative.

Element 9: Internal assets

When you consider the element of internal resources in the context of defining the future state, you will see that the role of the business analyst here is to assess the existing capabilities and resources the organization has and whether there is a need to increase or change those resources to support the future state. This also includes an assessment of whether the existing capabilities and resources can be reused as part of the desired future state.

Let's look at a straightforward practical example. *Consider a courier company that would like the capability to double the number of weekly deliveries as part of the desired future state. The question in terms of the internal assets or capabilities then becomes: To achieve these delivery numbers in the future, would the current number of courier vehicles and drivers be sufficient?*

In this example, the business analyst considers the internal assets within the current state to see whether it would be sufficient to support the desired future state.

Element 10: Identify assumptions

Most strategies are predicated on a set of assumptions that will determine whether or not the strategy can succeed, particularly when operating in a highly uncertain environment. It will often be difficult or impossible to prove that the delivery of a new capability will meet a business need, even in cases where it appears reasonable to assume that the new capability will have the desired effect.

It is important to be clear and have well-understood assumptions about what needs to be true in order for the desired future state to be successfully implemented or achieved. When assumptions are well defined, it enables the team to test any change strategies to validate assumptions or discover whether any assumptions are in fact incorrect. If critical assumptions are proven incorrect in the early stages of an initiative, it assists the team in redirecting or potentially terminating the initiative.

Let's consider a real-world scenario of an assumption made in a banking environment. *The assumption made was that if a loan application system was built in-house, rather than purchasing an existing solution off the shelf, it would be of more value to the bank because it would address the bank's specific business needs.*

However, once the solution has been built and tested, it is found that there are many problems that could not easily be solved in-house due to a lack of skills and know-how.

Unfortunately, in this scenario, the assumption that it would be more beneficial to develop the software solution in-house instead of buying a vendor's off-the-shelf solution was incorrect and not analyzed and validated in the early stages of the initiative. This invalid assumption has cost the bank a large amount of unplanned time and resource costs.

The last element to consider when the business analyst works to define the future state is assessing the potential value of the future state.

Element 11: Potential value

The element describing the potential value that the desired future state expects to deliver is about considering not only the implementation costs of the new solution or change but understanding the potential future value that the change will bring to the business. This could be expressed in terms of a financial return or it could be expressed in less tangible terms. A scenario may occur where an organization needs to implement a change to be able to continue to practice in business due to a legislative change. In this case, the business may even have a decline in overall value or return but is still able to operate as a business.

Let's continue with our dealership management system example. *The procurement costs, installation costs, and customization costs, as well as monthly running costs, must be considered when choosing a suitable vendor to replace the current dealer management system. This is necessary to be confident that the net benefit of proceeding with the new solution would outweigh any costs incurred to implement the change.*

Additional sources for potential value may be less tangible or quantifiable and in our example, could include the new vendor having a strong industry-aligned technology knowledge base and aligning their software with ongoing innovations happening within the industry.

Inputs and outputs

With the Define Future State strategy analysis task, there are the following key inputs and outputs:

- **Inputs**: Business requirements
- **Outputs**: Business objectives, future state description, and potential value

You have now learned about the task of defining a future state, which will result in business objectives, a future state description, and the potential value expected from the future state solution.

Let's now move on to the next strategy analysis task, Assess Risks.

Task: Assess Risks

The third task described as part of the strategy analysis knowledge area is to assess risks that exist in the context of moving into the future state or once the organization is in the future state.

As a business analyst, this is an important task to incorporate into your work because the business analyst is in a unique position to understand the business needs in detail as well as to have a broad understanding of the solution aspects being considered. This enables the business analyst to identify and assess risks during the course of an initiative. In this section, we will learn about the key elements to consider when assessing potential risks. We will address the key aspects of making suitable recommendations to stakeholders in terms of the best course of action once risks have been assessed for an initiative.

Let's start by understanding the purpose of the Assess Risks task.

Purpose

According to the BABOK® v3 guide, the purpose of the Assess Risks task is the following:

>*"to understand the undesirable consequences of internal and external forces on the enterprise during a transition to, or once in, the future state. An understanding of the potential impact of those forces can be used to make a recommendation about a course of action."*

 What is the definition of risk? The BABOK® v3 Guide definition is as follows: "Risk is the effect of uncertainty on the value of the change, a solution, or the enterprise."

Assessing risks is about analyzing the risks and also actively managing their potential impact on the solution underway. You might identify risks associated with the current state, the desired future state, a specific change or change strategy, or any other area within the enterprise.

The reasons why risks are analyzed is to understand the possible consequences if a potential risk should actually occur, to understand the real impact of those consequences, how likely it is for the risk to eventuate, and the timeframe of when this risk might occur.

If you understand the risks that exist within the context in which you are working, you are in a much better position to make decisions relating to the risk and you can prepare yourself for managing the risk if it should materialize.

Let's now consider a common example of identifying and managing risks:

Let's say you are required to implement a change to allow "card not present" type transactions within a banking environment. You are aware of the possible fraud risks associated with this transaction type and because of this you can document, prepare for, and manage those risks in a structured and controlled way.

In this case, you will also be able to make informed decisions when all the risks are known about whether the organization is willing to accept these risks by continuing with the implementation.

Now that we have an overview of the scope of assessing risks, we will delve into the key elements that you should consider when performing this task as a business analyst in practice.

Elements

There are five elements to consider when you assess risks:

- Unknowns
- Constraints, assumptions, and dependencies
- Negative impact on the value
- Risk tolerance
- Recommendations

Element 1: Unknowns

What if you don't know all the risks?

Often in an initiative, there is some uncertainty of the likelihood of any specific risk occurring and what the exact impact would be. The role of the business analyst is to work with stakeholders in relation to any identified risks and aim to elicit as much information as possible about the risk, its likelihood, and the potential impact. Even if this proves challenging, it is still worth documenting as much information as possible about the risks and to prepare a plan to mitigate or manage the risks should they occur.

Let's look at a real-world example. *Let's consider the risks associated with a point-of-sale device upgrade project. Within a retail organization, there is a requirement to upgrade to new point-of-sale devices. The new devices will be supplied by a different manufacturer than the current devices.*

As a business analyst, you identify some risks relating to the data integration and device communication aspects. You also realize that there might be other risks that you are not able to define yet that may occur or become known once the new devices have been installed and are functioning. This leads you to recommend a risk mitigation strategy, which is to do some testing on the new devices before rolling out all devices to the retail outlets.

Element 2: Constraints, assumptions, and dependencies

If we consider the task of assessing risks, it is worth understanding that any constraints, assumptions, or dependencies that have been defined for your change or initiative should also be analyzed in terms of identifying risks. This may result in reformulating the constraint, assumption, or dependency as a risk and then managing it as such going forward.

Let's clarify this scenario with a real-world example:

You have purchased a new property, but there is a condition on the purchase contract that says that it is dependent on the sale of your existing property. This dependency in itself can be seen as a risk to the property purchase process and needs to be identified and assessed.

It is also assumed that the purchase of the new property and the sale of the old property will happen at the same time and that you won't end up needing to look for alternative accommodation for a certain period of time. This assumption can be identified as a risk.

An additional risk in the context of this scenario could be the constraint that you will not be able to move into the new property until the current owners have moved out. The consequence of this risk occurring is that you may not have anywhere to live until the current owners have moved out of the new property.

Element 3: Negative impact on the value

One of the fundamental reasons it is important to identify risks while performing business analysis is because we need to know the conditions that will increase the likelihood of a negative impact on the value we are working toward delivering. It is important to determine the level of risk and the likelihood of the risk eventuating.

There is the possibility to be able to quantify the overall risk level in financial terms, by looking at the amount of time potentially lost or spent, or at the effort involved.

Let's consider the following example:

A company is required to move their server hosting from one hosting company to another. There are many risks associated with this type of move, but let's look at only a couple here in this example:

The risk of data loss: *If this risk does occur, it is possible to consider the financial impact this will have by estimating the costs involved in recovering the data. Another financial implication could be the potential loss of income if the server is down for a period of time.*

Element 4: Risk tolerance

What is risk tolerance and how is it measured?

Risk tolerance is a measure of how much uncertainty a stakeholder or an enterprise is willing to take on in exchange for potential value.

There are three broad ways of describing a company's attitude toward risk in general:

- **Risk aversion:** When a company is risk-averse, it means that their preference is to not take risks or there is an unwillingness to accept much uncertainty.
- **Neutrality**: When a company is risk-neutral, it means that their attitude toward risk allows some level of risk to be acceptable, just as long as when the risk does occur, there is no loss of any kind.
- **Risk seeking:** When a company is risk-seeking, it means that they are willing to take on more risk as long as a higher potential value will be achieved, perhaps even seeking higher risks for a higher-value return.

As you can imagine, an individual or company may express different risk tolerances at different times of their lives or in different circumstances.

These types of risk tolerance can often clearly be seen when it comes to making financial investments. However, they can also be applied within normal project environments.

Let's consider the following example: *A stakeholder group sponsoring a project is willing to take the risk of implementing a specific change without the change being fully tested because this change has the potential for high financial return in the short term. If they want to pursue this short-term financial gain, they have to accept the risk that it is an untested change that could negatively impact other aspects if problems arise. In this scenario, in order to potentially realize the financial benefits, higher risk tolerance is accepted.*

Element 5: Recommendations

This element describes the recommendations a business analyst would make in terms of a course of action to be taken after considering the overall risk level and the stakeholders' risk tolerance.

There are very common categories these recommendations would fall into:

- Continue to pursue the benefits of a change regardless of the risk level
- Pursue the benefits of a change while spending time and effort to reduce the likelihood and/or impact of that risk
- Aim to find more ways to increase the benefits of making a change to outweigh the risk
- Recommend not pursuing the benefits of a change due to the risk level

Inputs and outputs

With the Assess Risks strategy analysis task, there are the following key inputs and outputs:

- **Inputs**: Business objectives, elicitation results (confirmed), influences, potential value, requirements (prioritized)

- **Outputs**: Risk analysis results

You have now learned about the task of assessing risk, which results in comprehensive risk analysis results to share with the team and the stakeholders of your initiative.

Let's now move on to the next strategy analysis task, Define Change Strategy, in order to develop and assess alternative approaches and make recommendations for the next steps.

Task: Define Change Strategy

The fourth task described as part of the strategy analysis knowledge area is to define the change strategy. This task is about understanding alternative approaches that could be taken to a change and what is involved in making a choice about which alternative to moving forward with.

Defining the change strategy is a key task in the context of business analysis because it supports the transition from the current state to the desired future state in a planned and systematic way. It guides and ensures that the change strategy is supported by sound analysis of the elements that influence the success of an initiative. In this section, we will cover the analysis elements that are key to the successful execution of a change strategy.

Let's start by understanding the purpose of defining a change strategy.

Purpose

According to the BABOK® v3 Guide, the purpose of Define Change Strategy is the following:

> *"to develop and assess alternative approaches to the change, and then select the recommended approach."*

Let's consider a real-world example to give this task some context. *You can consider a scenario where the best implementation approach needs to be selected. You may need to make an assessment between whether a "big bang" approach to implementing a change would be most suitable, or whether a "phased approach" to implementing a change would be the most appropriate within a specific environment. A "big bang" approach refers to an implementation where all changes are implemented at once, and a "phased approach" refers to a more staggered approach to implementing changes over a period of time.*

You will be able to appreciate that it is easier to develop a change strategy when the current state and the future state are already defined because they provide some perspective on what the change is about.

When you develop a change strategy, you should describe the change in the context of answering key questions about the following aspects:

- What is the context of the change?
- What are the identified alternative change strategies?
- Include a justification for why a particular change strategy is the best approach.
- What investment and resources would be required to work toward the future state?
- How will the organization be able to realize value after the solution is delivered?
- Who are the key stakeholders in the change?
- What would the transition states be along the way?

Elements

There are five elements to consider when you define a change strategy:

- Solution scope
- Gap analysis
- Enterprise readiness assessment
- Change strategy
- Transition states and release planning

Let's now consider each of these elements in more detail.

Element 1: Solution scope

What is the solution scope and why is it required?

Let's start by defining the term solution in this context. The term solution here simply refers to the outcome or result once a change has been implemented in order to meet a particular business need.

Whereas the solution scope defines the new capabilities and functionality that will be included as part of the change. It also includes a description of how it will solve any identified current state issues or problems and how it will meet the goals set for the desired future state.

The solution scope can often also include descriptions of aspects that are not included in the scope and are deemed out-of-scope components.

Let's now consider a real-world example: *An architectural design company's stakeholders have identified that the company website is not generating the number of leads they need to grow the business effectively. They have determined that there is a need to improve the number of leads that are generated by the website and that a change needs to be made to the website to facilitate this change.*

A website development company is briefed on the current problems they are experiencing with the current website and asked to come back with a solution scope of what they believe needs to be changed in order to achieve the desired future state (more good leads). When the website development company provides the documented solution scope, they include the following:

- The look and feel aspects of the website to generate more leads
- Additional lead tracking software

- Additional online marketing options
- A better-structured website to assist in lead generation as part of the solution scope

In addition, they have suggested documenting internal business processes that should be enhanced to be able to process the incoming leads more effectively.

This example illustrates that the solution scope can be described in different ways and can include change aspects such as capabilities, technology, processes, and so forth.

Element 2: Gap analysis

The idea of a gap analysis is often used when describing a document or set of activities that identify all the differences between the current state and the future state capabilities. To be able to perform an effective gap analysis, it is important that both the current and future state is defined in detail.

Let's continue our real-world example of the architectural design company:

It is clear that a gap analysis will be a helpful activity to perform to determine the differences between the capabilities of the current website and the potential future website described by the website development company's solution scope.

It also enables the business analyst to see what would be required and the effort needed to move from the current state to the future state.

In our real-world example, *the effort could include things such as designing a new website, implementing additional software integrations, employing additional staff, and implementing changes in business processes.*

Element 3: Enterprise readiness assessment

The enterprise readiness assessment is about the activities performed to determine whether an organization has the capacity and ability to accept the change being proposed, as well as whether the organization will be able to sustain the solution and realize value from the solution. This is an important assessment to do in order to facilitate a successful project outcome.

In a real-world scenario, *the level of success of the implementation could be heavily affected if the following aspects have not been completed or agreed upon:*

- *The impacted recipient stakeholders are not ready to accept a new software solution.*
- *The business support operations division who has to consume the output generated by the new solution has not yet planned, documented, or tested any of the new operational support processes.*

This is why it is crucial to perform an enterprise readiness assessment to determine whether a new change or solution will be able to be sustained and valued in the organization.

Other aspects included in the enterprise readiness assessment are an analysis of the timeline from when the change will be implemented to when it is expected that value can be realized, as well as which resources are required to be available to support the change effort.

Element 4: Change strategy

When you formulate a change strategy, you are creating a high-level plan that describes the key activities that will be executed to move or transform the organization from their current situation to the future state. Change strategies are most commonly described either as a one-off (big-bang) implementation or a phased or iterative style implementation.

Before choosing the preferred change strategy, you should consider the following aspects:

How ready is the organization to make the change?

For example: *If the organization recently underwent restructuring, it may not be the most suitable time to introduce an additional change to the organization.*

Are there major costs and investments required to make the change?

For example: *Consider whether it is more costly to continuously do iterative smaller implementations or to do a one-off implementation.*

Is now a good time from an organizational timeline perspective to make a change?

For example: *If there is no strict deadline to have a fully functional solution, smaller more frequent implementations might be considered in order to implement the change over a longer period of time.*

Further considerations include the following:

Is the change strategy aligned with the business objectives?

For example: *If a business objective is to reduce the operational costs across the business and a change strategy recommendation is an implementation approach that is not cost-effective, then this could be considered as an unaligned change strategy.*

Is it optimal from a timeline to a value-realization perspective?

Does the change strategy minimize the time between implementation and when the business can start expecting a cost reduction or value increase? For example: *Consider a change strategy where it is decided to adopt an iterative cycle-based implementation. This approach is estimated to take 12 months to complete implementation whereas a "Big Bang" change strategy for the same implementation would take only 6 months. The business would need to consider all factors (associated risks, costs, people, and so on) as well as the timeline to value realization before they make a final decision to adopt an iterative change strategy.*

What are the opportunity costs of the change strategy?

The opportunity costs refer to the benefits that could have been realized if an alternative change strategy was adopted. For example: *If a business decides to adopt a "Big Bang" strategy for implementation, they can save money because they only need to fund a project implementation team for a short period of time. However, if they choose an iterative implementation approach that takes longer to be completed, they will need to fund a project implementation team for a longer period of time.*

Element 5: Transition states and release planning

A transition state is where the organization has to keep operating within a state where the change has not been fully implemented yet. It is often considered as part of the release planning, which is when it is decided which capabilities of the new solution will be included in which parts of the solution release for implementation. Other factors that determine which capabilities will be included in the releases are factors such as budget, time, and resource constraints.

It is important for the business analyst to know when changes will be implemented, what changes will be implemented, and how they will impact the business.

Let's consider the following real-world example to understand this concept further.

Consider implementing a new banking system that affects both the back-office systems and the frontline bank personnel and systems. From a change strategy point of view, it doesn't make sense to implement the entire change at once, because the impact on staff and on the business itself will be too significant. In this case, a phased implementation will be a better change strategy.

It is the responsibility of the business analyst to ensure that they know how the old and new systems will integrate or communicate during the transition state. The transition state will continuously change as new releases are implemented and will cease when the full solution has been implemented.

Additional planning considerations such as new training for staff members to facilitate the transition state should be incorporated as part of the release-planning tasks.

Inputs and outputs

With the Define Change Strategy strategy analysis task, there are the following key inputs and outputs:

- **Inputs**: Current state description, future state description, risk analysis results, and stakeholder engagement approach

- **Outputs**: Change strategy and solution scope

You have now learned about the task of defining a change strategy that results in a defined solution scope and a recommended change strategy.

Summary

In this chapter, you have learned about the strategy analysis knowledge area.

The following are the key concepts and tasks we covered during this chapter:

- The strategy analysis knowledge area
- Task: Analyze Current State
- Task: Define Future State
- Task: Assess Risks
- Task: Define Change Strategy

Make sure you revise these before completing the knowledge quiz at the end of this chapter.

You now have an understanding of the importance and purpose of the strategy analysis knowledge area and know the scope of performing analysis tasks for an initiative from a strategic analysis perspective.

Learning outcome: Strategy Analysis

You now have a holistic understanding of the importance and purpose of the strategy analysis knowledge area in terms of the role it plays in analyzing, planning, and completing the business analysis work you do. You are able to describe this knowledge area in the context of the BACCM™ using real-world practical situations. You are also able to visualize the key inputs and outputs to perform this task effectively.

Learning outcome: Analyze Current State

In this chapter, you learned about the task of analyzing the current state and you are now able to describe the purpose of this task and describe the key elements to consider when performing this task using real-world scenarios and concepts. You are also able to visualize the key inputs and outputs to perform this task effectively.

Learning outcome: Define Future State

In this chapter, you learned about the task of defining the future state and you are now able to describe the purpose of this task and describe the key elements to consider when doing this task using real-world scenarios and concepts. You are also able to visualize the key inputs and outputs to perform this task effectively.

Learning outcome: Assess Risks

Another key learning from this chapter is your understanding of and ability to describe the task of assessing risks in terms of its purpose and you are able to describe the key elements to consider when performing this task using real-world scenarios and concepts. You are also able to visualize the key inputs and outputs to perform this task effectively.

Learning outcome: Define Change Strategy

In this chapter, you learned about the task of defining the change strategy and you are now able to describe the purpose of this task and describe the key elements to consider when doing this task using real-world scenarios and concepts. You are also able to visualize the key inputs and outputs to perform this task effectively.

Knowledge quiz

Consider the following real-world scenario and complete the micro mock exam based on this chapter that follows.

Case Study: Police criminal record management system

Program initiative background: The Australian police force currently uses an old mainframe system to record any police incidents and criminal record information. This system is very outdated and not user-friendly at all. New, younger police officers find it particularly hard to learn because it is very unfamiliar, old-fashioned technology. Although this system contains a wealth of criminal record data, some of this data is inaccurate and it is very hard for police officers to find any critical information in a timely fashion. This means that due to all these limiting factors, police are less effective in their roles than they would be if they had the right information available at the right time. Other issues such as finding missing people using the information available is also very hard to match to new police information when it becomes available. The effect of this cumbersome, old-fashioned system is that police members feel disempowered and frustrated. There is a proposal being put forward by senior leaders within the police force to replace the current mainframe system with a new, up-to-date criminal record system that addresses the preceding problems. The new system will include all the current criminal record system's functionality as well as new out-of-the-box capabilities. The senior leaders have had a lot of recent pressure from a variety of sources and are now committed to driving this change through the organization. Some of these sources include the government, the community themselves, as well as the many proven technology solutions in the market, which leaves this police force with no excuse but to take action with this initiative.

The expectation is that implementing this new system will help police reduce crime, find more missing people, and boost the morale of police officers in general. It will also bring the police systems up to date with modern technology, which will enable them to respond much quicker to critical incidents. Although quantifying the benefits of this system is hard, the general belief is that the new system will save the taxpayer $5 million dollars in the next 5 years, with a big reduction in the system maintenance bill they currently have to pay to maintain the old technology. This initiative will include integration with other law enforcement agencies to enable information sharing to make policing in the general community more effective. They are proposing to include document management capabilities in the solution scope to reduce paper usage and to expedite the resolution of case records that are due in court.

Question 1

Consider the following extract from the provided case study: "This system is very outdated and not user-friendly at all." This leads to poor police officer performance and affects the ability of the police to be highly effective when policing the streets.

Which element of the "Analyze Current State" task is being described here?

Select the correct answer from the choices that follow:

A. Policies

B. Organizational structure

C. Business needs

D. Gap analysis

Question 2

Using the provided case study, from which level in the organization is the change being driven from implementing the new criminal records system?

Select the correct answer from the choices that follow:

A. From the bottom up

B. From middle management

C. From external drivers

D. From the top down

Question 3

Using the provided case study, which of the following is an example of an external influencer who is driving the need for this system change for the police force?

Select the correct answer from the choices that follow:

A. Customers / Community

B. Young police members

C. Internal Policy

D. Social media

Question 4

Using the provided case study, there are three main aspects mentioned to be included as part of the solution scope of the change:

1. **All existing functionality of the current system**
2. **Any additional out-of-the-box functionality a new system may include**

Select the description for the third capability to be included in the solution scope from the following:

A. Mobile devices to record criminal details

B. Document management system

C. Real-time "person of interest" search capability

D. Analytical reporting capabilities

Question 5

Using the provided case study, the following statement describes a business goal that they want to achieve by implementing the new system: "the new system will save the taxpayer $5 million dollars in the next 5 years."

This objective meets the common test for assessing goals and objectives. What does the acronym SMART stand for?

Select the correct answer from the choices that follow:

    A. Specific, Measurable, Actionable, Realistic, Time-bound.

    B. Specific, Measurable, Achievable, Realistic, Time-bound.

    C. Specific, Measurable, Achievable, Relevant, Time-bound.

    D. Specific, Measurable, Actionable, Relevant, Time-bound.

Question 6

Using the provided case study, when the old system is replaced by the new system, there is a risk that some critical incidents and criminal record data will be unavailable to police officers during the transition period. This transition period will only be for a couple of hours. Which other aspects should you analyze in relation to this risk?

Select the correct answer from the choices that follow:

    A. Likelihood, alternative solutions, and possible consequences if the risk occurs.

    B. Because it is only for a couple of hours, there is no need to analyze the risk further.

    C. Only analyze the likelihood of the risk occurring.

    D. Likelihood, impact, and possible consequences if the risk occurs.

Question 7

Using the provided case study, the police force is concerned that the planned future state may not include all capabilities currently available in the current state system. Which activity would you perform to compare the current state and future state capabilities to address this concern?

Select the correct answer from the choices that follow:

    A. Value analysis

    B. Functional analysis

    C. Risk analysis

    D. Gap analysis

Question 8

Using the provided case study, the police force is very open to the change that is planned with the new system but they have some considerations that will need to be taken into account before the change is implemented. Which of the following strategy analysis tasks will provide them with an assessment of alternative approaches that could be taken prior to selecting the recommended approach?

Select the correct answer from the choices that follow:

A. Define Future State

B. Define Change Strategy

C. Assess Risks

D. Define Change Approach Options

Question 9

Using the provided case study, due to the context of the police force, they will not be open to taking any risks that could endanger the community's safety in any way. They would therefore not take a project risk that could mean that they cannot get access to the required police information when they need it. Considering this, which risk tolerance level describes the police force in this scenario best?

Select the correct answer from the choices that follow:

A. Risk-seeking

B. Risk-accepting

C. Neutral

D. Risk-averse

Question 10

Using the provided case study, identify the intangible and subjective benefits mentioned that the new system could provide when it is implemented.

Select the correct answers from the choices that follow:

A. Boost the morale of police members

B. Reduce crime by 10%

C. Find more missing people

D. Save $5 million dollars in 5 years

Question 11

The strategy analysis knowledge area is described as consisting of four tasks. Which of the following options are NOT part of this knowledge area?

Select the correct answer from the choices that follow:

A. Define Future State

B. Assess Changes

C. Assess Risks

D. Analyze Current State

Question 12

The Analyze Current State task is described as part of the strategy analysis knowledge area. Which one of the following describes an output of the Analyze Current State task?

Select the correct answer from the choices that follow:

A. Stakeholder requirements

B. Future state description

C. Business needs

D. Business requirements

Question 13

The Assess Risks task is described as part of the strategy analysis knowledge area. Which one of the following describes an output of the Assess Risks task?

Select the correct answer from the choices that follow:

    A. Risk Analysis Response

    B. Risk Analysis Results

    C. Risk Analysis Assessment

    D. Risk Analysis Appetite

Question 14

Which one of the tasks in the strategy analysis knowledge area has the following purpose?

"...to understand the reasons why an enterprise needs to change some aspect of how it operates and what would be directly or indirectly affected by the change..."

Select the correct answer from the choices that follow:

    A. Analyze Current State

    B. Assess Risks

    C. Assess Change Strategy

    D. Define Future State

Question 15

Assessing risks includes analyzing and managing them. When you analyze risks as part of the Assess Risks task, you are doing it for one of the following reasons.

Select the most relevant reason from the choices that follow:

A. To understand the impact of the consequences better

B. To understand the possible consequences if the risk occurs better

C. To understand the likelihood of the risk occurring better

D. All of these reasons

Question 16

"The starting point for any change is an understanding of when the change is needed..."

Choose whether this statement is true or false:

A. True

B. False

Question 17

Let's consider the Analyze Current State task as part of the strategy analysis knowledge area: Which one of the following options describes an element of the Analyze Current State task?

Select the correct answer from the choices that follow:

A. Policies

B. Gap analysis

C. External assets

D. Unknowns

Question 18

Which of the following considerations should be included when selecting the preferred change strategy to follow when working in the strategy analysis context?

Select the correct answer from the choices that follow:

A. Costs and investments needed to make the change

B. Organizational readiness

C. Competitors approach to change

D. Alignment to business objectives

Question 19

Which of the following should be defined before a gap analysis can be performed?

Select the correct answer from the choices that follow:

A. Neither the current State or the future state

B. Only the future state

C. The current state and the future state

D. Only the current state

Question 20

"Business analysts analyze the enterprise to assess its capacity to make the change and to sustain the change in the future state."

Choose whether this statement is true or false:

A. True

B. False

Answers

Questions	Answers
1	C
2	D
3	A
4	B
5	C
6	D
7	D
8	B
9	D
10	A,C
11	B
12	D
13	B
14	A
15	D
16	B
17	A
18	A, B, D
19	C
20	A

10
Requirements Analysis and Design Definition

This chapter covers the tasks that are used to structure the requirements that we have elicited and gathered.

During this chapter, you will learn what it means to verify and validate requirements, define the requirements architecture, and define the possible solution options that could be pursued. We will also describe the task of analyzing the potential value and provide guidelines for recommending a solution.

This chapter dives into some of the BABOK® v3 guide tasks—specifying and modeling requirements, verifying requirements, validating requirements, defining the requirements architecture, defining solution options, and analyzing the potential value and recommending a solution. We will also bring each task into the real world with scenarios and examples.

By the end of this chapter, you will understand the following concepts and tasks:

- The purpose and context of this knowledge area
- Specifying and modeling requirements
- Verifying requirements
- Validating requirements
- Defining the requirements architecture
- Defining solution options
- Analyzing the potential value and recommending a solution
- A real-world case study quiz
- Testing your knowledge

The concepts you will learn are as follows:

- Understanding the context of this BABOK® v3 guide knowledge area in a real-world scenario
- Understanding and applying the specifying and modeling requirements task to real-world scenarios
- Understanding and applying the verifying requirements task to real-world scenarios
- Understanding and applying the validating requirements task to real-world scenarios
- Understanding and applying the defining the requirements architecture task to real-world scenarios
- Understanding and applying the defining solution options task to real-world scenarios
- Understanding and applying the analyzing the potential value and recommending a solution task to real-world scenarios
- Interpreting a real-world scenario and applying the knowledge learned in this chapter
- Trying a micro exam-style assessment

What is Requirements Analysis and Design Definition?

In the context of business analysis, the Requirements Analysis and Design Definition knowledge area describes the work involved in structuring and formulating the requirements information elicited during requirements elicitation activities.

Requirements and designs are important parts of an initiative where the business analyst has direct influence over supporting and guiding the changes that will be introduced. The level of detail of requirements and designs can vary depending on the purpose and the audience that will consume this information. It is imperative for the business analyst to model and captures the needs, requirements, and designs in an optimal way. This ensures effective communication of the required changes or solutions of the initiative to the appropriate stakeholders:

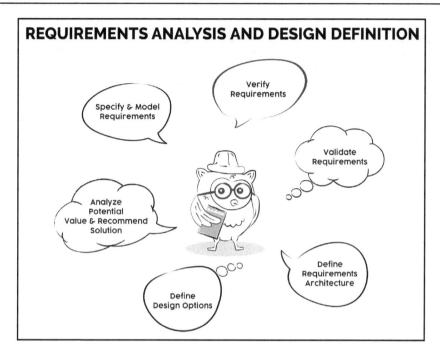

Requirements Analysis and Design Definition knowledge area and tasks

The Requirements Analysis and Design Definition knowledge area includes the following tasks:

- Specify and model the requirements.
- Verify the requirements.
- Validate the requirements.
- Define the requirements architecture.
- Define the solution options.
- Analyze the potential value and recommend a solution.

With the Requirements Analysis and Design Definition knowledge area, there are a few different types of output or deliverables that are typically produced. These include artifacts such as requirements (at different states), the requirements architecture, the design options, and solution recommendations.

Let's now explore how the Requirements Analysis and Design Definition aligns with the **Business Analysis Core Concept Model (BACCM)™**.

Business Analysis Core Concept Model™

Before we delve into each of the specific tasks in Requirements Analysis and Design Definition, let's understand how this knowledge area applies to BACCM™ with an example.

The six core concepts that are described in BACCM™ include the following:

- Change
- Need
- Solution
- Stakeholder
- Value
- Context

Here, we will consider how Requirements Analysis and Design Definition as a knowledge area applies to BACCM™ through the use of a practical example.

Change

This core concept refers to how elicitation results are transformed into requirements and designs in order to define change.

Let's look at an example to bring this concept around change to life.

Let's say you have just finished running a series of requirements elicitation workshops for an initiative to change a company's current manual payroll calculation procedures into an automated solution. Let's call this initiative the payroll calculation automation initiative.

You are now ready to start transforming your elicitation results into requirements and designs, such as process models, requirements documents, and potentially, user stories for the software development components of the initiative.

This example illustrates how the core concept of change is typically implemented during the Requirements Analysis and Design Definition.

Need

This core concept refers to how needs are analyzed in order to be able to recommend a solution that meets the needs.

Let's look at an example to bring this concept around need into the real world.

If we continue with the example of the payroll calculation automation initiative mentioned in the previous section, you will need to analyze the identified needs in order to be able to recommend the most effective solution to address those needs. This could, for example, be a change in the current business processes as well as the implementation of an automated payroll calculator, or it could potentially include outsourcing the manual payroll calculation so that it is performed by a specialist payroll provider. The recommended solution would be directly in line with the needs identified in collaboration with the stakeholders.

This example illustrates how the core concept of need is implemented during the Requirements Analysis and Design Definition by considering the needs identified and aligning the recommended solution with those needs.

Solution

This core concept refers to defining the solution options and recommending a solution that is most likely to meet the business needs as well as have the most value.

Let's look at an example to bring this concept around solution into the real world.

The needs identified during the payroll calculation automation initiative clearly align with a solution where the payroll calculation is outsourced rather than kept in-house. The needs are to reduce internal operating costs and reduce calculation errors caused by internal manual procedures. The best solution recommendation based on these needs would be to outsource the payroll calculation function. This will yield the best value for money as well as adhering to the need to reduce errors caused by cumbersome internal processes.

This example illustrates how the core concept of solution can be implemented during Requirements Analysis and Design Definition with a focus on providing solution options that meet the needs and maximize the value.

Stakeholder

This core concept refers to how stakeholders relate to the requirements and designs produced by business analysts.

Let's look at an example to bring this concept around stakeholders into the real world:

Let's now consider an example of two different types of stakeholder groups. The first stakeholder group is a group of product managers who have been closely involved in the requirements elicitation workshops you recently conducted. The second stakeholder group consists of the internal sales team, who have not been closely involved with the requirements and design work at all. It is important that you present the requirements and designs in a different way for each of these two groups. The product managers would be interested in the detailed requirements they have provided and, therefore, you could provide them with comprehensive requirements documentation using models and designs that they can understand and relate to.

With the sales managers' group, it is more suitable to present the main new features of the planned products in a summary. It might also work well to use a prototype-based format to ensure the sales managers can relate to the new products because they may not have been involved in the detailed requirements elicitation.

Therefore, it is important to realize during the Requirements Analysis and Design Definition that stakeholders relate to business analysis information in different ways.

Value

This core concept refers to analyzing and quantifying the potential value of solution options.

Let's look at an example to bring this concept around value into the real world:

In the example of the payroll calculation automation initiative, as the business analyst, not only are you assured that the recommended solution meets the identified needs but you also carry out an analysis of the potential value of the outsourcing solution, as well as the other solution options that are identified. You find that the outsourcing solution would add 30% more value to the business than any of the other solution options that existed.

Looking at this example, it is clear to see how the Requirements Analysis and Design Definition plays a key part in determining the potential value of a planned change.

Context

The final core concept refers to the business analyst models and describes their context in forms that are understandable and usable by all stakeholders.

Let's look at an example to bring this concept around context into the real world.

If we continue with our example where you have presented requirements and designs using different formats to the product manager and sales manager groups, it is important to emphasize that you should always describe requirements and designs with your audience in mind.

Now that we have an understanding of BACCM™ and how it relates to the Requirements Analysis and Design Definition knowledge area, it is time to move on to the specific tasks you need to perform. The next section covers the specific analysis tasks involved when working with the Requirements Analysis and Design Definition knowledge area.

Task: Specifying and modeling requirements

The first task described as part of the Requirements Analysis and Design Definition knowledge area is about analyzing the requirements information that the business analyst has elicited from stakeholders and then creating requirements and design artifacts of those results.

In this section, we will cover the purpose of this task and the different aspects of specifying and modeling requirements in the context of the task's core elements. You will also learn the difference between a requirement and a design and how to apply these terms in your role as a business analyst.

Let's start by considering the purpose of this task.

Purpose

According to the BABOK® v3 guide, the purpose of specifying and modeling requirements is as follows:

> *"...to analyze, synthesize, and refine elicitation results into requirements and designs."*

This task is all about the activities you perform to analyze and create representations (textual or visual) of this information in a format that is digestible by other stakeholders groups who need the information.

Before we delve deeper into the elements of this task, let's understand how you should use the terms "requirements" and "designs" in the business analysis world.

The term "**requirements**" is used when the focus of the "specify and model" activity is on understanding the business needs. The outputs that are generated as a result of these types of analysis activities are referred to as requirements.

The term "**designs**" is used when the focus of the "specify and model" activity is on understanding the solution. The outputs that are generated as a result of these types of analysis activities are referred to as designs.

Let's consider a practical real-world example of how these terms can be used appropriately.

An organization needs to increase its number of customers. The requirement here is to increase the new customer leads generated. Because there is a focus here on the business needs, the output of the activities to understand this business need would be referred to as the requirements.

However, part of the solution to this requirement is to build a new website and to add additional search engine campaigns. These solutions would be analyzed and modeled in the form of mock screen layouts, specific marketing campaign pages, and so on. These would be example outputs where the focus of the analysis activities are on the solution and would, therefore, be referred to as designs.

 The BABOK® v3 Guide makes a point to differentiate between these terms. It is important that you understand the distinction well so that you can answer exam questions effectively.

Let's now consider the core elements that a business analyst should include when performing this task.

Elements

There are four elements to consider when you specify and model requirements, which are as follows:

- The model requirements.
- Analyzing the requirements.
- Representing the requirements and attributes.
- Implementing the appropriate levels of abstraction.

We will now summarize each of these elements and describe each in the context of a practical example.

Element 1: The model requirements

What are model requirements and why are they used?

A model is any visual representation of information that has the specific purpose of supporting the understanding of analysis among different stakeholder groups.

Models are generally used to confirm the information and identify duplicates, or even identify information gaps that might exist.

Business analysts can use any of the following modeling formats to express and describe their business analysis information.

Matrices

A matrix is simply a type of table structure that is used to express business analysis information. It is often used when information lends itself to be categorized and when information shares a lot of similar attributes. A matrix is often the best way of displaying requirements information that needs to be sorted or prioritized.

Let's consider a real-world example.

If you have a set of requirements that all have a certain set of elements, such as a requirements identifier, a requirements category, a description, a priority, a source, and associated business rules, you can compile and manage these requirements in a matrix format.

Matrices may be used for data dictionaries or requirements traceability, or to support the stages of performing a gap analysis.

Diagrams

A diagram is a visual expression of a requirement or a set of requirements. Often, these sets of requirements are documented as a picture to help represent or convey something. Diagrams are an effective way of simplifying potentially complex concepts to help a wider audience of stakeholders understand them.

Diagrams are often included in requirements documentation, with some of the most popular diagrams being entity-relationship diagrams, process diagrams, and use case diagrams. Many other popular diagrams are used by business analysts and it is important to consider the purpose and audience of a diagram before choosing which one to use.

There are different categories where models are applied, depending on the category's main purpose and scope. Some model categories can include the following:

- People and roles
- Rationale
- Activity flow
- Capability
- Data and information

Let's now discuss each model category and understand how to apply it by considering a real-world example:

- **People and roles**: This model category represents organizations, groups of people, and roles, as well as their relationships within an organization and with a solution.

  A real-world example could be: *If the business analyst has to develop a people and roles model to show all the roles involved in a change management process or project. They may choose to develop a stakeholder map showing roles such as the key project team roles, the business stakeholders involved in the change, and any change implementation roles. The role of relationships in relation to the project will also be represented.*

  Techniques used to represent people and their roles include organizational modeling, roles and permissions matrices, stakeholder lists, maps, or personas.

- **Rationale**: This model category tends to represent the reasons for a change and answers the question of "why" in different ways.

Let's look at an example of a vehicle sales process:

Using the rational model category, a decision model can be used to illustrate the different decisions that must be made as part of the vehicle sales process. There will be multiple decision points within this process and each point will trigger a different flow. Some example decision points in the context of a vehicle sales process are as follows:

- *Is the client choosing a new or used vehicle?*
- *Will the client pay with cash or choose a different finance option?*
- *Did the client accept the vehicle quotation price or was it declined?*

There are a number of other modeling techniques that you can apply to depict the model category for showing a rationale; these include scope modeling, a business model canvas, root cause analysis, and business rules analysis.

- **Activity flow**: This model category represents a sequence of actions or events or a course of action that may be taken.

Let's continue the real-world example of a vehicle sales process by applying a process model to represent the activities in the vehicle sales process. Some of the high-level activities can include the following:

1. *The salesperson receives a customer inquiry.*
2. *The customer indicates whether they want a new or used vehicle.*
3. *The salesperson suggests a potential vehicle to the customer, including a price for the vehicle.*
4. *The client accepts or declines the offer.*
5. *If they accept the offer to purchase, then the purchase contract will be produced and signed. However, if they decline the offer, the transaction is closed and the process ends.*

All these activities or steps in the process will be documented with a visual activity flow model. There are a number of different techniques that can be used to represent activity flows. These include techniques such as process models, use cases and scenarios, and user stories.

- **Capability**: This model category is a visual representation of the features or functions of a solution or an organization.

  For example, *a capability model can be used to represent the different functions that an internet banking application should have. These functions may include the ability for a new user to sign up to the system, the ability to verify existing users, and the ability to enable password changes, as well as functionality to manage a bank account online.*

  Techniques that could be used to model the capabilities of a solution include business capability analysis, functional decomposition, and prototyping.

- **Data and information**: This model category represents the characteristics and the exchange of information within an organization or a solution.

  Techniques that are used to represent data and information include a data dictionary, data flow diagrams, data modeling, a glossary, state modeling, and interface analysis.

Element 2: Analyzing the requirements

Why do requirements need analysis?

Business analysis information needs to be further decomposed to understand the information from the following perspectives:

- To ensure that everything that might need to change to meet the business needs has been noted and documented
- Similarly, to ensure that everything that should stay the same to meet the business needs remains intact
- To identify any missing components that are not yet included or specified
- To remove any unnecessary components
- To decompose and document any constraints or assumptions that have an impact on the components under analysis

By performing an analysis of the business analysis information, the business analyst provides a basis for discussion to enable the team to reach a conclusion about potential solution options.

Element 3: Representing requirements and attributes

A business analyst is required to document and represent all the attributes identified for a requirement as part of the elicitation results information.

All requirements must be documented in enough detail so that they exhibit the characteristics of the requirements and design quality. As part of specifying the requirements, they can also be categorized according to the schema described in an earlier section. Typically, elicitation results contain information about different types of requirements, which means different types of requirements are specified at the same time during an initiative.

Let's imagine a real-world practical example scenario.

You are reviewing the elicitation results from a recent workshop and discover functional requirements describing the new online portal's required functional capabilities. You also find some non-functional requirements relating to the performance and security requirements for the online portal as part of the workshop output. You should document these requirements and clearly show which requirements are functional and non-functional in your documentation.

Element 4: Implementing the appropriate levels of abstraction

The level of abstraction for a requirement refers to the different perspectives, the level of detail, and the representation formats that are used for different stakeholder audiences. Not all stakeholders may require the same level of information or require information in the same format or representation. It is important for the business analyst to keep this in mind when preparing different models of requirements for different stakeholder groups.

Let's look at an example where we add a functional capability to validate a user during the login process of an existing online banking system.

The level of abstraction used when describing the requirements will be very different when communicating with the head of the organization compared to the development team who are building the new module:

- *The head of the organization prefers to only know whether the user experience is secure and whether there is a level of security verification included in the new module.*
- *The development team, however, would need to know, for example, the exact detail of the verification steps and rules, as well as any additional or updated field-level information in order to build the new module.*

Inputs and outputs

With the specify and model the requirements task, there are the following inputs and outputs:

- **Inputs**: The elicitation results (in any state)
- **Outputs**: The requirements (specified and modeled)

The task of specifying and modeling the requirements was all about taking your elicitation results and converting them into a set of requirements that have been modeled and specified using business analysis techniques and practices.

Let's now move on to the next Requirements Analysis and Design Definition task—verifying the requirements.

Task: Verifying the requirements

The second task described as part of the Requirements Analysis and Design Definition knowledge area is about verifying the requirements so that the business analyst can ensure that the quality standards have been met and that the requirements are fit for purpose.

In this section, we will cover the different aspects of verifying the requirements and ensuring the requirements have been defined correctly. You will also learn about the important characteristics that a good requirement should always have. Let's start by considering the purpose of this task.

Purpose

The BABOK® v3 guide defines the purpose of verifying the requirements as follows:

> *"to ensure that requirements and designs specifications and models meet quality standards and are usable for the purpose they serve..."*

If you ask yourself *"Am I building the solution correctly?"* you will ensure that you have always verified your requirements.

The task of verifying the requirements ensures that the requirements and designs have been defined in the correct way by the business analyst. A good-quality requirements specification is well written and easily understood by its intended audience. In a similar way, a good-quality model is a model that follows formal or informal notation standards and effectively represents reality.

It is essential that requirements and designs are prepared in a way that is effective and relevant to the intended purpose and meets the needs of the stakeholder.

Consider this real-world scenario:

The stakeholder's business need is to increase online customer sales. The business analyst analyzes this need and produces a requirements specification, showing some models to describe part of what will be required to build a new website. After a business analysis peer review of the requirements specification is carried out, it is found that the requirements specification is not complete and, in some parts, contains very inconsistent information in relation to the original needs of the stakeholders. After this verification activity, it is determined that these requirements are not yet ready to be presented to stakeholders for validation and some additional work is required.

Elements

There are three elements to consider when you verify requirements:

- The characteristics of the requirements and design quality.
- The verification activities.
- The checklists.

In the next section, we will summarize each of these elements and describe the meaning of these concepts in a practical way.

Element 1: The characteristics of the requirements and the design quality

What are the characteristics of the quality requirements and designs?

Good quality requirements and designs will exhibit certain characteristics. It is important for a business analyst to keep these characteristics in mind when formulating requirements and designs as part of their business analysis outputs:

- **Atomic**: When a requirement is atomic, it can be understood independently of other requirements or designs. It is also self-contained and can stand on its own as a statement or expression.
- **Complete**: The requirement must have enough detail to be able to work and continue. The level of completeness is not always the same and will depend on the perspective or methodology, as well as when in the life cycle the requirement is used.
- **Consistent**: When a requirement is considered consistent, it really means that it aligns with the identified needs of the stakeholders. It also means that the requirements do not contradict any other requirements.
- **Concise**: A requirement is considered concise when it uses just enough information to describe itself. It doesn't contain unnecessary explanations or content.
- **Feasible**: A requirement is considered feasible when it is in line with the expectations of the project in terms of risk, schedule, and budget or when it is considered worthy of being explored in more detail.
- **Unambiguous**: A requirement is considered unambiguous when it states in a clear and straightforward way whether a solution meets the associated need.
- **Testable**: A requirement is considered testable when it is clear to the reader whether a requirement or design has been fulfilled by a solution or not.
- **Prioritized**: A requirement is considered prioritized when it shows its relative importance and/or value in relation to the other requirements it is associated with.
- **Understandable**: A requirement is considered understandable when it uses terminology that the intended audience will recognize.

Element 2: The verification activities

What types of verification activities exist?

Activities to verify requirements are often performed iteratively throughout the requirement analysis process.

When requirements are verified, it is often done in an iterative and ongoing way.

Some verification types of activities include the following:

- The business analyst checks whether organizational business analysis standards, processes, and tools are used.
- The business analyst may check whether the correct use of modeling notation, templates, or forms are applied.
- Verification that common organization terminology is used when describing the requirements and that each requirement is understandable.
- Verifying that examples are included where additional clarification may be required.
- Verifying that all models included in the requirements are consistent and not missing any information.

Element 3: Checklists

Why would you use checklists when verifying requirements?

Checklists are used to assist with quality control when verifying requirements and designs.

Some example quality check questions that could be included on a checklist include the following:

- Have the correct and latest document templates been used?
- Have all the calculations and samples been used correctly?
- Have the training requirements been addressed?
- Have the report requirements been addressed?
- Have the policy changes been addressed?

It is good practice to agree to a standard checklist to use in your business analysis team to ensure a consistent standard is set for all the verified requirements.

Inputs and outputs

With the verify Requirements Analysis and Design Definition task, there are the following key inputs and outputs:

- **Inputs**: The requirements (specified and modeled)
- **Outputs**: The requirements (verified)

The result of verifying the requirements is that the requirements have a status of being verified. This allows the business analyst to move on to the next stage in the life cycle for the verified requirements.

In the next section of this chapter, we will discuss the validate the requirements task.

Task: Validating the requirements

The third task described as part of the Requirements Analysis and Design Definition knowledge area is about validating the requirements that align with the business needs and support the delivery of the anticipated value.

In this section, you will learn about the nature of validating requirements and designs as part of your role as a business analyst. We will also outline the importance of making and documenting assumptions to ensure clear communication with stakeholders, both upstream and downstream in the delivery cycle. We will discuss the role of evaluation criteria to ensure the measurability of the value that our implemented requirements and designs will bring to the business. Let's now consider the purpose of the validating requirements task.

Purpose

According to the BABOK® v3 Guide, the purpose of validating requirements is as follows:

> *"to ensure that all requirements and designs align to the business requirements and support the delivery of needed value..."*

If you ask yourself *"Am I building the correct solution?"*, you will ensure that you have always validated your requirements.

You will remember that in the previous section, where we addressed the verify the requirements task, we asked *"Am I building the solution correctly?"*

This is a simple way to differentiate between verifying and validating requirements.

Requirement validation is a task that is performed throughout the life cycle of the requirements and designs and is primarily concerned with ensuring that the requirements and designs remain aligned to the business needs. This includes stakeholder requirements, solutions, and transition requirements. Ultimately, the purpose of implementing requirements and designs is to achieve the business stakeholder's desired future state.

The task of validating requirements is also performed to ensure that all stakeholders remain in alignment with what is required and it helps identify any requirement conflicts that might exist.

Elements

There are three elements to consider when you validate requirements:

- Identify the assumptions.
- Define the measurable evaluation criteria.
- Evaluate the alignment with the solution scope.

The next section summarizes each of these elements and describes each one in the context of a practical example.

Element 1: Identifying assumptions

Why should you identify assumptions?

In some cases, it is necessary to identify assumptions that may have been made when requirements were raised or designs were completed. These assumptions can assist us in providing a basis for decision making, when information may not be available, or in managing any risks that might be associated with a particular solution.

Sometimes, a brand-new product or service is launched by making some assumptions. The assumptions can be about the customers' or stakeholders' responses, which can be used to help drive the project or initiative forward.

It could also be the case that stakeholders assume that certain benefits can be expected with the implementation of a certain requirement. These assumptions are defined and documented to allow the team to move ahead with a solution.

Let's look at a real-world example.

In the context of the vehicle manufacturing company we discussed earlier, where a need to save on software maintenance costs was identified, it is decided that the dealer management system of the company will be replaced with a solution that has lower software maintenance costs. The stakeholders, in this case, assume that this change will have an overall cost-saving benefit for the company.

Element 2: Defining measurable evaluation criteria

While the expected benefits are defined as part of the future state, the specific measurement criteria and evaluation process may not have been included. Business analysts define the evaluation criteria that will be used to evaluate how successful the change has been after the solution is implemented.

This element is about the business analyst defining the expected benefits a solution will bring to the business in a way that is measurable. It is often required for the business analyst to start by setting a baseline for the agreed measurable benefits identified and then track the benefits realization over an agreed period.

Let's look at a real-world example for identifying and capturing a baseline for an expected solution benefit:

There is a stakeholder requirement to change the current manufacturer of a specific product for a company. This requirement exists to address the need for a faster manufacturing process that also delivers at a reduced operational cost.

To measure the benefit of implementing this requirement, the baseline metrics of the current state should be defined and documented.

The baseline metrics for this product are that the current manufacturing process takes 3 business days, the delivery time for the product is documented as 2 days, and the cost to manufacture this product is $20 per unit.

Once the baseline metrics are defined, the business analyst should work with the business stakeholders to define a target or future state metrics that can be tracked over time to demonstrate the business value of the solution.

Element 3: Evaluating the alignment against the solution scope

This element is about ensuring that the solution that is delivered benefits the stakeholder and aligns with the stakeholder requirements. If it is determined that the requirement or the solution features are not aligned to the business needs, the respective requirement should be eliminated or the solution scope should be changed.

The purpose of this element is to ensure that the requirement delivers the required benefits to the stakeholder.

Let's look at a real-world example of how this might happen.

A stakeholder has received a new laptop and they need to install Microsoft Word and Microsoft PowerPoint on their machine.

The documented requirement is that a new mailbox should be set up on the new laptop. The scope of the solution is defined to include setting up the stakeholder's mailbox.

Clearly, neither the documented requirement nor the specified solution will meet the needs of this stakeholder and should, therefore, be re-evaluated. It is likely that the solution scope would need to be changed by eliminating the requirement to set up a new mailbox and replace it with the requirement to set up Microsoft Word and Microsoft PowerPoint. This also requires the design specification to be updated to ensure that the stakeholder's need is met.

Inputs and outputs

With the validate Requirements Analysis and Design Definition task, the following key inputs and outputs exist:

- **Inputs**: The requirements (specified and modeled)
- **Outputs**: The requirements (validated)

The result of completing the validating the requirements task is that the requirements have a validated status. Requirements and designs that are validated are those that will deliver benefits to the stakeholders and are in alignment with the business goals and objectives for the planned change.

In the next section of this chapter, we will discuss the define the requirements architecture task.

Task: Defining the requirements architecture

The fourth task described as part of the Requirements Analysis and Design Definition knowledge area is defining the requirements architecture. This task is about establishing the structure of all the requirements to form cohesive requirements that support the business objectives for the change.

In this section, you will learn about the different considerations when establishing a requirements architecture. You will also understand that a requirements architecture will assist the business analyst in all aspects of requirements management and communication throughout the life of the requirements. It will also become clear how the requirements architecture supports the successful delivery of the requirements. Let's start by defining the purpose of this task.

Purpose

According to the BABOK® v3 guide, the purpose of defining the requirements architecture is as follows:

> *"to ensure that the requirements collectively support one another to fully achieve the objectives..."*

The requirements architecture is the way that the requirements are put together as a holistic view of the requirements for a change. It describes how different requirements artifacts (such as models and textual descriptions) relate to each other to form an overall requirements view for an initiative or change.

A business analyst would use requirements architecture for the following reasons:

- The requirement architecture defines which models are appropriate for the domain, context, and solution scope; *for example, business process models to illustrate business processes and data models to describe data-related requirements.*
- The requirements architecture also organizes requirements into structures relevant to different stakeholders; *for example, the technology solutions department would want to see more detailed technical structures, whereas the head of the organization would just want a high-level overview, knowing enough to feel comfortable that the suggested solution meets the business needs identified.*

- The requirements architecture also illustrates how requirements and models interact with and relate to each other. Ultimately, the requirements architecture makes sure that the requirements are met as a whole and in alignment with the overall objectives of the initiative or planned change; *for example, if a requirement would not benefit the overall objective or is in contradiction with the objective, this should be discussed and potentially removed.*

Elements

There are five elements to consider when you define the requirements architecture:

- The requirements architecture viewpoints and views.
- The template architectures.
- The completeness.
- Relating and verifying the requirements relationships.
- The business analysis information architecture.

Now, we will describe each element with a real-world example.

Element 1: The requirements architecture viewpoints and views

How do viewpoints and views impact the requirements architecture?

A viewpoint is a set of standards or guidelines that defines how requirements will be represented and how these representations will be organized. It also shows how requirements are presented and communicated to stakeholders. A viewpoint provides a template to use to communicate requirements to a particular stakeholder group.

The following aspects are often expressed as standard or guidelines for a particular viewpoint:

- Which model types, notations, and attributes should be used for requirements documentation
- Which approaches should be used to identify and maintain relevant relationships between models

Let's look at a real-world example scenario.

An organization may have a standard business process notation that must be applied whenever business processes are documented as part of requirements. In a similar way, the organization may have requirement statement conventions in place, such as following the user story format when formulating textual requirements. These are both viewpoints that should be applied when performing requirements analysis and designing definition tasks.

No single viewpoint can form an entire architecture. It is normally a collection of different viewpoints that form the requirements architecture.

Certain viewpoints represent the information and architecture of a specific aspect better than others.

Some examples of viewpoints include the following:

- Business process models
- Data models and information
- User interactions, including use cases and/or the user experience
- Audit and security
- Business models

The specific requirements and designs for a solution from a chosen viewpoint are referred to as **views**. A collection of views makes up the requirements architecture for a specific solution or initiative.

It is the business analyst's responsibility to align, coordinate, and structure requirements into meaningful views for the various stakeholder groups to ensure each stakeholder group receives a meaningful view of the requirements that are relevant to them.

Therefore, a viewpoint consists of various standards and guidelines that a business analyst should follow when preparing a view of the actual requirements for a specific solution.

Element 2: Template architectures

What is the significance of template architectures?

In essence, an architectural framework, in this context, is described as a collection of viewpoints that is standard across industry, sector, or organization.

These frameworks can be used by business analysts as predefined templates to start from when defining their own requirements architecture.

For example, an organization has defined its own custom requirements architecture that was based on the industry architectural framework published by the International Institute of Business Analysis. This requirements architecture consists of various templates and notational modeling guidelines (viewpoints) that must be applied when a business analyst prepares the requirements documentation for a particular initiative of the organization.

Element 3: Completeness

Using requirements architecture as a guide can also assist in the requirements' level of completeness. This is because using provided templates can guide the author to ask pertinent, predefined questions that will assist them in ensuring all of the requirements and perspectives are captured.

When the requirements architecture is applied to complete an entire set of requirements, it increases the understandability and ensures that a cohesive and complete picture is captured when describing the requirements.

Element 4: Relating and verifying the requirements relationships

Requirements are often related to each other and there are various different ways that these relationships might exist. It is important that the business analyst identifies and analyzes these relationships clearly.

When a relationship is identified between requirements, the business analysts will examine the relationship and ensure that it satisfies the following quality criteria:

- The relationship is defined and the relationship type is described.
- The relationship is necessary in order for the requirements to be understood in a holistic way.
- The relationship is correctly described between the requirements.
- The relationship is unambiguous in that it is clear and there is no confusion or multiple interpretations about the relationship.
- The relationship is consistent in the way that it is described between the different requirements. This means that the relationship description follows a standard or guideline as outlined in the viewpoints of the requirements architecture.

Let's now look at what the business analysis information architecture is and why it is important to consider as part of this task.

Element 5: The business analysis information architecture

The structure of business analysis information is also referred to as information architecture and because it describes how business analysis information relates to each other in a structured way and forms part of the requirements architecture.

The information architecture helps the stakeholders to understand how the models, requirements, and designs are related and linked and how information is shared between them.

Inputs and outputs

With defining the requirements architecture Requirements Analysis and Design task, there are the following key inputs and outputs:

- **Inputs**: The information management approach, the requirements (in any state), and the solution scope

- **Outputs**: The requirements architecture

You have now learned that the define the requirements architecture for an initiative task includes taking the information management approach, the requirements, and designs, and the solution scope as key inputs to then be transformed into a requirements architecture that can help support the overall effectiveness and accuracy of the requirements for a given change.

In the following section, we will discuss the task where the business analyst defines the design options for an initiative.

Task: Defining the design options

The fifth task described as part of the Requirements Analysis and Design Definition knowledge area is defining the design options. This task is about defining the solution approach as well as allocating requirements and designs in a way that will support achieving the desired future state.

In this section, you will learn about the different considerations when defining the design options.

Purpose

According to the BABOK® v3 guide, the purpose of defining the design options is as follows:

> *"to define the solution approach, identify opportunities to improve the business, allocate requirements across solution components, and represent design options that achieve the desired future state..."*

In a practical way, you can look at this task as the activities you will perform when you are working out which way to go in terms of implementing the requirements you have prepared in order to achieve the business value. This is referred to as identifying the design options.

Design options generally refer to the steps that will be taken to ensure the solution is delivered.

Design options are not the specific solution functionality but rather the approach that will be taken to deliver the solution.

Let's look at this real-world example.

In this example, there are two design options identified for a small project.

The first design option describes the approach for implementing software changes to an existing system. A micro-phased approach follows, where only three software changes are implemented during every release cycle.

The second design option describes the decision for implementing a new vendor software component as part of the overall solution. With this design option, it was decided to purchase this vendor software component instead of developing it in-house. The business analyst should consider whether this design option will meet all the requirements for the business stakeholders and whether any trade-offs would need to be identified and managed accordingly.

If any of these tactical design options require any type of trade-offs to be made in order to successfully deliver the solution, the business analyst must aim to ensure that these trade-offs don't impact the requirements in an adverse way.

In the next section, we will discuss the specific elements that the business analyst must include when performing the task of defining the design options.

Elements

There are four elements to consider when you define the design options:

- Define the solution approaches.
- Identify improvement opportunities.
- The requirements allocation.
- Describe the design options.

Let's discuss each of these elements in more detail.

Element 1: Defining the solution approaches

When a solution approach is formulated, it is essentially a determination of whether a solution component will be purchased or created, or perhaps a combination of these two approaches.

When it is decided to follow an approach where the solution component is created, it means that the requirements will be used by experts to develop, construct, or assemble the solution. When this approach is chosen, the requirements are at a level of detail that allows this approach to be chosen. This solution approach also includes any modifications required to existing solutions.

Let's look at a real-world example of creating a solution component.

A vehicle finance application system already exists within a financial institution. Based on stakeholder requirements, it is decided to construct and develop a new module for this system.

When it is decided to purchase a solution component to fulfill the requirements, it means that a third party will be involved in executing this solution approach. In most cases, the third party will manage and own the solution component, regardless of whether it is a service or a product.

Let's look at a real-world example of purchasing a solution component.

An "off-the-shelf" accounting system is selected to meet the accounting requirements of the organization and will be delivered by a third-party vendor.

In most cases, however, the solution approach is a combination of creating and purchasing different parts of the overall solution and should be defined as such when defining the design options.

Element 2: Identifying the improvement opportunities

Part of the task of defining the design options often includes identifying opportunities to improve business operations. This section will look at some common examples of how this might occur.

Increasing efficiencies

A result of implementing a solution is often the automation of some processes or tasks in the business operational area.

An everyday real-world example could be that a new timesheet management solution is implemented that removes the need for employees to have their timesheets printed and signed by a line manager prior to submitting it to the payroll department. This results in cost- and time-saving efficiency.

Automate or simplify the work people perform by reengineering or sharing processes, changing responsibilities, or outsourcing.

Improving access to information

By providing more information access to staff who interface directly or indirectly with customers, the need for specialized personnel is reduced. This also helps prevent a customer from being sent from one customer service worker to another to get different types of services or information.

Identifying additional capabilities

Highlight the capabilities of a new solution that has the potential to provide future value to the business and can be supported by the solution.

Element 3: Requirements allocation

What is the requirements allocation?

Requirements allocation is an activity where requirements are assigned to specific solution components or planned releases to ensure that the requirements are delivered in the most efficient way while providing the highest business value.

A real-world example could be that it would be rather pointless to implement a special Christmas-themed product or service at the wrong time of the year!

Element 4: Describing the design options

Design options are described when considering the desired future state and the anticipated business value it must deliver. They are also described to ensure the design option is valid and feasible.

A design option is often described using design elements. These elements may describe the following types of information:

- Business policies and business rules that apply
- Business processes to be performed and managed
- People who operate and maintain the solution, including their job functions and responsibilities
- Operational business decisions that must be made
- Software applications and application components that are used in the solution
- Organizational structures, including interactions between the organization, its customers, and its suppliers

In this section, you learned about all the elements to consider when you perform the task of defining design options.

Inputs and outputs

With defining the design options Requirements Analysis and Design task, there are the following key inputs and outputs:

- **Inputs**: The change strategy, requirements (validated and prioritized), and requirements architecture

- **Outputs**: The design options

You have learned that the design options are formulated after considering various elements and utilizing inputs, such as the change strategy, the requirements, and the requirements architecture.

We will discuss the last task—analyzing the potential value and recommending a solution—in the next section of this chapter.

Task: Analyzing the potential value and recommending a solution

The sixth and final task described as part of the Requirements Analysis and Design Definition knowledge area is to analyze the potential value and recommend a solution. This task is about assessing the potential business value of each design option and recommending the best design option that will meet most of the business's defined requirements.

In this section, you will learn about the different considerations when analyzing the potential value of the design options, as well as what is involved when recommending a solution.

Purpose

According to the BABOK® v3 guide, the purpose of analyzing the potential value and recommending a solution is as follows:

> *"to estimate the potential value for each design option and to establish which one is most appropriate to meet the enterprise's requirements..."*

It is easy to understand, from the preceding quote, that this task is about working out the potential value of each design option. It is also about considering which option will be most appropriate for meeting the organization's requirements.

Let's use a practical everyday example to explain this further.

You are at point A and want to find a way to travel to point B. These points are all land-based, so you choose to travel by road.

You have different transportation options available, such as the following:

- *You can travel by bicycle.*
- *You can travel by motorcycle.*
- *You can travel by motor vehicle.*

These options are all recommended solutions to get from point A to point B; however, the value you will gain by using each possible solution option is very different. Let's now consider each option and what the potential of each could be:

- **Option 1**: *If you choose to travel by bicycle, it will be the most cost-efficient but it will take a long time to reach point B.*
- **Option 2**: *If you choose to travel by motorcycle, you can see that it would be very time-efficient; however, you will not be able to take all your luggage or any of your family members along.*
- **Option 3**: *If you choose to go by motor vehicle, you know it might not be as time-efficient as option 2 and a bit less cost-effective than both option 1 and option 2, but it brings additional value to you in the form of being able to carry all your luggage and you are able to take your family along with you. If being able to carry your luggage and bring your family is part of your requirements, then option 3 will meet all of your requirements without any additional costs for sending luggage or family separately from you.*

Even with this simple example, you can see that there are many factors that need to be considered when you assess the potential value that a design option will bring to the organization.

Different types of value can be identified and considered and typically include the value that is described in terms of finance, reputation, or even impacts on the marketplace.

In some cases, you need to build a proof of concept first to determine the best design option. It may also be that the best decision is to not implement the change at all.

Lets now discuss the key elements to consider when analyzing the potential value and recommending a solution.

Elements

There are four elements to consider when you analyze the potential value and recommend a solution:

- The expected benefits
- The expected costs
- Determine the value
- Assess the design options and recommend a solution

The following section will discuss each element and outline real-world examples to clarify each concept further.

Element 1: The expected benefits

When you consider the expected benefits of a solution, you focus on the positive value that a particular design option can bring to the business when it is delivered. The expected benefits can include financial benefits as well as benefits such as reduced risk, compliance with business policies and regulations, improved user experience, or any positive outcome for the organization.

A real-world example could be described as follows:

The stakeholders of an organization agree that a new website is required to represent the organization online and they would like an external website provider to manage and implement this solution.

It is expected that the new website will run on a faster hosting platform, which could improve traffic to the website and, therefore, also increase product sales.

It is expected that a new website will provide the company with a new market image that will make them more attractive to potential new clients. It is also expected that the user experience will be much better than using the current website.

In this example, there are two key expected benefits identified with a particular design option. These benefits relate to an increase in sales (financial benefit) and an improved reputation and brand image, which will attract more customers and satisfy existing customers from a user-experience perspective.

Element 2: The expected costs

When you consider the expected costs of a solution, you focus on the negative value a new solution may introduce to the organization.

A negative value can be described in different ways, including the cost to acquire the solution or any negative effects it might have on stakeholders. It can also include the cost to maintain the solution over time.

Some types of expected costs that should be considered when analyzing the potential value of each design option can include the timeline, the effort, operating costs, purchase and/or implementation costs, maintenance costs, physical resources, information resources, and human resources.

Element 3: Determining the value

Now that you have considered the expected benefits and the expected costs, it is time to look at determining the value of a particular design option. You do this by establishing whether the expected benefits outweigh the expected costs or vice versa.

Let's look at a real-world example.

Consider a new prepaid gift card project. The national post office decides to extend its service offering to the public by introducing a brand new product in the form of a prepaid gift card. This card will be sold in all the local post offices around the country. Some of the costs associated with this project include implementing a brand new team to establish and manage the product, establishing relationships with card payment processing and manufacturing third-party vendors, and an extensive marketing campaign for this new product to the public. The potential benefits to the overall business, however, are described as exceeding the costs of establishing a new product line within the first year.

After a few months into the project, a new card processing cost is introduced as a result of a legislative change. This means that the potential benefits will only be realized after the second year of operation.

This example describes some of the costs and benefits that exist in a real-world example. However, it also illustrates that the potential value can be affected when change is introduced and new requirements must be met. It is important to keep this analysis relevant to the current situation when design options are evaluated. This brings us to the last element for this task.

Element 4: Assessing the design options and recommending a solution

As we mentioned, each design option is assessed based on the potential value it is expected to deliver to the business. It is the role of the business analyst to analyze all the relevant benefits and costs associated with each design option for the solution. This includes an assessment of any trade-offs that a design option might include.

There are several factors to take into consideration when doing this assessment.

Available resources

It is important to assess the availability of the resources required for implementing any design option. If there is a limit on the resources that can be used to implement a solution, this must be highlighted and it should be determined whether there are any ways of changing this limiting factor (for example, can a larger budget be agreed on to help make more resources available?).

Constraints on the solution

The business analyst should be aware of any regulatory requirements or business decisions that may require requirements to be handled in a different way to other requirements in terms of how they are delivered.

Dependencies between requirements

Understanding the relationships between different requirements is important to ensure that there is an understanding that some capabilities may, in and of themselves, provide limited value to the organization but need to be delivered in order to support other high-value requirements.

Let's look at a real-world example.

An organization wants to implement a fully integrated call center solution. In order to be able to implement this solution, they need to replace all existing phone handsets because the existing handsets are not compatible with the special integration requirements for a fully integrated call center solution.

In this example, the organization has no need for new phone handsets as such; however, this has been identified as a requirement dependency. Therefore, it must be included in order for the call center solution to be fully functional when implemented.

Inputs and outputs

With the analyze a potential value and recommend a solution Requirements Analysis and Design Definition task, there are the following key inputs and outputs:

- **Inputs**: The potential value and the design options

- **Outputs**: A solution recommendation

You have learned that when analyzing the potential value and recommending a solution, there are a number of key elements to include as well as using the potential value information and design options available as key inputs. This results in a well-justified and sound solution recommendation as a key output of this task.

Summary

In this chapter, you learned about the Requirements Analysis and Design Definition knowledge area.

The following are the key concepts and tasks we covered in this chapter:

- The Requirements Analysis and Design Definition knowledge area
- Specifying and modeling requirements
- Verifying requirements
- Validating requirements
- Defining the requirements architecture
- Defining the solution options

Make sure you revise these key learnings before completing the knowledge quiz at the end of this chapter.

You now have an understanding of the importance and purpose of the Requirements Analysis and Design Definition knowledge area and know what the scope is of performing analysis tasks for an initiative from an analysis point of view.

The learning outcome for the Requirements Analysis and Design Definition knowledge area

You now have an overall understanding of the importance and purpose of the Requirements Analysis and Design Definition knowledge area in terms of the role it plays in analyzing, planning, and completing the business analysis work you do. You are able to describe this knowledge area in the context of BACCM™ using real-world practical situations. You are also able to visualize the key inputs and outputs to perform this task effectively.

The learning outcome for specifying and modeling requirements

In this chapter, you learned about specifying and modeling requirements and you are now able to describe the purpose of this task and describe the key elements to consider when performing this task using real-world scenarios and concepts. You are also able to visualize the key inputs and outputs to perform this task effectively.

The learning outcome for verifying requirements

During this chapter, you learned about verifying requirements and you are now able to describe the purpose of this task and describe the key elements to consider when carrying out this task using real-world scenarios and concepts. You are also able to interpret and outline the key inputs and outputs to perform this task effectively.

The learning outcome for validating requirements

Another key learning from this chapter is your understanding and ability to describe the task of validating requirements in terms of its purpose and you are able to describe the key elements to consider when performing this task using real-world scenarios and concepts. You are also able to describe the key inputs and outputs to perform this task effectively.

The learning outcome for defining the requirements architecture

In this chapter, you learned about defining the requirements architecture and you are now able to describe the purpose of this task and describe the key elements to consider when carrying out this task using real-world scenarios and concepts. You are also able to explain the key inputs and outputs to perform this task effectively.

The learning outcome for defining the solution options

In this chapter, you learned about defining solution options and you are now able to describe the purpose of this task and describe the key elements to consider when doing this task using real-world scenarios and concepts. You are also able to describe the key inputs and outputs to perform this task effectively.

In the next chapter, we will discuss the Solution Evaluation knowledge area. This chapter is about learning how to analyze a solution's performance, which measures to apply and how to assess limitations and make recommendations.

Knowledge quiz

Consider the following real-world scenario and complete the micro mock exam based on this chapter.

Case study – a health solutions company

A health solutions company has been asked to develop a system for a large corporate client that monitors the time employees spend on projects and other tasks. The client wants this timesheet system to capture timesheets every week and employees must be able to update their personal details to keep them up to date. Line managers must be able to approve or reject a timesheet, as well as view and print their employees' timesheets. They should also be able to run and print management reports. As part of the time capture functionality, the system must validate whether the employee is using a valid project code to assign time against. Every month, the system will run an overtime calculation to notify line managers of any employees who had to work overtime. The system will be used globally and employees must be able to capture their time from anywhere in the world.

Question 1

Consider the following extract from the case study provided: "As part of the time capture functionality, the system must validate whether the employee is using a valid project code to assign time against."

This requirement has been disputed by some of your stakeholders, who have said that this requirement has not been defined correctly.

Which of the following tasks do you need to do to check whether this requirement is, in fact, correct or incorrect?

    A. Define the requirements architecture

    B. Analyze the requirements

    C. Verify the requirements

    D. Validate the requirements

Question 2

Refer to the case study provided. These requirements were elicited about 2 months ago and as the business analyst, you are not sure that they still align with what the business requirements really are.

Which of the following tasks will assist you with achieving this goal of making sure the requirements elicited are still aligned to the business requirements and support the delivery of the required value?

Select the correct answer from the following choices:

    A. Review the requirements

    B. Validate the requirements

    C. Confirm the requirements

    D. Verify the requirements

Question 3

Refer to the case study provided. After reviewing the elicitation results (as per the case study), you realize that the stakeholders are assuming that the new solution will be able to cater to different time zones in the world and manage any time differences in the respective timesheet calculations. This was not explicitly stated, rather assumed. Which of the following elements of the "validate the requirements" task should you include this information in when completing the business analysis activities?

Select one or more correct answers from the following choices:

A. Define the measurable evaluation criteria

B. The expected benefits

C. Identify the assumptions

D. Evaluate the alignment against the solution scope

Question 4

Refer to the case study provided. You decided to make use of a model to describe the requirements. One of the models you are planning to use is a UML use case diagram. Which of the following options describes this modeling format best?

Select the correct answer from the following choices:

A. Matrices

B. Functions

C. Diagrams

D. Capability

Question 5

Refer to the case study provided. The following requirement statement must be checked for quality:

"Line managers must be able to approve or reject a timesheet."

Which of the following attributes should this statement have in order to be considered a good quality requirement statement?

   A. Atomic, complete, consistent, concise, feasible, unambiguous, testable, unclear

   B. Atomic, complete, consistent, concise, feasible, unambiguous, testable, generic

   C. Atomic, complete, consistent, concise, feasible, unambiguous, testable, free text

   D. Atomic, complete, consistent, concise, feasible, unambiguous, testable, understandable

Question 6

The Requirements Analysis and Design Definition knowledge area consists of six tasks. Which of the following tasks are NOT a part of this knowledge area?

Select one or more correct options from the following choices:

   A. Verify the requirements

   B. Validate the requirements

   C. Confirm the requirements

   D. Assess the risks

Question 7

Which of the following options describes the output of the specify and model requirements task?

Select the correct answer from the following choices:

   A. Requirements (specified and modeled)

   B. Requirements (modeled)

   C. Requirements (documented)

   D. Requirements (specified)

Question 8

Which one of the following options describes the output of the validate the requirements task?

Select the correct answer from the following choices:

    A. Requirements (validated)

    B. Requirements (verified)

    C. Designs (verified)

    D. Requirements and Designs (validated)

Question 9

Which one of the following Requirements Analysis and Design Definition tasks has the following purpose?

"..to ensure that all requirements and designs align with the business requirements and support the delivery of needed value."

Select the correct answer from the following choices:

    A. Align the requirements

    B. Validate the requirements

    C. Verify the requirements

    D. Confirm the requirements

Question 10

When assessing a requirement in terms of its quality, which of the following describes the quality characteristics to look out for? Only select the options that have two *valid* quality characteristics.

Select one or more correct answers from the following choices:

    A. Testability and validity

    B. Validity and completeness

    C. Consistency and feasibility

    D. Feasibility and testability

Question 11

"Checklists are used for quality control when verifying requirements and designs."

Choose whether this statement is true or false:

    A. True

    B. False

Question 12

Which one of the following options describes an element of the validate the requirements task?

Select the correct answer from the following choices:

    A. Define the measurable value options

    B. Define the measurable value parameters

    C. Define the measurable evaluation controls

    D. Define the measurable evaluation criteria

Question 13

A viewpoint is a set of conventions that defines how requirements will be represented, how these representations will be organized, and how they will be related. Viewpoints provide templates for addressing the concerns of particular stakeholder groups.

Requirements viewpoints frequently include standards and guidelines for certain aspects. Some of these aspects are listed here.

Select one or more correction options from the following choices:

A. Competitors' approach to viewpoints

B. Model types used for requirements

C. Model notations that are used

D. Attributes that are included and consistently used in different models

Question 14

Choose the most relevant reason for why a business analyst might use a requirements architecture.

Select the correct answer from the following choices:

A. To elicit requirements during workshops

B. To provide the software developers with the final specification for the requirements

C. To help make trade-off decisions about requirements

D. To organize their thoughts before a meeting

Question 15

"A design option usually consists of many design components. Some of these components can include business policies and business rules."

Choose whether this statement is true or false:

A. True

B. False

Question 16

The define the design options task defines three inputs. Which one of the following describes an input of this task?

Select the correct answer from the following choices:

A. Designs and requirements (validated and prioritized)

B. Requirements (validated and prioritized)

C. Designs (validated and documented)

D. Requirements (validated and documented)

Question 17

Which of the following options describe an element of the analyze the potential value and recommend a solution task?

Select the correct answer from the following choices:

A. The expected value

B. The expected benefits

C. The expected risks

D. The expected costs

Question 18

When analyzing the potential value of a design option, it considers the expected benefits and expected costs associated with that design option. Which of the following items describe an example of a type of an expected non-financial benefit?

Select the correct answer from the following choices:

A. Increased brand awareness

B. Increased sales

C. Reduced marketing costs

D. Employee salary increase

Question 19

When analyzing the potential value of a design option, it considers the expected benefits and expected costs associated with that design option. Which of the following items describe examples of cost types that should be included in your analysis?

Select all the correct answers from the following choices:

A. Solution maintenance costs

B. Initial software license costs

C. Vendor catering costs

D. Opportunity costs

Question 20

Which of the following types of costs and benefits should be included when analyzing the potential value of a design option?

Select all the correct answers from the following choices:

A. Intangible costs

B. Tangible costs

C. Intangible benefits

D. Tangible benefits

Answers

Questions	Answers
1	D
2	B
3	C
4	C
5	D
6	C, D
7	A
8	A
9	B
10	C, D
11	A
12	D
13	B, C, D
14	C
15	A
16	B
17	B
18	A
19	A, B, D
20	A, B, C, D

11
Solution Evaluation

V3Vn this chapter, we will cover the tasks that business analysts perform to analyze and assess a solution in terms of its ability to meet the business objectives in a way that delivers real business value to the organization. It also looks at the tasks a business analyst performs to formulate recommendations for removing barriers and constraints that inhibit the organization's ability to deliver the full business value.

This chapter will look at the BABOK® V3 Guide tasks—Measure Solution Performance, Analyze Performance Measures, Assess Solution Limitations, Assess Enterprise Limitations, and Recommend Actions to Increase the Solution Value—and will bring each into the real world with scenarios and examples.

By the end of this chapter, the reader will have knowledge about the following concepts and tasks:

- Purpose and context of solution evaluation
- Task: Measure Solution Performance
- Task: Analyze Performance Measures
- Task: Assess Solution Limitations
- Task: Assess Enterprise Limitations
- Task: Recommend Actions to Increase Solution Value
- Real-world case study quiz
- Test your knowledge

By the end of this chapter, you will be able to do the following:

- Understand the context of this BABOK® V3 guide knowledge area within a real-world scenario
- Understand and apply the measure solution performance task to real-world scenarios
- Understand and apply the analyze performance measures task to real-world scenarios
- Understand and apply the assess solution limitations task to real-world scenarios
- Understand and apply the assess enterprise limitations task to real-world scenarios
- Understand and apply the recommend actions to increase solution value task to real-world scenarios
- Interpret a real-world scenario and apply the knowledge learned in this chapter
- Do a micro exam-style assessment

What is Solution Evaluation?

Solution evaluation deals with the assessment and analysis of an actual solution that already exists within the organization. This knowledge area has some similarities to other knowledge areas, namely strategy analysis, requirement analysis, and design definition. The key distinction between these knowledge areas' activities and solution evaluation is that solution evaluation involves working with an existing solution that is already operational within the organization. It is also important to note that this could also include a solution that has been in production for a while after being implemented by the organization. This solution could now be evaluated in terms of its performance in relation to meeting expected benefits.

Solution evaluation tasks are often performed on parts of the solution during different stages of their development. These stages could include the following:

- **Prototypes or proofs of concept**: This is when a solution is not yet fully developed but has some limited functionality that can be evaluated and assessed in terms of the value it can offer to the organization.
- **Pilot or beta releases**: A pilot or beta release of a solution is when a limited version of a solution is implemented for the purposes of assessing or testing a solution to determine its viability and value to the organization.

- **Operational releases**: An operational release of a solution is a fully functional solution or solution component and is used to achieve a specific objective, achieve progress, or fulfill the desired outcome:

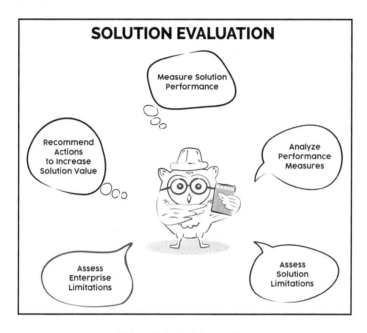

Solution evaluation knowledge area and tasks

The field of solution evaluation specifically consists of the following key tasks:

- Measuring solution performance
- Analyzing performance measures
- Assessing solution limitations
- Assessing enterprise limitations
- Recommending actions to increase solution value

With solution evaluation, there are a few different types of output or deliverable that typically get produced. These include artifacts, such as solution-performance measures, solution-performance analysis, solution limitations, enterprise limitations, and recommended actions.

Let's now explore how solution evaluation aligns with the Business Analysis Core Concept Model™.

Business Analysis Core Concept Model™

Before we delve into each of the specific tasks of solution evaluation, let's first understand how this knowledge area applies to the Business Analysis Core Concept Model with an example.

The six core concepts, which are described in the Business Analysis Core Concept Model, are as follows:

- Change
- Need
- Solution
- Stakeholder
- Value
- Context

In this section, we will consider how solution evaluation as a knowledge area applies to the Business Analysis Core Concept Model through the use of a practical example.

Change

The core concept of Change refers to a recommendation for a change to either a solution or the enterprise in order to realize the potential value of a solution.

Let's look at an example to bring the concept of Change to life:

A fashion retail company, Debby's Unique Dresses, currently sells most of its exclusive dress patterns using a mail-order system. Customers have to view designs by browsing the online website catalog and then make an offline mail order to purchase a design. As the business analyst who worked on the original website selling via mail order, you have come back to do a post-implementation review to analyze whether the company is getting the expected benefits and value. After reviewing their existing sales channels, you find that there are improvements that will help increase the business value of the current website. You recommend that they implement an e-commerce component to their existing website. This will enable the company to also sell designs using online payment options as well as using the existing mail-order channel. By making this change to their existing website solution, they will increase the value of their sales dramatically.

This example illustrates how the core concept of Change is typically implemented during solution evaluation.

Need

The core concept of Need refers to how a solution or a solution component fulfills a need.

Let's continue our example to see how the concept of Need works in the real world:

By adding the functionality to allow online payments on Debby's Unique Dresses' existing website, this action further helps to meet the need of increasing sales for the business.

This example illustrates how the core concept of Need is implemented during solution evaluation by considering how a solution or solution component fulfills business needs.

Solution

The core concept of Solution refers to the assessment of the performance of a solution and determining whether it is delivering the potential value. It is also about determining why a solution may or may not be delivering the value that was expected.

Let's continue our example of Debby's Unique Dresses to see how the concept of Solution works in the real world:

The potential value in the form of increased sales for Debby's Unique Dresses was not realized as expected when the new e-commerce solution component was added to the existing website. The role of the business analyst is to analyze why this value was not realized.

This example illustrates how the core concept of Solution should be assessed in terms of its performance when attempting to deliver the expected business value.

Stakeholder

The core concept of the Stakeholder refers to how the stakeholder can provide information about a solution's performance and value delivery.

Let's look at a new example to see how the concept of the Stakeholder works in the real world:

After the implementation of a new user interface to an existing call center solution, the stakeholders noticed an increase in the time that a call center agent spends to resolve customer inquiries. As the business analyst, your role is to elicit detailed information from stakeholders in relation to the performance of the new solution component—the new user interface in this case—and analyze the information to determine the cause of the increase in the call duration.

Therefore, during solution evaluation, it is important to realize that stakeholders are engaged to provide information about solution performance and value delivery.

Value

The core concept of Value refers to whether a solution is delivering the potential value that was expected, as well as the analysis that determines why the value may or may not be delivered.

In this case, the core concept of Solution and the core concept of Value are aiming to determine whether the value was delivered as expected.

In the example of Debby's Unique Dresses mentioned earlier, *the additional website functionality still did not deliver the expected value of increased sales. It is the role of the business analyst to analyze the solution to determine why this is the case.*

Context

The final core concept of Context refers to how the context could impact on the solution performance and potentially add limitations, which may prohibit value from being realized.

If we continue with the example of the new user interface, which was added to the existing call center solution, we can see how this concept of Context works in the real world:

The context of this implementation is that none of the call center staff received any training in how to use the new user interface that was introduced. Because of the lack of training, the call center staff took much longer to assist a customer with inquiries because they were unfamiliar with how to use the new user interface. This is why the value of the solution was not immediately realized. By providing adequate training to the call center staff, the potential value of the solution is likely to be realized sooner.

Now that we have an understanding of the Business Analysis Core Concept Model and how it relates to the solution evaluation knowledge area, it is time to move to the specific tasks that you need to perform. The next section covers the specific analysis tasks involved when working within the solution evaluation knowledge area.

Task: Measure Solution Performance

The first task that is described as part of solution evaluation is about determining what the measurements are for evaluating the performance of a solution.

In this section, we will cover the purpose of this task and the different aspects of measuring solution performance in the context of the task's core elements. For any solution to be a success, it is important to capture and track its performance using defined measures. In this section, we will discuss what considerations and elements a business analyst should apply when they measure a solution's performance.

Let's start by considering the purpose of this task.

Purpose

According to the BABOK® V3 Guide, the purpose of measuring solution performance is "*to define performance measures and use the data collected to evaluate the effectiveness of a solution in relation to the value it brings.*"

When we refer to performance measures, we are referring to those measures that can help us determine the value that a newly implemented or existing solution is bringing to the organization. In some cases, a solution may have built-in performance measures to track how much value is being generated by the solution, but in many cases, the business analyst needs to work with stakeholders to define these measures. Measures often take the form of key performance indicators that are in line with the overall organizational goals, targets, or predefined tests for a software solution.

Let's consider the following real-world example:

Consider the situation where a new call center software solution has been implemented. One measure to determine whether the solution is performing as expected could be to measure the time spent to resolve a customer inquiry. A decrease in the time spent supporting customers during a single support call will be a positive performance result for the new solution. Another performance measure could be the number of positive customer feedback ratings that are recorded after each successful call.

Let's now consider the core elements that a business analyst should include when performing this task.

Elements

There are three elements to consider when you measure solution performance. These include the following:

- Defining solution performance measures
- Validating performance measures
- Collecting performance measures

We will now summarize each of these elements and describe them in the context of a practical example.

Element 1: Defining solution performance measures

What should be considered when you define solution performance measures? The first thing to consider when defining solution performance measures is which performance measures already exist, or whether there are methods in place to capture these measures. If there are some performance measures in place, then it is the role of the business analyst to ensure that they are accurate and relevant, and if any further measures are needed. It is also the role of the business analyst to elicit this information from stakeholders.

If there is a need to define solution performance measures, then it is often a great idea to analyze business goals, objectives, and business processes that are relevant to the solution under discussion.

In some cases, some of the performance measures can be influenced or directed by third parties, such as solution vendors, government bodies, or other regulatory organizations.

The nature of the solution performance measures can be quantitative, qualitative, or a combination of both. The nature of the measures often depends on the type of value being measured.

Let's now learn what the different types of measures are.

Quantitative measures

A quantitative measure is the type of measure that can be measured with numbers, quantities, or ratings.

For example, a new website has been implemented for an organization. It was expected that the new site will generate 10% more new clients within the first 30 days of being operational and a 30% increase in existing customers returning to the website within the same period.

Qualitative measures

A qualitative measure is more subjective in nature and can include attitudes, perceptions, and any other subjective response. Customers, users, and others involved in the operation of a solution will have their own ideas and perceptions of how well they believe a solution is meeting their needs.

For example, a banking institution has always had major complaints from customers and staff members about the poor usability and low level of customer friendliness of the loan-application process. They also complained that it was a very time consuming and tedious process. These are examples of qualitative measures that exist within the context of this loan-application process.

Element 2: Validating performance measures

Why validate performance measures?

It is important to validate the performance measures with the stakeholders who are responsible for delivering business value from the solution. The performance measures that the business analyst proposes must make sense to them and their business objectives. It is therefore key for the business analyst to identify the most appropriate stakeholders (often the sponsor) to agree and validate that the proposed performance measures are good, relevant, and useful to the stakeholder group.

Continuing with the loan-application solution example we used in the previous section, let's say that the loan-application process has been enhanced to implement improved speed and usability.

If the success of this solution is being measured by the total loan amounts disbursed since the solution implementation, you will agree that this measure will not be an accurate reflection of the original customer needs. The original business need was concerned with improved customer experience when using the loan-application process. It will be much more appropriate to implement a measure that measures customer satisfaction once they have completed the loan-application process than measuring an aspect that is not in line with the original business needs.

Element 3: Collecting performance measures

Business Analysts can also use some basic statistical sampling concepts when defining the performance measures. Some of these basic concepts are related to the following considerations when formulating performance measures:

- **Volume or sample size:** If a statistical method is used to analyze performance for a particular solution, it is important that the business analyst considers the sample size or data volume that will be used. A sample size that is too small might skew the results and lead to inaccurate conclusions.
- **Frequency and timing:** It is important to also consider that the frequency and timing with which measurements are taken may have an effect on the outcome.
- **Currency**: This consideration refers to the fact that measurements that are taken more recently tend to be more representative than older data.

Let's now consider a real-world example:

A business analyst is required to collect performance measures for a national heating system company in order to rate customer satisfaction in terms of the effectiveness of the heating systems installed in people's homes.

It is recommended that the sample size of the performance measures should be an accurate reflection of the geographical location of customers. The analyst should also consider the season during which the sample will be taken and aim to base the results on recent customer data.

Inputs and outputs

The solution evaluation task of measuring the solution performance has the following key inputs and outputs:

- **Inputs**: Business objectives

Implemented solution (external)

- **Outputs**: Solution performance measures

The task of measuring solution performance was all about considering the business objectives in the context of finding ways to measure how well the implemented solution is delivering the expected business value.

Let's now move to the next solution evaluation task, analyzing performance measures. Now that we have identified and defined which performance measures will be used to measure a solution's effectiveness, we will now look at what a business analyst should consider when analyzing the performance measures received or collected.

Task: Analyzing Performance Measures

The second task described as part of the field of solution evaluation involves the business analyst providing insights and analysis of the results in terms of the business value being delivered by an existing implemented solution. We will discuss the key concepts around the desired value versus the actual value being delivered by the solution, the risks to consider, trends that may arise in our performance results, and the importance of considering the accuracy of our results.

During this section, we will cover the different aspects of providing these performance insights and outline some of the key considerations when performing this task. Let's now continue with the purpose of this task.

Purpose

According to the BABOK® V3 Guide, the purpose of analyzing performance measures is *"to provide insights into the performance of a solution in relation to the value it brings."*

Business analysts need to consider the goals and objectives of the business, as well as existing key performance indicators when working out what the expected business value is that the stakeholders are hoping to achieve. Once the business analyst has a view of the expected value that stakeholders would like to see, it is possible to compare this with the actual performance based on the performance measures used to measure the value of the solution.

If you consider the previous task, the performance of the solution was measured. In this task, the actual performance is compared to what was expected when the need was identified in the first place.

Let's consider a real-world example:

A business stakeholder group from a large enterprise had an expectation that when the network's data transmission capacity was increased, it would also increase the performance of their primary system in terms of its transaction processing time.

After the data transmission capacity is increased, the system performance should be measured again so that the actual improvements in processing times can be compared against the originally expected performance improvements.

Elements

There are five elements to consider when you analyze performance measures:

- Solution performance versus desired value
- Risks
- Trends
- Accuracy
- Performance variances

In the following sections, we summarize each of these elements and describe them in the context of real-world examples.

Element 1: Solution performance versus desired value

This element involves the business analyst working with the stakeholders to collect measurements that were previously identified in relation to the value that the organization desires from the solution.

It is important to understand that while a solution might be performing very well, such as an efficient online transaction processing system, the business value that it brings could still be fairly minimal. On the other hand, a lower-performing or less efficient system can potentially contribute more value to the business and would be considered to be more valuable as a solution. It might, therefore, make more business sense to simply aim to improve this core system's performance to continue receiving strong business value.

This illustrates that deciding what the true business value of a solution is can involve multiple aspects of the business, and therefore it is really important to understand the actual business value versus the desired business value. This is done by fully understanding the performance measures of a solution, as well as understanding the stakeholder's business value exceptions.

Element 2: Risks

Performance measures can also bring about new risks to solution performance and to the wider organization. These risks should be identified and managed like any other risks.

Let's consider a brief real-world example:

While analyzing performance measures for an existing loan-application system, it is discovered that certain data fields within the database are being prepopulated with test data (as opposed to real customer data). This faulty data population error skews the analysis done on customer data and makes the current customer data unreliable and incorrect.

This is identified and reported as a major data-integrity risk and is being managed in the same way as a business risk.

Element 3: Trends

When analyzing performance data, business analysts must consider the age of the data that is being used for trend analysis. If the data is out of date and deemed not relevant to the current analysis, it should be replaced with more relevant and timely datasets to prevent any skewed or misinterpreted findings. A larger sample size over a sufficiently long time period will provide a much more accurate depiction of solution performance on which to base decisions. This will also assist you in guarding against false signals brought about by incomplete data.

Let's consider a real-world example:

A sudden increase in the credit card transaction volumes at the same time of day recorded over a period of a couple of months could indicate a trend in abnormal spending behavior; however, when looking closer at this data sample, the business analyst might find that the data is only collected during a period of high spendings, such as the Christmas season. The results of this data-trend analysis cannot be used for general spending assumptions or measurements because the timing of this data sample is skewing the results.

Element 4: Accuracy

There is a simple way to determine whether the results obtained from performance measures are accurate, and this is to ensure that the same performance results are reproducible and repeatable using a different but similar dataset.

Let's consider a practical example:

Consider a speed test for websites at a web design company. The same website speed-testing tool should always be used to ensure that all websites are tested against the same benchmark, which will, therefore, make the results from different websites comparable.

If the same tool is consistently used, the test can be repeated as often as required and the stakeholders using the measures can be comfortable that the measure remains constant and accurate.

Element 5: Performance variations

The difference between the expected and actual performance represents a variance that is considered when analyzing solution performance. Root-cause analysis may be necessary to determine the underlying causes of significant variances within a solution.

One of the key aspects of this task is for the business analyst to understand the stakeholder's expectations in terms of the desired business value they seek and then compare this with the actual performance measure results. If there is a large variance between what the actual business value is that the solution is delivering and the desired business value, then it is the role of the business analyst to work out why there is a variance.

Let's consider a practical example:

The stakeholders of an enterprise had an expectation that the transaction processing times will increase by 20% when the network data transmission capacity is increased. This business value did not come about when analyzing the actual performance measurement results. It is therefore now the role of the business analyst to analyze the results and other factors to try to understand the variance in results. Some of the other factors that could be analyzed in this scenario might be the size of the server, the number of applications or processes running on the server, or perhaps even the age (and efficiency) of the surrounding hardware that is supporting this change.

It is a good practice to consider the holistic solution and the relevant business processes, goals, and other key relevant factors when diagnosing the root cause of such variances.

Inputs and outputs

With the solution evaluation task of analyzing performance measures, there are the following key inputs and outputs:

- **Inputs**: Potential value, solution performance measures

- **Outputs**: Solution performance analysis

The task of analyzing performance measures is about understanding the business value when comparing the expected value and the actual value being delivered by a solution.

Let's now discuss the next solution evaluation task of assessing solution limitations so that we can gain a deeper appreciation of why a solution may or may not perform as was expected.

Task: Assessing Solution Limitations

We have just learned how to define performance measures and what to consider when we analyze the performance results. This section will help the business analyst to understand what the solution limitations could be that will have an effect on the performance results.

The third task described as part of solution evaluation is about investigating any internal solution factors that may impact the solution's ability to realize its full business value.

In this section, you will learn about the root causes of ineffective or underperformance in existing solutions. You will also learn that this type of assessment can be performed at any stage of the solution's life cycle, from development to being an operational implemented solution.

Let's now consider the purpose of the task: assessing solution limitations.

Purpose

According to the BABOK® V3 Guide, the purpose of assessing the solution limitations is "*to determine the factors internal to the solution that restricts the full realization of value.*"

The tasks of assessing solution limitations and assessing enterprise limitations are similar in nature and can be performed at the same time. Assessing solution limitations looks at internal factors that may limit the solution's ability to deliver value, whereas assessing enterprise limitations looks at factors that are external to the solution but limit its ability to deliver value.

It is the business analyst's role to assess both the internal and external factors that have an impact on the solution's ability to deliver the expected value. Regardless of when this assessment is performed during the life cycle, the activities for internal and external factor assessments are similar and involve the same considerations.

Let's consider a real-world example:

A new online e-commerce solution has been implemented for a global shoe company. After the implementation of the e-commerce store, the performance was measured for a few months and the actual value was far below the expected value. The business analyst looked at this variance closely and noticed that it was specifically the total amount of international sales that had decreased substantially. After further investigation, the business analyst discovered that the solution didn't have the capability to change the currency of the shopping cart when dealing with different countries' customers. This resulted in a lot of abandoned carts and missed revenue from international sales. This was deemed an internal solution limitation that prevented the solution from realizing its full business value potential.

Elements

There are three elements to consider when you assess a solution's limitations:

- Identify internal solution component dependencies
- Investigate solution problems
- Impact assessment

The next sections discuss each of these three elements in the context of a practical example.

Element 1: Identify internal solution component dependencies

This element is about assessing the solution components from the perspective of efficiency and identifying which parts of the solution are dependent on each other and which of those parts are the least effective. Once the business analyst understands these dependencies and inefficiencies, it is possible to determine which parts of the solution are responsible for limiting a solution's ability to realize its fullest potential business value.

Let's consider a real-world scenario to explore this concept further:

A new workflow is implemented to improve customer communications; however, when the performance is measured, it is found that the new end-to-end workflow process now takes three days longer than before.

Upon analysis of the solution, it is identified that part of the new workflow process is a manual email communication step, which, if not managed correctly by the staff members facilitating the process, causes this time delay. There is, therefore, a direct performance dependency of the total solution on this specific manual component, which in turn limits the solution in realizing the full potential value it was implemented for.

Element 2: Investigate solution problems

This element of the task is about the different aspects that a business analyst should consider when performing problem analysis. Sometimes a solution will repeatedly produce ineffective or incorrect outputs that clearly point to a problem somewhere in the solution.

When performing problem analysis, a business analyst will identify the problems in a solution or solution component by analyzing the instances where the outputs from the solution are below an acceptable level of quality or where the potential value is not being realized.

Problems may show up in different ways, which could include an inability to meet a business goal, objective, or a specific stakeholder requirement. It could also be a failure to realize a benefit that was projected during a past analysis of the tasks.

Let's continue with the example we started in the previous section:

A new online e-commerce solution has been implemented for a global shoe company. After the implementation of the e-commerce store, the performance was measured for a few months and the actual value was far below the expected value. The business analyst looked at this variance closely and noticed that it was specifically the total amount of international sales that had decreased substantially. After further investigation, the business analyst discovered that the solution didn't have the ability to change the currency of the shopping cart when dealing with different countries' customers. This caused a lot of abandoned carts and missed revenue from international sales. This was deemed an internal solution limitation that prevented the solution from realizing its full business value potential.

One recommended solution here would be to request location information from the customer visiting the online store. Depending on the location provided, the customer would then be redirected to the appropriate country-specific instance of the online store that can then sell to the customer in their local currency.

Element 3: Impact assessment

Now that the business analyst identified some problem areas in relation to the solution, it is important to review the impact that these problems have on the wider organization or the ability for the solution to deliver its potential business value.

As with most impact assessments, this is about understanding the severity of the problem, as well as the probability of the problem reoccurring, the impact it may have on the business operations, and also the capacity of the business to absorb the impact overall.

The business analyst will also then identify which of the problems needs to be resolved, which problems can be mitigated through other activities or perhaps workarounds, and which problems can be lived with and therefore accepted.

Let's consider a real-world example:

A problem has been identified in a customer-management solution that is used in a retail organization. Every time the customer search function is used to search for a specific customer, Mr. B Brown, his customer record is not found.

However, if a check is done within the database, the customer record for Mr. B Brown is found to exist and the search criteria used were correct.

This has been identified as a one-off problem and has not reoccurred with any other customer; however, additional quality control measures have been put in place to ensure that this does not happen with any other customer records again.

The business risk posed by this problem has also been identified as low, and so no specific mitigation plan is required in this case. It is also decided to accept this instance of the problem.

Inputs and outputs

With the solution evaluation task of assessing solution limitations, there are the following key inputs and outputs:

- **Inputs**: Implemented solution (external)
- Solution performance analysis
- **Outputs**: Solution limitation

The task of assessing solution limitation is about understanding the factors that are internal to the solution that is limiting its ability to realize its full business value. The primary output of this task is any identified solution limitations, including an impact assessment.

Now that we have considered the solution's limitations, it is time to look at the wider enterprise limitations that may exist and influence the environment of the solution being analyzed. Let's now discuss the next solution evaluation task, assessing enterprise limitations.

Task: Assessing Enterprise Limitations

When we assess the enterprise limitations, we do this in the context of the performance results for the solution we are analyzing.

The fourth task described as part of the field of solution evaluation is to assess enterprise limitations. This task describes the activities involved in assessing the factors external to the solution that limit its potential to deliver its full business value.

In this section, you will learn about the nature of enterprise limitations and what to consider when performing an enterprise culture assessment, stakeholder impact analysis, and organizational structure change. You will also learn about what is included in an operational assessment.

Let's continue this section by learning about the overarching purpose of assessing enterprise limitations in the context of solution evaluation.

Purpose

According to the BABOK® V3 Guide, the purpose of assessing enterprise limitations is "*to determine how factors external to the solution are restricting value realization.*"

When we consider the external environment of a solution, we should consider its interactions and interdependencies, as well as other environmental factors that exist outside of the enterprise.

Enterprise limitations can even include factors such as culture, operations, technical components, stakeholder interests, or organizational reporting structures.

In a nutshell, when assessing enterprise limitations, you identify the root causes and describe how enterprise factors limit value realization for the organization.

Let's consider the following real-world example:

A complete paperless publishing solution is implemented within a traditional publishing house. The idea is that all core business processes will now only be executed electronically and no more printing of drafts or review copies will be allowed. Therefore, manuscripts that are received into the publishing house will be electronically scanned and recorded, then all editing should be done on-screen. This solution works perfectly on the receiving side of the business; however, the editors are very unsatisfied with the solution as they have always been able to print all the manuscripts to review and edit on paper. They believe that paper-based editing is much more productive and creative and they are threatening to stop work unless they are able to print as they did before.

The core business process here, as well as the organizational culture, is causing a limitation to the effectiveness of the solution, thereby limiting the realization of potential business value.

Elements

There are four elements to consider when you assess enterprise limitations:

- Enterprise culture assessment
- Stakeholder impact analysis
- Organizational structure changes
- Operational assessment

Let's now consider each element in terms of a practical example.

Element 1: Enterprise culture assessment

When the business analyst performs an enterprise culture assessment, they try to gain a level of understanding of what makes an enterprise 'tick', as it were. The business analyst needs to understand hat the deeply rooted beliefs, values, and norms that are shared between the members of the organization. This is important because often the culture of an organization will directly impact the actions they take.

A business analyst will perform a cultural assessment so that they can do the following:

- Identify whether stakeholders have an appreciation for why a solution exists within the organization
- Work out whether the stakeholders see the solution as a beneficial change that brings potential or actual business value into the business
- Understand whether any cultural changes are required to help realize better business value from a solution.

Ultimately the enterprise culture assessment evaluates the level to which a current culture is able to accept a new solution. If it is found that there are some cultural adjustments needed for a solution to be accepted and successful, the assessment is used to judge the enterprise's ability and willingness to adapt to these cultural changes.

Let's consider a real-world example:

In an attempt to cut operational costs within a company, a new office hot-desk solution is being considered. The idea is that each day, all staff can sit wherever they find an open desk and no one will have a dedicated desk to go to anymore. This requires staff to move all their belongings into allocated locker space because they will sit at a different desk every day.

Although most of the staff understands that the change is proposed to save money for the company, they do not see the benefits for themselves and believe this will be very disruptive. They are reluctant to accept the change and therefore are not very supportive. In this scenario, it will be relevant to perform an enterprise culture assessment so that the initiative can identify what cultural changes can be made to enhance the acceptance of the solution. This will also enable the solution to realize the expected value.

Element 2: Stakeholder impact analysis

When performing the task of assessing enterprise limitations, it is important to do a stakeholder impact analysis. This entails gaining insights into how the solution impacts a particular stakeholder group. There are some specific factors to consider when you perform the stakeholder impact analysis, which we will look at in the following sections.

Function

The concept of function is concerned with how the stakeholder groups use the solution from input, process, and output perspective. The business analyst will consider the inputs that the stakeholders provide to the solution's processes, and how they then use the solutions processes to generate specific outputs.

Let's consider the following real-world example:

A stakeholder group might have a primary function of analyzing daily sales for a company. They use a daily sales report to execute their tasks. If a new solution provides a new report format as part of a change and this doesn't include the team's information requirements to perform their daily sales analysis, then this will impact their group's function directly and should be included as part of a stakeholder impact analysis.

Location

When you consider the location as a key factor in a stakeholder impact analysis, this involves considering the physical location of a stakeholder group in relation to a solution.

Let's consider the following real-world example:

Consider the scenario where a new video-conferencing solution is installed in the head office, but it is not implemented in the company's satellite offices. This means that only stakeholders based in the head office can realize the value of the new solution.

Concerns

It is important to pay attention to the stakeholder groups' potential concerns in relation to a new solution. These can come in the format of issues, risks, and general concerns relating to a solution's potential value to the group. The group may be concerned about using the solution and this may impact their ability to perform their roles effectively.

Let's consider the following real-world example:

If a stakeholder is concerned that the new video-conferencing solution will cause ineffective and unproductive meetings because of less in-person communication, then this will inhibit their ability to embrace the new solution. If they don't use the new solution often, then the business value of the new solution will be diminished. It is therefore important to consider this concern from this stakeholder group to ensure that activities are planned to demonstrate the effectiveness and increase the productivity of this solution to this stakeholder group.

Element 3: Organizational structure changes

In some situations, depending on the solution being implemented, there may be an impact on the organizational structure of the organization. These are referred to as the formal structures or relationships of the organizations. These formal relationships can cause blocks or obstacles when implementing a new solution. It is important to also keep in mind that informal relationships in an organization can also cause blockers.

Business analysts consider informal and formal relationships as part of assessing the potential for the solution to realize its full business value.

Element 4: Operational assessment

Why is an operational assessment performed?

Firstly, an operational assessment is about considering whether the organization is able to adapt to or use a solution effectively. This is done by identifying the relevant tools and procedures within the organization that will potentially benefit from the solution and ensuring that the appropriate assets are in place to support it.

When an operational assessment is being conducted, the business analyst should consider the following:

- Policies and procedures
- Capabilities and processes that enable other capabilities
- Skill and training needs
- Human resources practices
- Risk tolerance and management approaches
- Tools and technology that support a solution

As a result of this type of assessment, it highlights whether there are training and knowledge limitations that need to be addressed. It could also identify a policy or procedure that will limit the success of the new solution.

Let's consider the following real-world example:

A new telephone call tracking and recording solution are being planned for the organization's call center. To enable detailed phone call tracking and recording, it was determined as part of the operational assessment that new telephone handsets need to be purchased and installed. This illustrates an example of an instance where the organization didn't have the necessary assets to support the new solution for the call center and will need to be addressed before the full business value of the solution can be realized.

Inputs and outputs

With the solution evaluation task of assessing enterprise limitations, there are the following key inputs and outputs:

- **Inputs**: Current state description, implemented (or constructed) solution (external), and solution performance analysis

- **Outputs**: Enterprise limitation

The task of assessing enterprise limitations is about understanding the factors that are external to the solution and limit its ability to realize its full business value. The primary output of this task is any identified enterprise limitations, including an impact and operational assessment.

Let's now discuss the last solution evaluation task, recommending actions to increase the solution value. At this stage of the analysis work, you have defined the factors that are impacting the solution's ability to perform as expected or intended by the business stakeholders. In the next section, we will look at how to recommend actions that could be taken to increase the solution's performance as a result of the analysis work done.

Task: Recommending Actions to Increase the Solution Value

The fifth and final task described as part of solution evaluation is recommending actions to increase the solution value. This task describes the elements and considerations that a business analyst needs to include when preparing to recommend actions to the organization to ensure better solution value.

In this section, you will learn about the different types of recommendation that a business analyst could make when presenting the results of assessing the solution and enterprise in the context of analyzing a solution's value to the organization.

Let's continue this section by learning about the primary purpose of recommending actions to increase the solution value in the context of solution evaluation.

Purpose

According to the BABOK® V3 Guide, the purpose of recommending actions to increase the solution value is *"to understand the factors that create differences between potential value and actual value, and to recommend a course of action to align them."*

Up until now, we have discussed the tasks that assist the business analyst in measuring, analyzing, and understanding the root causes of unacceptable solution performance. During this part of the chapter, we will discuss what is involved when you recommend specific changes or courses of action to help increase the realization of full business benefits and value.

In a lot of cases, the recommendations are about how a solution could potentially be replaced, retired, or improved. These recommendations may also consider long-term impacts and contributions of the solution to stakeholders.

Consider the previously discussed example scenario:

A new online e-commerce solution has been implemented for a global shoe company. After the implementation of the e-commerce store, the performance was measured for a few months and the actual value was far below the expected value. The business analyst looked at this variance closely and noticed that it was specifically the total amount of international sales that had decreased substantially. After further investigation, the business analyst discovered that the e-commerce solution didn't have the ability to change the currency of the shopping cart when dealing with customers from different countries. This resulted in a lot of abandoned carts and missed revenue from international sales.

Because of the long-term effect that this would have on the overall company revenue, a recommended solution here could be to replace the existing online store with an online store that can sell in the currency that is automatically derived from an end user's geographic location.

Elements

There are two elements to consider when you recommend actions to increase the solution value:

- Adjust solution performance measures
- Recommendations

Let's now consider each element in terms of a practical example.

Element 1: Adjust solution performance measures

The adjustment of solution performance measures describes the consideration that in some cases, a solution may be acceptable, but the measures that are used to track its performance are inadequate or not aligned for business goals or objectives. In these cases, it may simply be a matter of redefining the performance measures to track the business value in alignment with business objectives.

Element 2: Recommendations

Although in many cases, a recommendation would encompass a series of activities to enable an increase in a solution's performance, this may not always be the case. In some cases, the business analyst may decide not to do anything different or to potentially change or adjust external aspects that may impact the performance of a solution instead of changing the solution itself. In other cases, all that might be required is a simple change in the expectations of stakeholders in terms of business value goals for this solution.

In the following list, you will find some common examples of recommendations that a business analyst may propose:

- **Do nothing:** This option is the most likely recommendation when the value of a change is relatively small in relation to the effort it will take to make the change. It is also often the recommendation that is proposed when the risks associated with making a change outweigh the potential increase in value derived from the change.
- **Organizational change:** This type of recommendation is about proposing changes to the organizational culture in terms of attitudes, perceptions of the solution, or participation levels to ensure that the solution is successful. Although much of this work will be undertaken by the change management function, it is often the business analyst who will provide input into potential organizational structural changes or any changes to job functions to help achieve maximum business benefit.
- **Reduce the complexity of interfaces:** This recommendation is about reducing the complexity of interfaces between systems or people.
- **Eliminate redundancy:** This recommendation is about highlighting the different stakeholder groups that may have common business needs and requirements, and that these can be met with a single solution. This can, therefore, reduce the cost of implementation and, in turn, contribute to the overall business value that is gained.
- **Avoid waste:** This type of recommendation aims to avoid unnecessary activities that don't add any value.

- **Identify additional capabilities**: This is when the business analyst recommends a solution option that may offer additional capabilities to the organization above and beyond those identified in the requirements. These capabilities may not be of immediate value to the organization, but they do have the potential to provide future value—for example, a software application may have features that the organization anticipates using in the future.
- **Retire the solution**: Another recommendation might be to get rid of the existing solution and completely replace it with a better more value-adding solution or solution component. This may be needed because the existing technology has reached the end of its life, the business processes are being outsourced, or the solution is simply not keeping up with business goals and cannot fulfill the needs of the organization any longer.

There are some more factors that may impact the decision regarding the replacement or retirement of a solution. These include the following considerations:

- **What is the ongoing cost versus the initial investment?** Often, an existing solution might have increased maintenance costs over a period of time, while some other more modern alternatives might have a higher initial investment cost but lower long-term maintenance costs. In a real-world scenario, we might see older mainframe solutions in some banks that have very high maintenance costs because of additional challenges, such as the fact that very few professionals have the skills to support these technology solutions and require really high service fees. Such systems are also very inflexible, limiting the number and degree of changes that are made to them.
- **Opportunity cost:** The opportunity cost factor represents the potential value that could be realized when pursuing an alternative course of action—for example, it might be more beneficial to purchase a tried and tested timesheet system than building a custom solution in house.
- **Necessity:** This factor considers whether a solution is still fulfilling a function that is necessary. In most situations, a solution has a limited lifespan (because of obsolescence, changing market conditions, and other factors). After a certain point in the life cycle of a solution, it will become impractical or impossible to maintain the existing component and a recommendation might be to replace a solution. For example, say that a government has always required certain business tax reports to be submitted through a manual process each month. Should the government streamline and automate its system, then this process will no longer be required, making the bulk printing of these reports redundant and obsolete.

- **Sunken cost:** The last type of factor to consider with these recommendations are sunk costs. This refers to the money and effort already committed to an initiative, which often leads stakeholders to feel like they should keep implementing a solution because so much money, time, and effort has already been invested. This type of situation affects objectivity and often affects the decision making process when considering future investment and identifying the future benefits that can realistically be gained.

Inputs and outputs

With the solution evaluation task of recommending actions to increase the solution value, there are the following key inputs and outputs:

- **Inputs**: Enterprise limitation and solution limitation

- **Outputs**: Recommended actions

The task of recommending actions to increase the solution value is about providing the business with the best recommendations for increasing the business value of a particular solution. The primary output of this task is the recommended actions that incorporate all results from the tasks performed during the analysis of performance measures, as well as the internal and external assessments.

Summary

In this chapter, you learned about solution evaluation.

The following are the key concepts and tasks that we covered during this chapter:

- The purpose and context of this knowledge area
- Task: Measuring solution performance
- Task: Analyzing performance measures
- Task: Assessing solution limitations
- Task: Assessing enterprise limitations
- Task: Recommending actions to increase the solution value

In the next chapter, we will learn about the underlying competencies that every business analyst should develop and improve during the course of their professional business analysis careers.

Make sure that you revise these key pieces of information before completing the knowledge quiz at the end of this chapter.

You should now have an understanding of the importance and purpose of the field of solution evaluation and know the scope of performing analysis tasks from the perspective of solution evaluation.

Learning outcome: Solution evaluation

You should now have a holistic understanding of the importance and purpose of the practice of business analysis planning and monitoring in terms of the role it plays in defining, planning, and completing the business analysis work that you do. You should be able to describe this practice in the context of the BACCM™ using real-world practical situations. You should also be able to visualize the key inputs and outputs to perform this task effectively.

Learning outcome: Task – Measuring solution performance

In this chapter, you learned about the task of measuring a solution's performance, and you should now be able to describe the purpose of this task and the key elements to consider when performing this task using real-world scenarios and concepts. You should also be able to visualize the key inputs and outputs to perform this task effectively.

Learning outcome: Task – Analyzing performance measures

In this chapter, you learned about the task of analyzing performance measures, and you should now be able to describe the purpose of this task and describe the key elements to consider when performing this task using real-world scenarios and concepts. You should also be able to visualize the key inputs and outputs to perform this task effectively.

Learning outcome: Task – Assessing solution limitations

In this chapter, you learned about the task of assessing solution limitations in terms of its purpose, and you should now be able to describe the key elements to consider when performing this task using real-world scenarios and concepts. You should also be able to visualize the key inputs and outputs to perform this task effectively.

Learning outcome: Task – Assessing enterprise limitations

In this chapter, you learned about the task of assessing enterprise limitations, and you should now be able to describe the purpose of this task and the key elements to consider when performing this task using real-world scenarios and concepts. You should also be able to visualize the key inputs and outputs to perform this task effectively.

Learning outcome: Task – Recommending actions to increase the solution value

In this chapter, you learned about the task of recommending actions to increase a solution's value to the organization, and you should now be able to describe the purpose of this task and the key elements to consider when performing this task using real-world scenarios and concepts. You should also be able to visualize the key inputs and outputs to perform this task effectively.

Knowledge quiz

Consider the following real-world scenario and complete the micro mock exam based on this chapter that follows.

Case study: Mobile pay

You are part of a project team working for the country's largest bank. Your team has just launched the first mobile phone payment application in partnership with the world's most advanced end-user technology company, Oranges Inc. The solution you implemented allows people to pay for everyday transactions using their mobile phones instead of plastic credit and debit cards. People simply need to pass their phone over the payment terminal and the transaction is completed. The bank's stakeholders expect that the number of transactions will increase dramatically and that customers will absolutely love this application. As the business analyst on this project, you have defined some performance measures prior to this launch and cannot wait to track the results. Some of the performance measures you agreed with the stakeholders are (a.) the number of sales processed using the new mobile application versus the regular plastic cards within the first three months and (b.) the number of customers that download and install the new application onto their mobile phones and the actual usage of the application when processing transactions. You also suggested that a survey is done two months after the launch date to determine what people think and feel in relation to the new application's usability and security features. After the first three months, when you analyzed the performance measures that you agreed before, you noticed that during the last two weeks of the three-month period, the number of sales transactions dropped suddenly and quite significantly. The application downloads also declined and quite a number of customers have reverted back to using the card only transactions. The stakeholders are asking you to work out what could be the cause of this significant change in mobile phone spending behavior.

Question 1

Using the provided case study, while measuring solution performance, which one of the following considerations should you take into account when you collect performance measures?

Select the correct answers from the following choices:

A. Purpose of measure

B. Volume or sample size

C. Customer culture

D. Enterprise environment

Question 2

There are examples of quantitative and qualification performance measures given in the provided case study.

Choose whether this statement is True or False:

A. True

B. False

Question 3

Refer to the provided case study. Considering that the two-week period that is showing different performance data than the rest of the period makes you wonder whether the data was collected over a long enough period, you are also concerned that the sample size of the data might not be adequate to make a sound judgment on performance. You are wondering if the data is perhaps a false signal of poor performance.

Which one of the following elements of the analyzing performance measures are you considering here?

Select the correct answers from the following choices:

A. Accuracy

B. Risks

C. Trends

D. Solution performance versus desired value

Question 4

Using the provided case study, which of the following tasks will you perform to track the agreed performance measures in relation to the solution after launch?

Select the correct answer from the following choices:

    A. Review performance aspects

    B. Assess solution limitations

    C. Measure solution performance

    D. Assess enterprise limitations

Question 5

Refer to the provided case study. After you sent the survey to the agreed sample size of customers, you received an overwhelmingly positive response, where almost all customers said that they love the new mobile payment application. What type of measure is this a response too?

Select the correct answers from the following choices:

    A. Quantitative measure

    B. Quantity measure

    C. Qualitative measure

    D. Positive measure

Question 6

Refer to the provided case study. After you did some analysis of the cause of the significant reduction in sales during the last two weeks of the three-month period, you established some external factors that could be to blame. The bank recently announced that they will become the sponsor of a new industrial plant that received a lot of negative publicity in the media. They lost a number of customers bank-wide and you believe this might be the reason the performance data was affected during the last two weeks. Which of the following elements of assessing enterprise limitations could have resulted in you discovering this information?

Select the correct answer from the following choices:

A. Stakeholder impact analysis

B. Risks

C. Organizational structure changes

D. Trends

Question 7

Refer to the provided case study. After discussing the performance data collected after the three-month period, the stakeholders ask you to do some analysis on the solution itself. Which of the following elements of assessing solution limitations should you execute?

Select one or more correct answers from the following choices:

A. Identify internal solution component dependencies

B. Identify internal solution component abnormalities

C. Investigate solution problems

D. Investigate solution options

Question 8

Which of the following is a key input to measuring solution performance?

Select the correct answer from the following choices:

    A. Business requirements

    B. Business value

    C. Business scope

    D. Business objectives

Question 9

Which of the following is a key output to measuring solution performance?

Select the correct answer from the following choices:

    A. Solution result metrics

    B. Solution performance measures

    C. Solution performance value

    D. Solution performance results

Question 10

The business analyst only needs to validate the performance measures and any influencing criteria with other business analysts and do not need to involve other stakeholders.

Choose whether this statement is True or False:

    A. True

    B. False

Question 11

When business analysts analyze performance measures, which elements do they need to take into account?

Select one or more correct answers from the following choices:

A. Accuracy

B. Solution performance versus desired value

C. Risks

D. Solution scope

Question 12

The purpose of this task is to determine the factors that are internal to the solution that restricts the full realization of value. Which task are we referring to here?

Select the correct answer from the following choices:

A. Assessing solution options

B. Assessing solution functionality

C. Assessing solution boundaries

D. Assessing solution limitations

Question 13

A stakeholder impact analysis provides insight into how the solution affects a particular stakeholder group. When conducting a stakeholder impact analysis, what must business analysts consider?

Select one or more correct answers from the following choices:

A. The processes that don't use the solution to execute.

B. The processes where the stakeholders use the solution.

C. The issues, risks, and overall concerns that the stakeholders have with the solution.

D. The geographic locations of the stakeholders interacting with the solution.

Question 14

In the context of common recommendations that a business analyst may make about what action to take in relation to a solution after analyzing its performance, what does the term "sunk cost" refer to?

Select the correct answer from the following choices:

A. The money and effort that is scoped for the implementation of an initiative

B. The money and effort planned for an initiative

C. The money and effort already committed and spent towards part of an initiative

D. The estimated money and effort to be committed to an initiative

Question 15

When collecting performance measures, the timing and frequency with which measurements are taken may have an effect on the outcome.

Choose whether this statement is True or False:

A. True

B. False

Question 16

When defining performance measures, it is not recommended that you use qualitative and quantitative measures. You should only use one type of measure per solution that you analyze.

Choose whether this statement is True or False:

A. True

B. False

Question 17

Solution evaluation consists of five key tasks. Choose all the appropriate tasks from the following list:

A. Assess solution limitations

B. Define solution measures

C. Assess enterprise limitations

D. Measure solution performance

Question 18

Which of the following is a key output of recommending actions to increase solution value?

Select the correct answer from the following choices:

A. Recommended actions

B. Recommended options

C. Recommended steps

D. Recommended solutions

Question 19

During which one of the following solution evaluation tasks is the business analyst most likely to do an impact assessment?

Select the correct answer from the following choices:

A. Analyze performance impacts

B. Analyze performance measures

C. Assess solution limitations

D. Assess solution impacts

Answers

Questions	Answers
1	B
2	A
3	C
4	C
5	C
6	A
7	A, C
8	D
9	B
10	B
11	A, B, C
12	D
13	B, C, D
14	C
15	A
16	B
17	A, C, D
18	A
19	C

12
Underlying Competencies

This chapter discusses the underlying competencies that support the successful execution of business analysis as a discipline in the workplace. It outlines the key behaviors, characteristics, knowledge, and personal qualities that every business analyst should aspire to express in their role.

By the end of this chapter, you will know what the underlying competencies are and understand each core competency that a business analyst should include in their daily work. More specifically, we will cover the following key topics in this chapter:

- The purpose and context of the underlying competencies
- Analytical thinking and problem-solving
- Behavioral characteristics
- Business knowledge
- Communication skills
- Interaction skills
- Tools and technology
- A real-world case study
- Testing your knowledge

The concepts you will learn are as follows:

- Understanding the context of this BABOK®-related chapter with a real-world scenario
- Understanding and applying the competencies of analytical thinking and problem-solving to real-world scenarios
- Understanding and applying the competencies of behavioral characteristics to real-world scenarios
- Understanding and applying the competencies of business knowledge to real-world scenarios
- Understanding and applying the competencies of communication skills to real-world scenarios
- Understanding and applying the competencies of interaction skills to real-world scenarios
- Understanding and applying the competencies of tools and technology to real-world scenarios

Let's now start our journey by understanding what underlying competencies you should know how to apply in your everyday role as a professional business analyst.

What are the underlying competencies?

You may be tempted to pass through this section of the study material quickly, but I suggest you stop and absorb the true scope of the underlying competencies in order to gain a much deeper and more well-rounded understanding of what this chapter is trying to teach you about business analysis as a whole.

This chapter outlines the core behaviors, observable characteristics, and inherent—and sometimes assumed—knowledge and personal attributes that underline the entire practice of business analysis.

Although these underlying competencies are not necessarily unique to business analysis, they are described here to help you fully appreciate the fundamental skills and knowledge required to be a genuinely successful business analyst.

There are six main categories of underlying competencies to be aware of, shown in the following diagram:

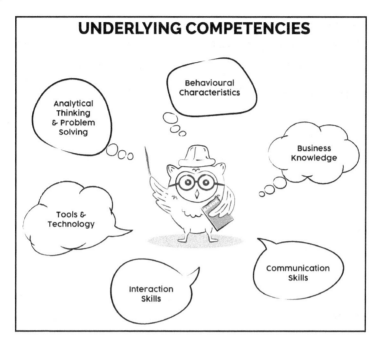

The underlying competencies categories

The list of competencies includes the following:

- Analytical thinking and problem-solving
- Behavioral characteristics
- Business knowledge
- Communication skills
- Interaction skills
- Tools and technology

Let's now dive into more detail about each category of the underlying competencies and understand what they mean and include.

Analytical thinking and problem-solving

As a business analyst, you need to develop your ability to apply analytical thinking and problem-solving in order to resolve the challenges and opportunities that you encounter as part of your role. These competencies are fundamental when identifying the best opportunities for delivering the most value to a business. They are also of key importance when helping your stakeholders understand the changing impacts within their business when pursuing these opportunities.

The analytical thinking and problem-solving core competencies include the following:

- Creative thinking
- Decision-making
- Learning
- Problem-solving
- Systems thinking
- Conceptual thinking
- Visual thinking

Let's now consider each of these core competencies and understand what they mean and how to apply them effectively when performing business analysis functions.

Core competency 1: Creative thinking

The first core competency in analytical thinking and problem-solving is the ability to think in a creative way. This involves being able to find ways of generating new ideas and approaches when considering problems and opportunities. Creative thinking also includes the ability to find new connections and associations between existing ideas and concepts.

Core competency 2: Decision-making

Being able to make effective decisions is about developing your ability to understand the criteria involved when making a decision and supporting other people to make better decisions by applying the criteria in a suitable way.

Ultimately, decision-making is about finding the path that will be most beneficial to the stakeholders and the organization as a whole.

Effective decision-making requires having all the relevant information and having an agreed set of criteria. Then, it is about analyzing the information and selecting the best option based on the criteria in order to reach the best outcome. Often, this involves developing comparisons and trade-offs in a way that yields the most desired option.

Core competency 3: Learning

Learning is central to practicing business analysis because it means being able to absorb new and different types of information efficiently and correctly. It is also about being adaptable and being able to adjust existing knowledge to suit new environments.

Learning is essentially the process of gaining knowledge or skills.

Learning about a new topic involves going through a set of different phases. It starts with you acquiring new information and learning raw facts. Once you have acquired this new information and facts, your learning progresses to deeper comprehension and understanding of its meaning. Once you achieve a level of deeper understanding, your learning moves on to applying it to your day-to-day work. Once a certain level of proficiency is achieved, it is possible to analyze, synthesize, and evaluate the information you have learned in a way that adds value to your new knowledge.

Learning is most effective when it considers the following representational systems that we all use:

- **Visual learning**: This includes learning through the presentation of pictures, photographs, diagrams, models, and videos.
- **Auditory learning**: This includes learning through verbal and written language and text.
- **Kinesthetic learning**: This is includes learning by doing something practically ourselves.

Most people will experience faster understanding and longer retention of information when more than one of the preceding learning representations are used.

Let's consider a real-world scenario where multiple representational systems are considered for learning new information.

Presenting a presentation-style summary of all the requirements of a project to a group of stakeholders would be very effective if the presentation includes graphs, pictures, diagrams, and a verbal summary of key points. This way, the people in the audience who prefer learning through visual presentations will relate to the information, as well as the people who prefer listening to information.

Core competency 4: Problem-solving

This competency is key to the practice of business analysis. It is about finding the true root cause of any problem so that the solution options you consider indeed address the real cause of the problem at hand.

Another key aspect of problem-solving is ensuring that all stakeholders have a common understanding of the underlying issues. It ensures that all points of view are addressed and identifies any conflicts that might exist between the stakeholder group's individual goals and objectives.

An easy way to remember what problem-solving is to remember that in the context of business analysis, it can almost be described as just another phrase for business analysis. Think of all the requirements you develop, analyze, and find solutions for as a form of problem-solving.

Another part of problem-solving is ensuring all assumptions are identified and validated. The final part of problem-solving is ensuring alternative solutions to a problem are considered and potentially developed further.

Core competency 5: Systems thinking

Systems thinking refers to the ability to understand an organization holistically in terms of the people, processes, and technology within it. When you develop your ability to apply systems thinking, you aim to understand not only the individual components within an organization but also how they are all interconnected. You look at not only the components that are isolated entities but also the people and the entire internal and external organizational environment. A key part of the role of business analysis is to analyze an entire system and all the components involved in order to have a full and meaningful picture of it as a whole.

Let's consider a real-world scenario.

When an employee decides to resign from their position in a company, it is not just a matter of stopping their salary payments after a certain date. The business analyst should analyze this process by applying systems thinking. By doing so, they look at all the components and processes, as well as other employees that may potentially be impacted by the employee's decision to resign.

Some example processes that could be impacted and require analysis are revoking access to an office building, stopping any pension payments, re-assigning roles and responsibilities, or triggering the recruitment process for a replacement employee. All of these (and more) are surrounding processes that form part of the whole process that is impacted when an employee makes the decision to leave an organization.

Core competency 6: Conceptual thinking

Conceptual thinking is the ability to make sense of large amounts of information on a conceptual level. When you are presented with a large amount of new information, your ability to make sense of this information by linking contexts, solutions, needs, changes, stakeholders, and value in an abstract way is called conceptual thinking. This includes the ability to link information, see patterns that may not be obvious, and connect this information in a way that makes sense. It is about taking details and making them fit into the bigger picture.

You apply conceptual thinking by using your past experiences, knowledge, creativity, intuition, and abstract thinking to generate alternative options and ideas that are not easily defined or related.

Let's consider a real-world scenario.

A business analyst may be faced with a lot of detailed information relating to a payroll department for a retail firm. The payroll manager has left the company and there is very little known about how all this information fits into the larger company. A business analyst has been assigned to this project to make sense of the detailed information and provide a conceptual overview of what information exists, how it all relates to each other, and what information is missing. This business analyst has past experience of working with a payroll function and can draw on this experience to make sense of the detailed information. The business analyst will also draw on their ability to be creative and use some intuition to help clarify any gaps in information. This will enable the business analyst to conceptualize the information and present options at a conceptual level. This information can then be used to assist the team in deciding which solution options to consider to help improve the payroll function for the company.

Core competency 7: Visual thinking

The core competency of visual thinking refers to the business analysts' ability to transform complex ideas, concepts, or information into clear, straightforward visual representations. The purpose of this activity is to effectively communicate new or complex concepts to a wide audience through the use of visualization. Visual representations allow stakeholders to quickly and easily understand complex or brand new ideas and are a very effective communication tool.

An example of when a business analyst applies visual thinking includes creating simple visual concepts, graphics, models, diagrams, and constructs to convey and integrate non-visual information.

Some popular real-world examples of visualization techniques include *process diagrams, use case diagrams, and scope models.*

You have now learned that the analytical thinking and problem-solving underlying competency category consists of different ways to think about information and distill that information to provide solutions. In the next section, we will learn which core competencies the behavioral characteristics underlying competency category consist of and how to apply it in the daily practice of business analysis.

Exploring behavioral characteristics

Behavioral characteristics are common to everyone and are not exclusive to business analysis. They improve personal and professional effectiveness in the practice of business analysis.

The underlying competency category referred to as behavioral characteristics refer to a core set of personal characteristics that every professional in the workplace should have in order to support themselves in a way that will guarantee positive outcomes.

The behavioral characteristics of core competencies include the following:

- Ethics
- Personal accountability
- Trustworthiness
- Organization and time management
- Adaptability

Let's now outline each of these core competencies in more detail to gain an understanding of what skills they describe for a business analyst to perform effectively.

Core competency 1: Ethics

Ethics as a core competency has two main applications. Firstly, when a business analyst behaves ethically it means that they are respected by stakeholders and they demonstrate fairness, consideration, and moral behavior in their work effort.

The second application of this core competency is concerned with the ethical impacts on others that the business analyst might discover during requirements analysis activities. They may find that certain aspects of requirements have an ethical consideration that must be presented to the business for resolution. This could be a case where stakeholders may be affected in an unfair way by a change that will be introduced by the business, or perhaps safeguarding the organization against unjust criticism. It is also the role of the business analyst to bring solutions to the business for any identified ethical dilemmas.

Core competency 2: Personal accountability

The core competency of personal accountability is about making sure that the business analysis tasks are completed on time and to the expectations of peers and stakeholders. A strong ability to demonstrate personal accountability enables a business analyst to establish credibility within their role.

This core competency includes the ability to effectively plan business analysis work, including setting clear goals and ensuring value is delivered in alignment with business needs. It is the core competency that ensures that the business analyst always strives to complete analysis work in an accurate and traceable way.

Core competency 3: Trustworthiness

Just as it is important to be trustworthy in your personal life, it is of equal importance to building a reputation of trustworthiness in the workplace. Business analysts are often referred to as the agents of change in an organization and change is often associated with uncertainty and even fear among stakeholders. This means it is very important for a business analyst to build a strong level of trustworthiness among stakeholders so that they can assist the stakeholder in accepting and working with any new changes that are introduced with new initiatives.

Core competency 4: Organization and time management

The core competency of organization and time management skills is about having the ability to carry out tasks effectively and use your work time efficiently. This also includes being able to prioritize work in an effective and time-efficient manner so that tasks are executed in an optimal way. This competency is also important because it enables a business analyst to manage large quantities of information and organize it in a way that is logical and reusable throughout an initiative.

Core competency 5: Adaptability

A business analyst's ability to adapt to changing environments, stakeholders and work priorities is essential to performing effectively. Adaptability is the ability to change communication styles, formats, and approaches on the go in order to suit changing environments and meet demands. Adaptability requires a business analyst to be curious and interested in the needs of their stakeholders, which will enable them to adjust their interactions to suit the stakeholder's requirements. It is, therefore, an important skill for a business analyst to develop by regularly tuning into the stakeholders' preferences in terms of communication, information needs, and general style and approach.

Let's consider a real-world scenario.

If a business analyst is employed to work in a financial institution where high-level stakeholders are involved, it would be important for them to adapt their way of communicating, their own personal style of interaction, and their general approach to be structured and follow the formal procedures and etiquette often followed within traditional financial institutions. However, should the business analyst be re-assigned to work in an agile software development environment, they must adapt. In this type of environment, the communication protocols and general work procedures are much less formal and are more fluid in nature. The business analyst should be able to adapt to suit the new environment's requirements by being less formal in their communication style, be able to follow less prescribed processes, and be flexible in the manner and approach that they follow in their work.

Business knowledge

The underlying competency of business knowledge refers to the ability of a business analyst to make sense of and perform well in their business, industry, solution, and methodology. It is an important competency because it enables the business analyst to relate their work in a change initiative back to the higher-level context of the business in terms of its benefits, structure, and the value delivered.

There are a number of specific core competencies identified as part of the category of business knowledge. These include the following:

- Business acumen
- Industry knowledge
- Organization knowledge
- Solution knowledge
- Methodology knowledge

Let's now consider each of these core competencies and understand what they mean and how to apply them effectively when performing business analysis functions.

Core competency 1: Business acumen

Business analysis requires an understanding of fundamental business principles and best practices in order to ensure they are considered as solutions and reviewed.

Business acumen refers to the requirement for a business analyst to have a fundamental understanding of business principles. This is so that the business analyst is able to consider these principles when working with stakeholders to develop solutions to business needs. As the business analyst becomes more experienced and knowledgeable, their level of business acumen develops and becomes more valuable and complete. Having a strong business acumen enables the business analyst to operate within different organizations, applying common business principles and knowledge gained from past experiences.

Let's consider a real-world scenario.

A business analyst worked on an initiative within a finance department in the automotive industry. They gained business acumen around the financial processes and systems used. When they then chose to move to a new industry but stayed within the financial arena, they had strong business acumen within the area of finance and were able to add value to their new role by applying their business acumen capabilities.

Core competency 2: Industry knowledge

Industry knowledge refers to the knowledge and understanding that a business analyst collects and learns by working within a particular industry. It can include knowledge of current practices in a particular industry or similar business processes performed across industries (for example, financial processes such as payroll processes).

Having industry knowledge involves gaining an understanding of aspects such as the following:

- Current trends
- Market forces
- Market drivers
- Key processes
- Services
- Products
- Definitions
- Customer segments
- Suppliers
- Practices
- Regulations

Industry knowledge also includes having knowledge and understanding of where a company is positioned within an industry and what the primary impacts and dependencies that exist within a market and people are.

Core competency 3: Organization knowledge

Organization knowledge is all about a business analyst's level of understanding of an organization's structure, architecture, and enterprise as a whole. With this competency, it is important for the business analyst to have an understanding of the organizational strategy and goals, how they generate profits, and generally, what business they are in. It is also crucial to develop an understanding of the different business units within an organization and how they relate to each other. This includes learning about the people occupying senior positions and understanding the formal and informal communication channels (which could be political aspects that influence decision-making) of the organization.

Core competency 4: Solution knowledge

Solution knowledge is about the knowledge and experience a business analyst has within a particular solution space. In some cases, a business analyst may have gained previous experience when working within a specific solution arena, which becomes a strong core competency to assist them in their next, similar initiative.

Let's consider a real-world scenario.

If a business analyst worked on an initiative to implement a new gift card solution for a retail organization, they would have gained strong solution knowledge as part of this initiative. When they decide to move to a new role in a new organization, they can make a valuable contribution to a similar initiative where a new gift card solution is implemented by drawing from the solution knowledge they gained in the previous role. By utilizing their existing solution knowledge of the gift card domain, they will save themselves (and their new team) significant time and effort in terms of analysis and research of potential vendors or technology solutions in the marketplace.

Core competency 5: Methodology knowledge

Methodology knowledge refers to the knowledge a business analyst has of different methodologies that are followed by different organizations. This knowledge is about understanding the context, dependencies, opportunities, and constraints that are defined so that a suitable business analysis approach can be developed.

Having strong methodology knowledge enables a business analyst to quickly grasp roles and responsibilities, the accepted risk level, and a general understanding of how a change will be approached and managed for an initiative. It enables the business analyst to also be adaptable, which as we previously learned is another important core competency for a business analyst to master.

Communication skills

Let's start by considering a basic definition of what communication skills are:

> *"Communication is the act of a sender conveying information to a receiver in a method that delivers the meaning the sender intended."*

Being able to communicate effectively as a business analyst is of vital importance and a clear success measure is having a truly consistent and agreed-upon understanding of the requirements. To be an effective communicator requires a business analyst to be an active listener, being able to adapt their communication styles to suit stakeholder audiences and have an understanding of tone, body language, and context when attaching meaning to words.

There are a number of specific core competencies identified as part of the communication skills category. These include the following:

- Verbal communication
- Non-verbal communication
- Written communication
- Listening

Let's now consider each of these core competencies and try to understand them in more detail, as well as learn how to apply them effectively when performing business analysis functions.

Core competency 1: Verbal communication

Verbal communication means simply using words and language to convey ideas, concepts, facts, and opinions to different stakeholders. These are spoken words and are often viewed as an effective and efficient form of communication that can be supported by written and non-verbal communication.

Core competency 2: Non-verbal communication

Non-verbal communication is the most powerful yet most understated form of communication. More than 93% of our communication is non-verbal; in other words, not using words. Non-verbal communication consists of all body language, tone of voice, eye contact, gestures, facial expressions, and more.

Although on the surface we tend to think that communication is focused on words that are written or spoken, it is with non-verbal communication that most of the meaning of words is conveyed. This can include information about moods, attitudes, and feelings, which has an impact on body movement and facial expressions. Learning to be more tuned into the non-verbal communication clues of another person enables a business analyst to build a stronger rapport and, as a result, more trusted relationships. The more aware a business analyst can be of these non-verbal clues, the better they are able to respond to the unspoken issues, fears, and concerns of their stakeholders.

Core competency 3: Written communication

Just as a business analyst can use verbal communication to convey ideas, concepts, facts, and opinions to different stakeholders, they can also use written communication to do the same. Often, these two forms of communication are used together to support each other, thereby producing a stronger and more effective message.

If we consider the basic concept of what written communication is, it is simply the practice of using text, symbols, models (formal or informal), and pictures to communicate information.

It is important for a business analyst to consider who the audience of their written communication will be and to adapt their writing style to suit that audience. It is important to use terminology that is familiar to the audience and match the format and style of written communication to meet the stakeholder group's preferred way of receiving written communication.

Let's consider a real-world scenario.

If a business analyst has to provide a summary of key requirements, which requires the resolution to be in a written format, it would be important for the business analyst to consider the stakeholders they will be presenting to. Some important considerations would include the following:

- *Do the stakeholders have previous knowledge of the subject that will be presented to them?*
- *What is the level of interest that they have in the requirements? Is it only a general level of interest or do they have a deep interest in the analysis results?*

- *How are the requirements usually presented? Are the stakeholders used to review diagrams, presentation-style key points, executive summaries, or a combination of all?*
- *Will this audience require any supplementary information to help them digest the written summaries?*

These are only some examples of considerations to keep in mind when a business analyst prepares a written piece of work for a stakeholder audience.

Core competency 4: Listening

Listening is about a business analyst's ability to actively listen and interpret the meaning of the words they hear. It is about being engaged with the stakeholder in a way that supports effective communication, building a sense of rapport, and distilling information so that it presents a clear meaning.

Active listening includes being able to summarize and confirm that what the business analyst heard is, in fact, the message and meaning of the sender of the information. This fosters a sense of common understanding, which could be used to build and develop stronger and more robust information sharing.

Interaction skills

When we refer to interaction skills, we are referring to all types of interaction with every type of stakeholder across every level of an organization. A business analyst is placed in a unique position where their role requires them to be able to engage with different types of stakeholders in ways that are most suitable to the individual. Interaction often involves demonstrating leadership and encouragement and promoting the value of a particular change or initiative.

There are a number of specific core competencies identified as part of interaction skills. They include the following:

- Facilitation
- Leadership and influencing
- Teamwork
- Negotiation and conflict resolution
- Teaching

Let's now consider each of these core competencies and learn how to apply them effectively when performing business analysis functions.

Core competency 1: Facilitation

Facilitation refers to the ability to interact with stakeholders in a way that helps them to make decisions, exchange ideas, or reach an agreement on priorities or the need for a certain set of requirements.

It is about moderating discussions and enabling a group of people to come to constructive conclusions while fostering an atmosphere where people appreciate different viewpoints and perspectives on different topics.

Core competency 2: Leadership and influencing

Leadership and influencing is the ability to guide stakeholders during business analysis activities toward a common-aligned goal. This often takes the format of an agreed set of requirements, a resolved set of requirements conflicts, or another analysis activity that requires influencing skills and leadership toward shared objectives.

This competency also includes the ability to understand each stakeholder's individual needs, motives, and capabilities in a way that enables the business analyst to steer stakeholders toward a consensus-based set of clear requirements aligned to the initiative and organizational goals.

Core competency 3: Teamwork

Teamwork is about a business analyst's ability to work effectively within a team, which includes directing team members as well as wider stakeholders involved within an initiative. A business analyst's ability to foster strong relationships and work well in a team is critical to the success of any initiative and, ultimately, the success of the enterprise as a whole.

A part of this competency is for the business analyst to understand the team structure as well as the team dynamics and their specific role in the team. It is important for the business analyst to flow with the team in a flexible and adaptable way by changing their attitude, being flexible, and embracing new challenges as the team progresses through different project stages.

Core competency 4: Negotiation and conflict resolution

Negotiation and conflict resolution are about a business analyst's ability to help mediate discussions between stakeholders where a requirements conflict has been identified. The business analyst aims to mediate the conflict in a way that will build stronger relationships and clearer understandings of different viewpoints, as well as resolve any conflict that might exist.

In some cases, a business analyst might identify that stakeholders might have unrelated or indirect interests, that may impact their views on requirements. When the business analyst is able to identify those interests during a mediation session, this often helps in finding alternative solutions or a consensus on requirements that remains aligned with the initiative's objectives.

Core competency 5: Teaching

Teaching is about being able to share business analysis information with stakeholders in a way that increases their knowledge and understanding on a certain topic. Teaching also aims to help stakeholders retain information so that they can use it in the future to help develop and finalize requirements.

Teaching skills also require a business analyst to consider and include different learning styles in the way they choose to share information. This can include using visual, verbal, written, and kinaesthetic (hands-on and practical) methods as part of their teaching approach. By doing this, they include the preferred learning styles of all the stakeholders and have the best chance of having a successful learning outcome for their audience.

Exploring tools and technology

In order for a business analyst to be effective in their daily roles, there are certain types of tools and technology that they should master in order to convey the results of the information they discover in an effective and efficient way. They need these tools and technology to convey information in the form of artifacts, models, and diagrams; to track issues and risks, and to increase their overall productivity.

There are a number of specific core competencies identified as part of the tools and technology category. These include the following:

- Office productivity tools and technology
- Business analysis tools and technology
- Communication tools and technology

Let's now consider each of these core competencies and learn how to apply them effectively when performing business analysis functions.

Core competency 1: Office productivity tools and technology

Office productivity tools and technology refers to all the tools a business analyst needs to use to prepare business analysis information artifacts. A business analyst uses these tools and technology to organize, dissect, edit, understand, and ultimately, communicate business analysis information to stakeholders.

Some examples of office productivity tools and technology include the following:

- *Word processing and presentation programs. An example would be Microsoft Word.*
- *Presentation software. An example would be Microsoft PowerPoint or Apple Keynote.*
- *Spreadsheets.* **An example would be Microsoft Excel or Apple Numbers**.
- *Communication tools (such as email and instant messaging programs). Some examples would be Gmail or Office 365.*
- *Hardware. An example would be your laptop computer.*

Core competency 2: Business analysis tools and technology

Business analysis tools and technology refers more specifically to the tools that a business analyst uses to produce business analysis-specific information, such as diagrams, mapping requirements, or other specialized tools designed to help document and track the life cycle of requirements.

Tools that are specific to the field of business analysis have specialized functionality in the areas of creating diagrams and models, tracking requirements, identifying relationships between requirements, and communicating with all upstream and downstream stakeholders and teams. This includes JIRA, SharePoint, and Microsoft Visio.

Core competency 3: Communication tools and technology

The last core competency, referred to as communication tools and technology, includes all the tools that a business analyst needs to use to communicate with stakeholders and peers.

These communication tools are used to plan and complete tasks related to conversational interactions and collaborative interactions and also allow business analysts to work with virtual and co-located teams.

Some examples of conversation interaction tools include *voice communication, instant messaging, online chat, email, and blogging*.

Some examples of collaboration tools include *video conferencing, electronic whiteboarding, wikis, electronic calendars, online brainstorming tools, electronic decision-making, electronic voting, document sharing, and idea-sharing*.

Summary

In this chapter, you learned about the underlying competencies that every business analyst must possess and develop during their career.

The following are the key concepts and tasks we covered in this chapter:

- The purpose and context of the underlying competencies
- Analytical thinking and problem-solving
- Behavioral characteristics
- Business knowledge
- Communication skills
- Interaction skills
- Tools and technology

In the next chapter, we will learn about the techniques that every business analyst should master and improve during the course of their professional business analysis careers.

Make sure you revise these key learnings before completing the knowledge quiz at the end of this chapter.

You now have an understanding of the importance and purpose of the underlying competencies and know what the scope of each core competency is, as well as the importance of developing these skills through the course of your career as a business analyst.

Learning outcome – underlying competencies

You now have a good understanding of the importance and purpose of the underlying competencies that assist a business analyst in their success in their role. You can now describe the contents of this chapter in the context of business analysis using real-world practical situations.

Learning outcome – analytical thinking and problem-solving

In this chapter, you learned about the analytical thinking and problem-solving underlying competency category. You are now able to describe the purpose of this competency category and the core competencies that need to be developed and demonstrated when performing business analysis by using real-world scenarios and concepts.

Learning outcome – behavioral characteristics

In this chapter, you learned about the behavioral characteristics underlying competency category. You can now describe the purpose of this competency category and the core competencies that need to be developed and demonstrated when performing business analysis by using real-world scenarios and concepts.

Learning outcome – business knowledge

In this chapter, you learned about the business knowledge underlying competency category. You can now describe the purpose of this competency category and the core competencies that need to be developed and demonstrated when performing business analysis by using real-world scenarios and concepts.

Learning outcome – communication skills

In this chapter, you learned about the communication skills underlying competency category. You can now describe the purpose of this competency category and the core competencies that need to be developed and demonstrated when performing business analysis by using real-world scenarios and concepts.

Learning outcome – interaction skills

In this chapter, you learned about the interaction skills underlying competency category. You can now describe the purpose of this competency category and the core competencies that need to be developed and demonstrated when performing business analysis by using real-world scenarios and concepts.

Learning outcome – tools and technology

In this chapter, you learned about the tools and technology underlying competency category. You can now describe the purpose of this competency category and the core competencies that need to be developed and demonstrated when performing business analysis by using real-world scenarios and concepts.

Knowledge quiz

Consider the following real-world scenario and complete the micro mock exam based on this chapter.

Case study – a day in the life of a business analyst

As business analysts, we encounter a variety of different situations every day that require us to perform and apply different core competencies. Consider each of the following situations that you have had to respond to today.

Situation 1

You are faced with a business problem that requires you to apply new ideas and approaches in order to solve it.

Situation 2

You are running a workshop at 9 am, where you will be presenting three different solution options for the user interface of a new mobile application to stakeholders. You are going to ask the group to consider the key benefits and disadvantages of each solution option. You also need them to identify any trade-offs that they are willing to consider before they choose their preferred option as a group.

Situation 3

You decide that video conferencing would be the best way of communicating a summary of the key design options for the new mobile application. The stakeholders are dispersed around the globe and using a video conference will allow everyone to see what you have prepared. You plan to include lots of visual aids, including diagrams and screen mockups to enhance the audience's ability to learn all the key features of the new design quickly.

Situation 4

One of the stakeholders you met with today wants to change the way the order of transactions is reported on every day. You said you would get back to them about the impacts of making the change.

Questions

Question 1

Consider scenario 1 from the case study:

"You are faced with a business problem that requires you to apply new ideas and approaches in order to solve it."

Which core competency do you need to apply to find a solution to this business problem?

    A. Verbal communication

    B. Decision-making

    C. Systems thinking

    D. Creative thinking

Question 2

Consider scenario 2 from the case study. Which core competency do you need to apply in order to achieve the desired outcome for your workshop?

Select the correct answer from the following choices:

    A. Visual thinking

    B. Business acumen

    C. Decision-making

    D. Systems thinking

Question 3

Consider scenario 2 from the case study. Which of the following core competencies can you positively apply to contribute to the delivery of a successful workshop?

Select one or more correct answers from the following choices:

    A. Flexibility

    B. Facilitation

    C. Solution knowledge

    D. Non-verbal communication

Question 4

Consider scenario 3 from the case study. You identified video conferencing as the most effective way of communicating with your stakeholders in this situation. Which core competency describes the use of collaboration tools such as video conferencing?

Select the correct answer from the following choices:

A. Office productivity tools and technology

B. Communication tools and technology

C. Business analysis tools and technology

D. Collaboration tools and technology

Question 5

Consider scenario 3 from the case study. You want the stakeholders to learn the features of the new design quickly and efficiently. Apart from making sure you use "visual" tools, such as diagrams and screen mockups, during the session, you also decide to send them a prototype solution before the session so that they can try out the new features themselves while they are listening to and watching the video conference presentation.

What other learning technique are you applying by sending the prototype solution to the stakeholders?

Select the correct answer from the following choices:

A. Auditory digital

B. Visual

C. Kinaesthetic

D. Auditory

Question 6

Consider scenario 2 from the case study. At 8:15 am, you receive a phone call from your project manager asking you whether it is possible to delay the workshop you have scheduled for 9 am the next day. They explain that a few more stakeholders are coming from another office the next day and it would be great if they could be part of it, too. A lot of things run through your mind, such as the logistics and preparation materials, and whether the format of the workshop would still be suitable. By agreeing to the request from your project manager, which of the following core competencies are you demonstrating?

Select the correct answer from the following choices:

A. Patience

B. Adaptability

C. Trustworthiness

D. Business acumen

Question 7

Consider scenario 4 from the case study. Which one of the following core competencies are you primarily applying in this situation?

Select the correct answer from the following choices:

A. Systems thinking

B. Industry knowledge

C. Creative thinking

D. Analyzing the problem

Question 8

Consider scenario 4 from the case study. Although there are many other reasons why the stakeholder chose to approach you about the required change, one of these reasons could be because you exhibit the core competency of trustworthiness and they felt comfortable that they could trust you with this request.

Is this statement true or false?

    A. True

    B. False

Question 9

Consider scenario 1 from the case study. One aspect of the business problem that you face is making you feel uncomfortable because some of the solutions to this problem involve implementing a change that will adversely affect another department, and you know that they have not been told about this. You want to do the right thing—which of the following options is the best way to deal with this situation?

Select the correct answer from the following choices:

    A. Ask the project manager what to do and if they say there isn't a problem, then just leave it

    B. Identify and resolve this ethical dilemma by engaging with the team and stakeholders

    C. Don't do anything; it is not your place to address these types of issues

    D. Go and tell the other department about this change and that it will affect them in an adverse way.

Question 10

This chapter describes six core competency categories. Which of the following categories are *not* included in the underlying competencies?

Select one or more correct options from the following choices:

    A. Communication skills

    B. Business skills

    C. Analytical thinking and problem-solving

    D. Tips and tools

Question 11

The analytical thinking and problem-solving competency category consist of seven core competencies. Which of the following options describes those seven core competencies?

Select the correct answer from the following choices:

A. Creative thinking, decision-making, learning, problem-solving, systems thinking, conceptual thinking, and visual thinking.

B. Creative thinking, decision-making, learning, problem-solving, systems thinking, numerical thinking, and agnostic thinking.

C. Creative thinking, decision-making, learning, problem-solving, systems thinking, conceptual thinking, and agnostic thinking.

D. Creative thinking, decision-making, learning, problem-solving, systems thinking, numerical thinking, and visual thinking.

Question 12

The behavioral characteristics competency category consists of five core competencies. Which of the following options describes some of those core competencies?

Select the correct answer from the following choices:

A. Ethics, personal acknowledgment, delivery, and time management

B. Ethics, personal acknowledgment, organization, and time management

C. Ethics, personal accountability, delivery, and time management

D. Ethics, personal accountability, organization, and time management

Question 13:

Which core competency is described in the following statement:

"...they adjust their behavior style and method of approach to increase their effectiveness when interacting with different stakeholders, organizations, and situations."

Select the correct answer from the following choices:

    A. Flexibility

    B. A behavioral approach

    C. Creative thinking

    D. Adaptability

Question 14

Which knowledge area allows business analysts to leverage their understanding of existing departments, environments, or technology to efficiently identify the most effective means of implementing a change?

Select the correct answer from the following choices:

    A. Solution

    B. Industry

    C. Methodology

    D. Organization

Question 15

Which core competencies does the interaction skills core competency category consist of?

Select one or more correct answers from the following choices:

    A. Teamwork, negotiation, and conflict resolution

    B. Adaptability and trustworthiness

    C. Facilitation, leadership, and influencing

    D. Flexibility, creativity, and problem-solving

Question 16

Which core competencies does the communication skills core competency category consist of?

Select one or more correct answers from the following choices:

A. Listening and written communication

B. Verbal communication and non-verbal communication

C. Facilitation and teaching

D. Active communication and electronic communication

Question 17

Which core competency describes the tools and technology you use to model, document, and manage outputs of business analysis activities?

Select the correct answer from the following choices:

A. Business analysis tools and technology

B. Modeling tools and technology

C. Communication tools and technology

D. Productivity tools and technology

Question 18

"Visual thinking is about the understanding of how people, processes, and technology within an organization interact, which allows a business analyst to understand the enterprise from a holistic point of view."

Choose whether this statement is true or false:

A. True

B. False

Question 19

Which core competency does the ability to work out how information fits into a larger picture and what details are important, as well as to connect seemingly abstract information, demonstrate?

Select the correct answer from the following choices:

 A. Visual thinking

 B. Holistic thinking

 C. Conceptual thinking

 D. Business acumen

Question 20

"Having a strong _____ knowledge enables a business analyst to quickly grasp their roles and responsibilities, as well as the accepted risk level. It also means they have a general understanding of how a change should be approached and managed for an initiative. This means the business analyst is also adaptable, which is another important core competency for a business analyst to master."

Which of the following choices best completes the preceding statement?

 A. Solution

 B. Industry

 C. Methodology

 D. Organization

Answers

Questions	Answers
1	D
2	C
3	B, C, and D
4	B
5	C
6	B
7	A
8	A
9	B
10	B and D
11	A
12	D
13	D
14	A
15	A and C
16	A and B
17	A
18	B
19	C
20	C

Techniques (Part 1) 13

This chapter discusses the techniques that support the successful execution of business analysis tasks in the workplace. It outlines the purpose of each technique and what it entails as well as some example tasks that use each technique to achieve a particular goal.

By the end of this chapter, you will know what these techniques are and understand the common purposes of each technique in the context of practical business analysis tasks.

More specifically, we will cover the following primary techniques:

- Acceptance and evaluation criteria
- Backlog management
- Balanced scorecards
- Benchmarking and market analysis
- Brainstorming
- Business capability analysis
- Business cases
- Business model canvas
- Business rules analysis
- Collaborative games
- Concept modeling
- Data dictionary
- Data flow diagrams
- Data mining

- Data modeling
- Decision analysis
- Decision modeling
- Document analysis
- Estimation
- Financial analysis
- Focus groups
- Functional decomposition
- Glossary
- Interface analysis
- Interviews

You will also understand when to apply each of these techniques as part of different knowledge area tasks and in the context of real-world scenarios.

 Ensure you understand each technique's purpose, key aspects, and when it can be applied in practice. Visualize your own practical experiences of business analysis and apply each technique to that context to bring it to life. This will help you gain a deeper comprehension of the content and, therefore, a stronger ability to answer scenario-based exam questions.

Let's now start our journey by understanding each technique in terms of its primary purpose and applicability to everyday business analysis tasks.

Techniques for the exam

As you know, there are many analysis techniques that are applicable to many different contexts and scenarios of business analysis. It is quite a vast topic area and so it can be quite challenging to prepare for the CCBA®/CBAP® exam.

There are a few things to keep in mind in terms of technique when preparing for the exam:

- You don't necessarily have to be proficient in using every technique but it is *essential* that you understand the purpose of each technique and have a good understanding of what the elements of each technique are. You should be able to tell someone what the technique is, why you use it, and when it should be used.
- You may need to carry out some financial analysis calculations in the exam. Make sure you can apply the formulas described as part of each technique.
- Understand the techniques well enough so that you are able to group them together to apply in a practical scenario or exclude the "odd one out" in a multiple-choice selection.
- The best way to learn about each technique is to try to apply each one to a real-world scenario you have personal and practical experience of; this way, you know you understand it and you can apply it in its relevant context.

Let's now start by taking each technique and understanding its purpose, scope, and when you might use it within the practice of business analysis.

Acceptance and evaluation criteria

When learning about acceptance and evaluation criteria, you need to make sure you are well versed in its primary purpose. You should know what it entails and be able to explain when (that is, in what types of scenarios related to business analysis tasks) it is relevant to apply this technique.

Let's start with the purpose of this technique.

What is the purpose of this technique?

According to the BABOK® v3 guide, the purpose of acceptance and evaluation criteria is as follows:

"Acceptance criteria are used to define the requirements, outcomes, or conditions that must be met in order for a solution to be considered acceptable to key stakeholders...Evaluation criteria are the measures used to assess a set of requirements in order to choose between multiple solutions."

Key things to know when using this technique

The key idea that is portrayed with this technique is that although there are some similarities between acceptance and evaluation criteria (such as value attributes), the way each aspect of acceptance criteria versus evaluation criteria is applied is fundamentally quite different. Review the following diagrams to understand the purpose of this technique and the differences between acceptance criteria and evaluation criteria. The following image shows the diagram for one solution:

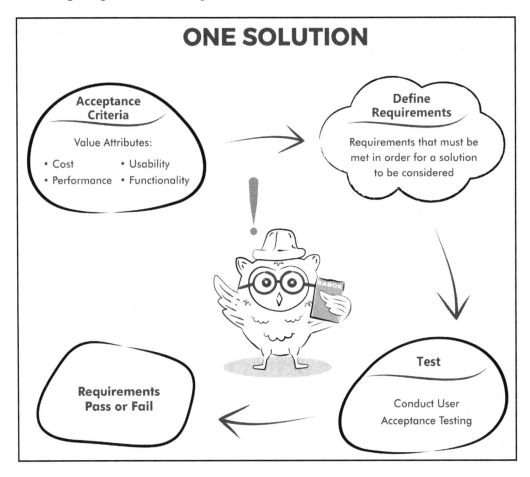

The following image shows a diagram for multiple solutions:

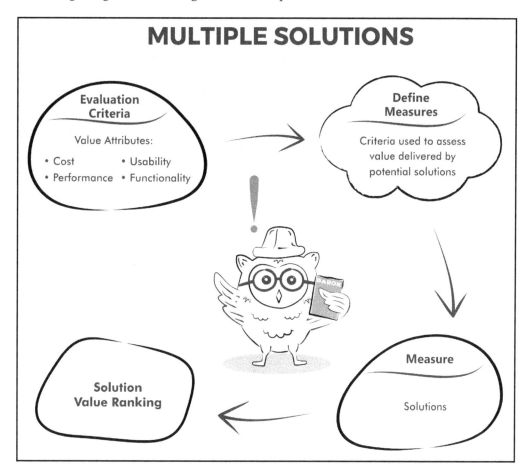

Pay attention to the differences between acceptance criteria and evaluation criteria. They are grouped together here but there are some differences to take note of. The preceding diagram which outlines these key differences. You will note that the key difference is that acceptance criteria are always developed with one solution in mind, whereas evaluation criteria are developed to assess multiple solutions.

When should you apply this technique?

This technique is used in a few different business analysis tasks in the knowledge areas described in the BABOK® v3 guide. These tasks include the following:

Task	The reason the technique is used
Approve requirements	To define the approval criteria for the requirements
Define future state	To define criteria to evaluate options
Specify and model requirements	To represent the acceptance and evaluation criteria for the requirements themselves
Verify requirements	To make sure a requirement is stated clearly enough to be tested to ensure a requirement has been met
Validate requirements	To define some quality metrics that the requirement should achieve before it is accepted by stakeholders
Analyze potential value and recommend a solution	To define requirements as acceptance criteria so that it is easier to determine whether a solution option meets the business's needs or not
Measure solution performance	To define criteria that stipulate acceptable solution performance metrics
Analyze performance measures	To define criteria that stipulate acceptable solution performance metrics
Assess solution limitations	To determine criteria that indicate the level that a solution meets or doesn't

Acceptance and evaluation criteria is an important technique to apply in your role as a business analyst and help define the acceptable solution behavior and characteristics. This helps to ensure that all the stakeholder requirements are delivered in the intended way.

The next technique you need to include in your preparation is backlog management.

Backlog management

When learning about backlog management, you need to make sure you are well versed in its primary purpose. You should know what it entails and be able to explain when (that is, in what types of scenarios related to business analysis tasks) it is relevant to apply this technique.

Let's start with the purpose of this technique.

What is the purpose of this technique?

According to the BABOK® v3 guide, the purpose of backlog management is "to record, track, and prioritize remaining work items."

Key things to know when using this technique

Backlog items can be anything, not just requirements. They can be tasks, defects, planned work, risk items, and much more.

It is important to know that items in the backlog are prioritized relative to the others.

The level of detail used to describe a backlog item can vary. Most of the time, backlog items at the top of the list are described in more detail than other items.

Backlog items are reviewed in terms of available capacity, dependencies, the size of the item, and relative complexity.

When should you apply this technique?

This technique is used in a few different business analysis tasks in some knowledge areas in the BABOK® v3 guide. These tasks include the following:

Task	The reason for the technique
Prioritize requirements	To compare requirements to be prioritized
Analyze potential value and recommend a solution	To sequence the potential value

Backlog management is an effective method of managing team workloads. This technique helps to ensure that all the team members are always aware of the upcoming work and their priorities.

The next technique you need to include in your preparation is balanced scorecards.

Balanced scorecards

When learning about balanced scorecards, you need to make sure you are well versed in its primary purpose. You should know what it entails and be able to explain when (that is, in what types of scenarios related to business analysis tasks) it is relevant to apply this technique.

Let's consider the purpose of this technique.

What is the purpose of this technique?

According to the BABOK® v3 guide, the purpose of backlog management is "to manage performance in any business model, organizational structure, or business process."

Key things to know when using this technique

It is important to know that the balanced scorecard technique is a strategic management technique that aims to measure an organization's performance beyond purely considering the financial metrics. The four dimensions it measures are as follows:

- Learning and growth: This dimension captures measures relating to employee training and learning, corporate culture, and/or product innovations.
- Business process: This dimension is interested in metrics that show how well the organization's products meet the customers' needs.
- Customer: This dimension captures metrics relating to customer satisfaction, focus, and the delivery of value from their perspective.
- Financial: This dimension represents key financial metrics, such as profitability and revenue growth.

 Understand the differences between a lagging indicator and a leading indicator. A lagging indicator is an indicator of results already achieved whereas a leading indicator is about providing information about future performance.

When should you apply this technique?

This technique is used in a few different business analysis tasks in some knowledge areas in the BABOK® v3 guide. These tasks include the following:

Task	The reason the technique is used
Define the future state	As a way to set or define targets for measuring the success of the future state
Define the change strategy	To define metrics to measure the effectiveness of the change strategy

The balanced scorecard technique is important to strategy analysis and overall business growth. As a business analyst, it enables you to come up with a measurable way to analyze the organization holistically.

The next technique you need to include in your preparation is benchmarking and market analysis.

Benchmarking and market analysis

When you learn about benchmarking and market analysis, you need to make sure you are well versed in its primary purpose. You should know what it entails and be able to explain when (that is, in what types of scenarios related to business analysis tasks) it is relevant to apply this technique.

Let's consider the purpose of this technique.

What is the purpose of this technique?

According to the BABOK® v3 guide, the purpose of benchmarking and market analysis is "to improve organizational operations, increase customer satisfaction, and increase value to stakeholders."

Key things to know when using this technique

With this technique, is it is important that you understand that benchmarking is related to market analysis but these are really two different aspects.

Benchmarking is concerned with the activities performed to compare an organization against the best-in-class practices, whereas market analysis is about researching the needs and wants of customers in terms of the products and services they want.

When should you apply this technique?

This technique is used in a few different business analysis tasks in some knowledge areas in the BABOK® v3 guide. These tasks include the following:

Task	The reason this technique is used
Conduct elicitation	To source business analysis information (such as process-, system-, product-, or service-related information) and to determine what customers want by looking at what competitors provide
Analyze the current state	To understand where the opportunities for improvement may be
Define the future state	To assist stakeholders in making decisions about future state business goals
Define the change strategy	To help decide which change strategy is the most appropriate for a particular situation
Define the design options	To find and analyze existing solutions in the market and to spot any trends that exist
Measure solution performance	To find out what the acceptable levels for the performance of a solution are
Analyze the performance measures	To review the results of similar solutions used by other organizations when assessing trends, risks, and any other variances
Assess the solution limitations	To try and find out what the challenges that other organizations experience are and how they address them
Assess the enterprise limitations	To find any existing solutions in the market that may provide insight into which external factors affect solution value realization

Benchmarking and market analysis is becoming more important to businesses and plays a pivotal role in customer-centric analysis and design.

The next technique you need to include in your preparation is brainstorming.

Brainstorming

When learning about brainstorming, you need to make sure you are well versed in its primary purpose. You should know what it entails and be able to explain when (that is, in what types of scenarios related to business analysis tasks) it is relevant to apply this technique.

Let's consider the purpose of this technique.

What is the purpose of this technique?

According to the BABOK® v3 guide, brainstorming is "an excellent way to foster creative thinking about a problem. The aim of brainstorming is to produce numerous new ideas, and to derive from them themes for further analysis."

Key things to know when using this technique

A couple of important aspects to keep in mind when using the brainstorming technique are that the session should be thoroughly prepared and executed and there should be wrap-up activities to ensure results are captured and communicated.

When should you apply this technique?

This technique is used in a few different business analysis tasks in some knowledge areas in the BABOK® v3 guide. These tasks include the following:

Task	The reason this technique is used
Plan the business analysis approach	To help find all the possible business analysis activities, risks, and other things in the formulation of the business analysis approach
Plan stakeholder engagement	To generate a stakeholder list and help define all the roles and responsibilities
Plan business analysis governance	To help generate the names of people who may need to be identified as approvers in the governance process

Plan business analysis information management	To identify business analysis information management needs
Identify business analysis performance improvements	To create a list of ideas of improvement opportunities
Prepare for elicitation	As a collaboration technique to solicit ideas for the best techniques to use during elicitation and to identify potential sources of business analysis information
Conduct elicitation	To facilitate a group of stakeholders to come up with a list of many ideas and to potentially organize and also prioritize those ideas
Define the future state	To come up with ideas for the future state
Assess the risks	To identify the potential risks to assess
Define the change strategy	To come up with ideas for the change strategy
Define the design options	To help identify opportunities for improvement and the design options
Analyze the potential value and recommend a solution	To collectively identify potential benefits of requirements
Assess the enterprise limitations	To identify organizational gaps or any concerns from stakeholders

It is important to remember that although brainstorming is a very common technique, it should still be treated as a formal technique to ensure the best results. As a business analyst, you should structure this activity when you apply this technique to achieve the desired outcome.

The next technique you need to include in your preparation is business capability analysis.

Business capability analysis

When you learn about business capability analysis, you need to make sure you are well versed in its primary purpose. You should know what it entails and be able to explain when (that is, in what types of scenarios related to business analysis tasks) it is relevant to apply this technique.

Let's consider the purpose of this technique.

What is the purpose of this technique?

According to the BABOK® v3 guide, the purpose of business capability analysis is to provide "a framework for scoping and planning by generating a shared understanding of outcomes, identifying alignment with strategy, and providing a scope and prioritization filter."

Key things to know when using this technique

The primary thing to understand about business capability analysis is that it is about assessing what an organization is able to do. This is assessed in terms of performance gaps and any risks in the capabilities to determine where to invest to improve the overall organization in terms of growth.

Make sure you understand the concept of a capability and the relationship a capability has to the value it creates within an organization.

Business capability analysis is often used as part of current and future state analysis to help an organization determine where to focus their efforts to achieve their organizational goals and objectives.

Business capability analysis is also used to determine the performance of a certain capability and to assess the risks that exist within a capability.

The final important point to take note of is that business capability analysis is often carried out by using capability maps to visually describe the different considerations of a capability within the context of the organization.

When should you apply this technique?

This technique is used in a few different business analysis tasks in some knowledge areas in the BABOK® v3 guide. These tasks include the following:

Task	The reasons this technique is used
Analyze the current state	To help find capability gaps and then prioritize them in terms of value and risk
Define the future state	To help prioritize capability gaps in terms of value and risk
Define the change strategy	To help prioritize capability gaps in terms of value and risk
Specify and model the requirements	To assist in showing the features and functions of an organization

Business capability analysis is most often applied as part of strategy analysis activities and provides a shared view of the outcomes, strategy, and performance of an organization.

The next technique you need to include in your preparation is business cases.

Business cases

When you learn about business cases, you need to make sure you are well versed in their primary purpose. You should know what they entail and be able to explain when (that is, in what types of scenarios related to business analysis tasks) it is relevant to apply this technique.

Let's consider the purpose of this technique.

What is the purpose of this technique?

According to the BABOK® v3 guide, the purpose of business cases is to provide "justification for a course of action based on the benefits to be realized by using the proposed solution, as compared to the cost, effort, and other considerations to acquire and live with that solution."

Key things to know when using this technique

This technique consists of a series of stages that must be followed when preparing a business case. It is important that you know the different stages and have an understanding of what they entail.

Need assessment

During this stage, the reason for preparing the business case must be made clear and understood. What is the goal of the business case and what problem is it trying to solve?

Desired outcomes

These are the anticipated benefits that an organization is hoping to achieve if the business case solution is implemented successfully. This should be defined independently from any specific solution and the benefits must be stated in a way that is measurable.

Assessing the alternatives

This part of business case development is about considering alternative solutions that could meet the desired outcomes. The scope, feasibility, assumptions, risks and constraints, financial analysis, and value assessment should all be defined.

Make sure you always include an option to "do nothing" as one of the alternative solutions.

Recommending a solution

This is the final stage of business case development and includes recommending a solution with enough supporting information for business decision-makers to be able to make a decision.

When should you apply this technique?

This technique is used in a few different business analysis tasks in some knowledge areas in the BABOK® v3 guide. These tasks include the following:

Task	The reason this technique is used
Plan the business analysis approach	To assess whether any parts of the problem or business need is particularly time-sensitive or high value or whether more than the usual uncertainties exist
Prioritize requirements	To assess the requirements in terms of how well they align to the business goals and objectives
Assess requirement changes	To justify a proposed change
Analyze the current state	To capture information in relation to the business need or business opportunity
Define the future state	To describe the desired outcomes of a change or initiative
Assess the risks	To describe the risks associated with the different change strategies considered
Define the change strategy	To describe information about the recommended and not recommended change strategies.
Analyze the potential value and recommend a solution	To analyze and assess recommendations by comparing them against the goals and objectives
Measure solution performance	To define and capture the business goals and any performance measures for a solution

Business cases provide a clear view of the complex facts, issues, and analyses that are required before making an investment decision. They also provide ongoing guidance to any decision-making required during an initiative.

The next technique you need to include in your preparation is business model canvases.

Business model canvas

When you learn about business model canvases, you need to make sure you are well versed in their primary purpose. You should know what they entail and be able to explain when (that is, in what types of scenarios related to business analysis tasks) it is relevant to apply this technique.

Let's consider the purpose of this technique.

What is the purpose of this technique?

According to the BABOK® v3 guide, the purpose of a business model canvas is to describe "how an enterprise creates, delivers, and captures value for and from its customers."

Key things to know when using this technique

This technique is a way of demonstrating how an organization intends to or currently delivers value and it is often depicted as a visual map. It is important to understand the nine key building blocks used to describe an organization in this way. These blocks are key partnerships, key activities, key resources, value proposition, customer relationships, channels, customer segments, cost structure, and revenue streams.

By using these blocks, you show the relationships that exist between an organization's operation, finance, customer, and product/service offerings. It is important to understand that this technique can also be used as a blueprint for implementing a strategy.

When should you apply this technique?

This technique is used in a few different business analysis tasks in some knowledge areas in the BABOK® v3 guide. These tasks include the following:

Task	The reason this technique is used
Analyze the current state	To help understand the context of any change and help to highlight problems or opportunities that will have a potentially large impact
Define the future state	To describe and plan a strategy for an organization by mapping out the required infrastructure, target customer base, and cost structures, as well as the revenue streams required to fulfill the planned value proposition for customers
Define the change strategy	To define and capture the required changes to the infrastructure, customer base, and financial structures in order to achieve the potential value for the organization
Specify and model the requirements	As a way of helping to describe the rationale for requirements
Analyze the potential value and recommend a solution	To help stakeholders understand the strategy and context of initiatives

The business model canvas technique is a straightforward and easy-to-apply technique that provides an effective framework to understand and optimize a business model.

The next technique you need to include in your preparation is business rules analysis.

Business rules analysis

When you learn about business rules analysis, you need to make sure you are well versed in its primary purpose. You should know what it entails and be able to explain when (that is, in what types of scenarios related to business analysis tasks) it is relevant to apply this technique.

Let's consider the purpose of this technique.

What is the purpose of this technique?

According to the BABOK® v3 guide, the purpose of business rules analysis is "to identify, express, validate, refine, and organize the rules that shape day-to-day business behavior and guide operational business decision making."

Key things to know when using this technique

Business rules and policies govern the day-to-day operation of an organization at different levels of the organization. These policies and rules also play a key role in business decision-making.

There is a difference between business rules and business policies.

Business policies are a general directive that an overall organization or business unit has to adhere too. They control, influence, and regulate the activities of the organization and its people. Business rules are different from business policies in that they are specific, testable directives that play the role of criteria for making decisions, guiding judgments, and guiding behavior.

There are two types of business rules, which are as follows:

- **Definitional rules:** This type of business rule is either true or untrue and can often be calculated.

  An example of this type of rule is that a product must be considered a well-selling product if more than 25 units of that product are sold per month.

- **Behavioral rules:** Behavioral rules are rules that people should follow when performing a particular task. These rules are often a policy that must be adhered to.

  An example of this type of rule is that an order must not be placed if the customer is not registered as a supplier with the organization.

When should you apply this technique?

This technique is used in a few different business analysis tasks in some knowledge areas in the BABOK® v3 guide. These tasks include the following:

Task	The reason this technique is used
Plan stakeholder engagement	To determine which stakeholders are the source of the existing business rules
Conduct elicitation	To determine what rules govern the decisions in an organization. Also used to understand the rules that define, constrain, or enable operations
Maintain the requirements	To find any business rules that may be relevant and reuseable on other initiatives
Assess the requirement changes	As information to guide changes to policies and business rules
Specify and model the requirements	To analyze the business rules themselves so that they can be developed alongside the requirements
Assess the solution limitations	To depict the currently existing business rules and determine whether there is a need for change

When business rules are applied as a formal technique and managed centrally, it provides an organization with the ability to change any business rules efficiently and effectively. This technique provides the organization with the structure to manage and govern business behavior.

The next technique you need to include in your preparation is collaborative games.

Collaborative games

When you learn about collaborative games, you need to make sure you are well versed in its primary purpose. You should know what it entails and be able to explain when (that is, in what types of scenarios related to business analysis tasks) it is relevant to apply this technique.

Let's consider the purpose of this technique.

What is the purpose of this technique?

According to the BABOK® v3 guide, the purpose of collaborative games is to "encourage participants in an elicitation activity to collaborate in building a joint understanding of a problem or a solution."

Key things to know when using this technique

The key aspect to keep in mind when applying collaborative games as an analysis technique is that the focus is on stimulating creative thinking and uncovering hidden assumptions or ideas that have not been thought of before. It is also important to realize that there are many different collaborative games that exist and most of these games have clear rules that follow specific steps.

When should you apply this technique?

This technique is used in a few different business analysis tasks in some knowledge areas in the BABOK® v3 guide. These tasks include the following:

Task	The reason this technique is used
Conduct elicitation	To gain a better understanding of the business need or problem. Also used to generate creative solutions
Manage stakeholder collaboration	To stimulate creative thinking within a group environment

Collaborative games are an effective technique that can reveal hidden assumptions or differences of opinion that might exist within a team or group. It encourages creative thinking and can sometimes expose business needs that may otherwise have been missed.

The next technique you need to include in your preparation is concept modeling.

Concept modeling

When you learn about concept modeling, you need to make sure you are well versed in its primary purpose. You should know what it entails and be able to explain when (that is, in what types of scenarios related to business analysis tasks) it is relevant to apply this technique.

Let's consider the purpose of this technique.

What is the purpose of this technique?

According to the BABOK® v3 guide, the purpose of concept modelling is "to organize the business vocabulary needed to consistently and thoroughly communicate the knowledge of a domain."

Key things to know when using this technique

The nature of a concept model is similar to that of a glossary (and a glossary often forms part of a concept model), although the focus is on providing the information-rich and specific meanings of nouns and verbs. The aim is to establish a content-rich and semantic-focused source of information about how natural language is used in a specific context.

You should understand that concept models are often illustrated graphically. There are two primary types of concept model expressions—noun concepts and verb concepts.

Noun concepts describe the specific meaning and common language used for a specific noun whereas verb concepts describe the relationships between noun concepts. Note that a concept model is not the same as a data model.

When should you apply this technique?

This technique is used in a few different business analysis tasks in some knowledge areas in the BABOK® v3 guide. These tasks include the following:

Task	The reason this technique is used
Conduct elicitation	To identify the key terms in a particular domain and define the relationships between them
Analyze the current state	To identify the key terms in a particular domain and define the relationships between them
Specify and model the requirements	To identify the key terms and relationships relevant to the context or domain under analysis

Concept modeling as a technique provides a business-friendly way to collaborate with stakeholders on working out some of the subtleties in terms and business concepts. This prevents unnecessary ambiguity and is a useful technique to build knowledge-rich processes.

The next technique you need to include in your preparation is a data dictionary.

Data dictionary

When you learn about data dictionaries, you need to make sure you are well versed in their primary purpose. You should know what they entail and be able to explain when (that is, in what types of scenarios related to business analysis tasks) it is relevant to apply this technique.

Let's consider the purpose of this technique.

What is the purpose of this technique?

According to the BABOK® v3 guide, the purpose of a data dictionary is "to standardize a definition of a data element and enable a common interpretation of data elements."

Key things to know when using this technique

A data dictionary contains standard definitions for the different data elements in a solution. It captures the common understanding of the meanings of data elements between stakeholders and solution teams.

Data dictionaries capture the data elements, primitive data elements, and composite elements. The differences between these three dimensions are best described through an example:

Primitive data elements	Data element 1	Data element 2	Data element 3
Name (the name referenced by data elements)	First name	Middle name	Last name
Alias (alternative names referenced by stakeholders)	Given name	Middle name	Family name
Values/meanings (a description of the data element)	A minimum of 2 characters and a maximum of 20 characters	Optional, can be omitted	A minimum of 2 characters and a maximum of 30 characters
Description (a definition)	First name	Middle name	Surname

Composite element: Customer name = first name + middle name + surname

It is important to share and collaborate with stakeholders when developing the data dictionary so that the meaning of the information is agreed upon and validated.

When should you apply this technique?

This technique is used in a few different business analysis tasks in some knowledge areas in the BABOK® v3 guide. These tasks include the following:

Task	The reason this technique is used
Specify and model requirements	To document the definitions of the data that is involved in change or initiative

A data dictionary is a useful technique to use when there is a need to establish a common and shared understanding of the meaning of information. It clarifies the format and intention of information at a low level of detail to ensure a consistent and accurate reference point of information for the organization.

The next technique you need to include in your preparation is data flow diagrams.

Data flow diagrams

When you learn about data flow diagrams, you need to make sure you are well versed in their primary purpose. You should know what they entail and be able to explain when (that is, in what types of scenarios related to business analysis tasks) it is relevant to apply this technique.

Let's consider the purpose of this technique.

What is the purpose of this technique?

According to the BABOK® v3 guide, the purpose of data flow diagrams is to "show where data comes from, which activities process the data, and if the output results are stored or utilized by another activity or external entity."

Key things to know when using this technique

Data flow diagrams are used to show the flow of data. They show the transformation of data between processes and the external entities an organization, system, or function work with. There are a few key concepts to understand.

A context diagram is a data flow diagram that shows an entire system and how it exchanges information with external entities. It is like the big-picture view and is often used to describe the high-level context of net input flow and output flows of a system.

A level 1 data flow diagram shows the processes, input flows, output flows, and any data stores. It is a very common type of data flow diagram. More detailed levels of data flow diagrams exist—namely, level 2, level 3, and so on.

The key components of every data flow diagram are external entities (such as the entity, source, and sink), the data store, processes, and the data flow. A summary of these terms are as follows:

- **External entities (such as the entity, source, and sink)**: An external entity is a place outside the system where information is either received from (known as the source) or where the system sends information to (known as the sink).
- **Data store**: This is a repository where data is stored. This can be a table in a database, where data is at rest. Information flows into and out of data stores.

- **Process**: This is where information that flows into a process is transformed, then sent out of the process in a different state or format, and is ready for consumption by the next process or data store.
- **Data flow**: This is the information that is sent from one process or data store to the next. It is indicated by arrows showing the direction of flow and is described with a noun.

When should you apply this technique?

This technique is used in a few different business analysis tasks in some knowledge areas in the BABOK® v3 guide. These tasks include the following:

Task	The reason this technique is used
Maintain requirements	To identify the types of information that flow between multiple processes in an organization with the expectation of potential reuse
Specify and model the requirements	To illustrate the flow of information in a visual way to stakeholders and solution professionals

Data flow diagrams are often used as a way of helping to discover processes and data and are generally a technique that is easy to understand for most stakeholders. Using a data flow diagram is also a good way of defining the system boundaries and demonstrates where any interactions with other systems may exist.

The next technique you need to include in your preparation is data mining.

Data mining

When you learn about data mining, you need to make sure you are well versed in its primary purpose. You should know what it entails and be able to explain when (that is, in what types of scenarios related to business analysis tasks) it is relevant to apply this technique.

Let's consider the purpose of this technique.

What is the purpose of this technique?

According to the BABOK® v3 guide, the purpose of data mining is "to improve decision making by finding useful patterns and insights from data."

Key things to know when using this technique

Data mining is all about identifying patterns in large amounts of data to find meaningful information to guide decision making. The output of data mining is depicted in visual dashboards, reports, or other decision-making systems.

Data mining is a general term that describes different descriptive, diagnostic, and predictive techniques:

- **Description data mining techniques**: This type of data mining is concerned with finding patterns in data that can highlight information, such as similarities between customers, employees, or products (to name a few).
- **Diagnostic data mining techniques**: This type of data mining is concerned with showing why a certain pattern exists and is often used in the format of decision trees or other segmentation techniques.
- **Predictive data mining techniques**: This type of data mining is concerned with regression- or neural network-based techniques that can show the likelihood of something being true.

Let's now consider when you can use these techniques as part of your role as a business analyst.

When should you apply this technique?

This technique is used in a few different business analysis tasks in some knowledge areas in the BABOK® v3 guide. These tasks include the following:

Task	The reason this technique is used
Prepare for elicitation	To identify information or patterns that can be used to carry out further analysis
Conduct elicitation	To find relevant information and patterns of information
Analyze the current state	To help find performance-related information about an organization

Measure the solution performance	To help find performance-related information about a solution
Analyze the performance measures	To help find information relating to performance, trends, and common issues in order to find meaningful patterns in data.
Assess the solution limitations	To help find the factors that potentially constrain the performance of a solution
Recommend actions to increase the solution value	To develop predictive estimates of solution performance

Data mining reveals hidden patterns of information, which provides valuable insight and behavioral information to a business. Effective data mining can also act as a method of validating any human viewpoints that may exist within a specific topic area.

The next technique you need to include in your preparation is data modeling.

Data modeling

When you learn about data modeling, you need to make sure you are well versed in its primary purpose. You should know what it entails and be able to explain when (that is, in what types of scenarios related to business analysis tasks) it is relevant to apply this technique.

Let's consider the purpose of this technique.

What is the purpose of this technique?

According to the BABOK® v3 guide, the purpose of data modeling is to describe "the entities, classes or data objects relevant to a domain, the attributes that are used to describe them, and the relationships among them to provide a common set of semantics for analysis and implementation."

Key things to know when using this technique

The main thing to understand about this technique is that a data model visually represents the aspects that are of significance to the business (for example, the people, places, and things). It describes the attributes associated with those aspects and shows the most important relationships between them.

There are three variations of data models to understand:

- **A conceptual data model**: This type of model is independent of any technology or solution and is intended to depict the way a business perceives information.
- **A logical data model**: This type of model is another interpretation of a conceptual model with the addition of showing data entities and their relationships. It also shows rules of normalization.
- **A physical data model**: This type of model is the actual depiction of how data is physically implemented in the form of a database. It also considers factors such as performance, concurrency, and security.

Key concepts

Key concepts that a business analyst should understand about data modeling include the following:

- **Entity (or class)**: An entity (sometimes referred to as a class) represents the element of a database that information is stored in. It is most commonly a person or a thing that the organization wants to store information about.

  Some examples of entities are an employee, customer, product, or order name.

- **Attribute**: An attribute is a piece of information that describes an entity.

  Some examples of attributes are a first name, last name, order number, date, or amount of something.

- **Relationships (or associations)**: A relationship shows whether two entities relate to each other and what their relationship is.

  An example of a relationship is an entity called `Employee` is related to another entity called `Salary`. The nature of this relationship can be that each `Employee` entity in a database has one-to-many `Salary` records.

- **Diagrams**: When you create a data model diagram, you show the entities and attributes and their relationship on the diagram. You should also show the nature of the relationships on the diagram. This is referred to as cardinality.

- **Metadata**: In cases where more detail is included, you can also show metadata on your model. This type of information shows why an entity is created, how it is used, how often it is used, when it is used, and who it is used by.

  Some examples of metadata are privacy setting, the creation date, and the date something should be updated by.

In what situations should you apply this technique?

This technique is used in a few different business analysis tasks in some knowledge areas in the BABOK® v3 guide. These tasks include the following:

Task	The reason this technique is used
Conduct elicitation	To help understand the relationship between entities, which often also highlights business rules that exist between entities
Maintain requirements	To identify a potential data structure that is similar across an organization, with the intention to reuse it
Specify and model requirements	To model requirements in a way that shows how data will be used in a business or solution
Define the requirements architecture	To describe the requirements structure of an initiative in relation to the data

This technique is a consistent way of analyzing and documenting data and the relationships that exist between data entities. There is flexibility in the level of detail that is included and it can be used as a communication tool between both business and technical stakeholder groups.

The next technique you need to include in your preparation is decision analysis.

Decision analysis

When you learn about decision analysis, you need to make sure you are well versed in its primary purpose. You should know what it entails and be able to explain when (that is, in what types of scenarios related to business analysis tasks) it is relevant to apply this technique.

Let's consider the purpose of this technique.

What is the purpose of this technique?

According to the BABOK® v3 guide, the purpose of decision analysis is to formally assess "a problem and possible decisions in order to determine the value of alternate outcomes under conditions of uncertainty."

Key things to know when using this technique

Decision analysis is about modeling the consequences or alternative paths that result in certain courses of action being followed for a particular business problem or opportunity.

Decision analysis always includes the following key stages, regardless of which modeling technique is followed:

- Stage 1: Define the problem statement.
- Stage 2: Define the alternatives.
- Stage 3: Evaluate the alternatives.
- Stage 4: Choose an alternative to implement.
- Stage 5: Implement a choice.

The information about a problem, the alternatives, the evaluation criteria, and the recommended options to proceed with are depicted in multiple different types of models. Some of the key models to be familiar with for the exam include decision trees and decision matrices:

- **Decision trees**: More information about these is available in the *Decision modeling* section of this chapter.
- **Decision matrices**: There are two primary types of decision matrices—simple and weighted. A simple decision matrix simply compares criteria between alternatives and there is no weighting or prioritization applied to any of the criteria options. In this case, the alternative with the most criteria met is the preferred option to proceed with. A weighted decision matrix expands on a simple decision matrix by adding a weighting against each criterion in the matrix. This means that criterion 1 may weigh more than criterion 2.

So, to explain this concept further with an example, if alternative A meets criterion 2 but not criterion 1, and alternative B meets criterion 1 but not criterion 2, then alternative 1 will have a higher total score due to the weighting of criterion 2 being more than that of criterion 1.

A weighted matrix is often used in vendor selection processes to ensure that criteria of higher importance are represented in a fair and just way when alternatives are considered.

When should you apply this technique?

This technique is used in a few different business analysis tasks in some knowledge areas in the BABOK® v3 guide. These tasks include the following:

Task	The reason this technique is used
Prioritize the requirements	To help identify the high-value requirements
Assess the requirement changes	To help facilitate the change assessment process as it guides decisions based on criteria
Approve the requirements	To remove any issues or conflicts and help to gain agreement on requirements and priorities and decisions that impact them
Define the future state	To help compare alternative solutions and choose the most suitable solution to implement on the future state
Assess the risks	To assess the problems that are identified by risk assessments
Define the change strategy	To determine which change strategy is the most suitable to implement
Analyze the potential value and recommend a solution	To help with the analysis and prioritization of different design options
Measure the solution performance	To help stakeholders make decisions on how to measure solution performance
Assess the solution limitations	To define current business decisions and help to outline the changes needed to achieve business value
Assess the enterprise limitations	To help make decisions under conditions of uncertainty
Recommend actions to increase the solution value	To determine the impact of acting on any potential value or performance-related issues

This technique provides the framework to assist a business analyst when guiding conversations related to making decisions. It is logical and comprehensive and provides clarity in complex situations.

The next technique you need to include in your preparation is decision modeling.

Decision modeling

When you learn about decision modeling, you need to make sure you are well versed in its primary purpose. You should know what it entails and be able to explain when (that is, in what types of scenarios related to business analysis tasks) it is relevant to apply this technique.

Let's consider the purpose of this technique.

What is the purpose of this technique?

According to the BABOK® v3 guide, the purpose of decision modeling is to show "how repeatable business decisions are made."

Key things to know when using this technique

A decision model is a method used to show how data and knowledge are combined in a way that results in a specific outcome. These models can be applied to simple or complex decisions and are always specific and repeatable in nature.

Some key decision models to be aware of include the following:

- **Decision tables**: Each row (or column) in the table shows a rule and each column (or row) shows a condition for that rule. Once the rule and condition are considered together, there is a clear, acceptable "decision" or outcome.
- **Decision trees**: Similar to decision tables, decision trees show rules (as leaf nodes) and conditions (as branches). These are repeated until all the rules are considered against conditions to result in a specified outcome or "decision."

  Both decision tables and decision trees are effective methods to apply when defining business rules for a business solution.

- **Decision requirements diagrams**: A decision requirements diagram is a model used to show much more complex business decisions that need to be made by a business or team. It shows information, knowledge, and decision-making using specific notation. It can be considered the bigger picture of decision analysis, and decision trees and decision tables often contribute to defining the elements of a decision requirements diagram.

When should you apply this technique?

This technique is used in a few different business analysis tasks in some knowledge areas in the BABOK® v3 guide. These tasks include the following:

Task	The reason this technique is used
Define the future state	To model the more complex decisions that are required during the definition of the future state for a solution or initiative
Specify and model the requirements	To demonstrate a decision path by showing it in a decision model, such as a decision tree, table, or diagram

Decision modeling is an effective way to share information with stakeholders when discussing impacts, decision flows, and dependencies. It also helps to simplify complex decision-making.

The next technique you need to include in your preparation is document analysis.

Document analysis

When you learn about document analysis, you need to make sure you are well versed in its primary purpose. You should know what it entails and be able to explain when (that is, in what types of scenarios related to business analysis tasks) it is relevant to apply this technique.

Let's consider the purpose of this technique.

What is the purpose of this technique?

According to the BABOK® v3 guide, the purpose of document analysis is "to elicit business analysis information, including contextual understanding and requirements, by examining available materials that describe either the business environment or existing organizational assets."

Key things to know when using this technique

The key thing to know is that it can include the form of research, analysis, or assessments where information is found in documents within or outside of an organization. There are many ways a business analyst can utilize this technique to gather information and knowledge about the business solution or problem under analysis.

Some key aspects to include when performing document analysis activities include the following:

- **Preparation**: Ensure the documents you are planning to analyze are still relevant enough to add value. Also, ensure the information is credible and valid. Ensure this source of information is understandable and translatable.
- **Execution**: During analysis and review, ensure that you keep detailed notes and records of key findings. Identify gaps in information and ensure you drill down into the detail of the information and whether it will add value to your purpose.
- **Record**: You should record your findings in a relevant format that is suitable to be read by the stakeholders and peers involved in your initiative.

When should you apply this technique?

This technique is used in a few different business analysis tasks in some knowledge areas in the BABOK® v3 guide. These tasks include the following:

Task	The reason this technique is used
Plan the business analysis approach	To review any existing organizational documents that might be useful when defining the business analysis approach
Plan stakeholder engagement	To review any existing organizational documents that might be useful when defining the stakeholder engagement plan
Plan business analysis governance	To review any existing organizational documents that might be useful when defining the governance aspects of business analysis activities
Prepare for elicitation	To identify and consider some sources of relevant documents and information to support elicitation activities
Conduct elicitation	To analyze sources of relevant documents and information to support elicitation activities
Confirm the elicitation results	To confirm the elicitation results by comparing them to the source information (where available)

Maintain the requirements	To analyze existing documents and sources of information that can be used to maintain or reuse requirements in the future
Assess the requirement changes	To analyze existing documents and sources of information that could help analyze the impact of change
Analyze the current state	To analyze existing documents and sources of information that could assist in the understanding and definition of the current state
Assess the risks	To analyze existing documents and sources of information that could help identify potential risks, assumptions, constraints, or dependencies of the requirements.
Validate the requirements	To refer to and validate requirements by comparing them to existing documents and sources of information that define the business needs
Define the design options	To find the information required to assist in the definition of design options (or similar elements)
Assess the enterprise limitations	To analyze existing documents and sources of information that could help provide insight into the company culture, operations, and structure

Document analysis provides a business analyst with content and a point of reference when performing analysis and elicitation work. The documents sourced when applying this technique can be used as a basis for further analysis work.

The next technique you need to include in your preparation is estimation.

Estimation

When you learn about estimation, you need to make sure you are well versed in its primary purpose. You should know what it entails and be able to explain when (that is, in what types of scenarios related to business analysis tasks) it is relevant to apply this technique.

Let's consider the purpose of this technique.

What is the purpose of this technique?

According to the BABOK® v3 guide, the purpose of estimation is to be "used by business analysts and other stakeholders to forecast the cost and effort involved in pursuing a course of action."

Key things to know when using this technique

Estimation is about considering the available information and making a judgment that most often relates to the costs, expected benefits, or value in a different form. It can be presented as a single number but is often shown as a minimum and maximum value. The range of values between the minimum and maximum values is referred to as the confidence interval.

The more information that is available to the estimator, the smaller the confidence interval (and the higher its percentage) and the more accurate the estimation.

There are many different methods for estimation, which include top-down, bottom-up, and parametric estimation; along with **Rough Order of Magnitude** (**ROM**), rolling wave, PERT, and Delphi.

When should you apply this technique?

This technique is used in a few different business analysis tasks in some knowledge areas in the BABOK® v3 guide. These tasks include the following:

Task	The reason this technique is used
Plan a business analysis approach	To determine how long it might take to perform business analysis activities on an initiative
Prepare for elicitation	To estimate the time and effort required to perform the elicitation activities
Prioritize the requirements	To estimate the time and effort required to implement a particular requirement. Also plays a role in deciding what the priority will be for a requirement
Assess the requirement changes	To estimate the time and effort required to make the requested change
Define the change strategy	To estimate the time and effort required to implement a change strategy
Analyze the potential value and recommend a solution	To estimate the time and effort required to realize the potential value of a requirement

This technique provides the team with the rationale for managing the resources of a project. It helps teams to create realistic plans.

The next technique you need to include in your preparation is financial analysis.

Financial analysis

When you learn about financial analysis, you need to make sure you are well versed in its primary purpose. You should know what it entails and be able to explain when (that is, in what types of scenarios related to business analysis tasks) it is relevant to apply this technique.

Let's consider the purpose of this technique.

What is the purpose of this technique?

According to the BABOK® v3 guide, the purpose of financial analysis is "to understand the financial aspects of an investment, a solution, or a solution approach."

Key things to know when using this technique

Financial analysis is a broad term that describes the assessment of the expected financial viability, stability, and benefits of an investment option. A business analyst uses this technique to make solution recommendations in terms of initial costs during the timeframe of implementation, the expected financial benefits, the timeframes for implementing the benefits, and the ongoing costs required to continue to support a solution.

You may be required to carry out financial analysis calculations in the exam. Make sure you can apply the formulas described as part of this technique.

It is important to understand the following key elements of financial analysis:

- **The cost of the change**: This describes the cost to build or acquire a solution.
- **The total cost of ownership**: This includes the cost of building or acquiring a solution, as well as the cost for using and supporting the solution for the foreseeable future.
- **Value realization**: This is about expressing how value will be realized over time.
- **Cost-benefit analysis**: This is an analysis that predicts the expected benefits (in financial value terms) and the expected total costs.

Financial calculations

There are a few key financial calculations that you must be able to practically apply and understand.

These calculations include the following:

- **Return on Investment (ROI)**: This is expressed as a percentage of the net benefits divided by the cost of the change. The formula to calculate ROI is as follows:

  ROI = (Total Benefits - Cost of Investment)/Cost of Investment) x 100

  An example is as follows:

  ROI = ($300,000 - $200,00)/($200,000) X 100 = 50%

- **Discount rate**: This is the assumed interest rate used in present value calculations. This value is determined by the organization and made available for any **Present Value (PV)** calculations.
- **PV**: This calculates the present-day value of the expected benefits. PV is expressed in currency format and doesn't take the cost of the investment into account. The formula to calculate PV is as follows:

  Present Value = Sum of (Net benefits in that period / (1 + Discount rate for that period)) for all periods in the cost-benefit analysis.

  An example is as follows:

Net benefits	Discount rate	Period
$50,000	1%	Year 1
$40,000	1.3%	Year 2
$35,000	1.5%	Year 3

  PV = ($50,000/(1+1%))+($40,000/(1+1.3%))+($35,000/1+1.5%)

  = $49,504.95 + $39,486.67 + $34,482.76 = $123,474.38 = PV

- **Net Present Value** (**NPV**): NPV is the PV value minus the cost of the original investment. The formula to calculate NPV is as follows:

    NPV = PV - Cost of investment

    Let's see an example. Assume a cost of investment of $50,000 and the PV from the previous example:

    NPV = $123,474.38 - $50,000 = $73,474.38

- **Internal Rate of Return** (**IRR**): This is the interest rate that an investment breaks even at. This assists us in determining whether an investment is worth investing in and can be used to compare different solutions. The formula to calculate the IRR is as follows:

    NPV = (-1 x Original investment) + Sum of (Net benefit for that period / (1 + IRR) for all periods) = 0

    The IRR calculation is complex and is often calculated in different ways. It is the value that will make the NPV zero in the preceding equation.

 The exam has been known to include practical calculations as part of some of the questions. Make sure you practice with some examples and learn these calculation formulas off by heart!

- **Payback period**: The payback period provides a projection on the time period that is required to generate enough benefit to recover the original cost of the change, irrespective of the discount rate. There is no standard formula for the payback period and it is expressed in years when calculated.

When should you apply this technique?

This technique is used in a few different business analysis tasks in some knowledge areas in the BABOK® v3 guide. These tasks include the following:

Task	The reason this technique is used
Plan the business analysis approach	To assess how different business analysis approaches can affect the value delivered. For example, one approach may cost a lot more to execute and the additional value delivered by using this approach may not be justifiable.
Prioritize the requirements	To assess the value of the requirements and how the timing (and sequence) of delivery might affect that value.
Assess the requirement changes	To estimate the financial impact of making a particular change.
Analyze the current state	To get an understanding of the profitability of the current state as well as whether there is enough financial capability to make the proposed changes.
Define the future state	To estimate the expected financial benefits of a proposed future state.
Assess the risks	To consider what impact the risks of the potential effects could have on the financial value of an initiative.
Define the change strategy	To value and the return on investment for the different change strategies that are considered.
Validate the requirements	To define the financial benefits associated with the requirements.
Analyze the potential value and recommend a solution	To analyze the financial return of different options and to be able to choose the option with the best return on investment.
Recommend actions to increase the solution value	To assess and analyze the financial costs and benefits associated with a considered change.

The financial analysis technique provides business stakeholders with clear, comparative information to make investment decisions by assessing information from different perspectives. It also helps to reduce uncertainty around investment decisions.

The next technique you need to include in your preparation is focus groups.

Focus groups

When you learn about focus groups, you need to make sure you are well versed in their primary purpose. You need to know what they entail and be able to explain when (that is, in what types of scenarios related to business analysis tasks) it is relevant to apply this technique.

Let's consider the purpose of this technique.

What is the purpose of this technique?

According to the BABOK® v3 guide, the purpose of focus groups is "to elicit ideas and opinions about a specific product, service, or opportunity in an interactive group environment. The participants, guided by a moderator, share their impressions, preferences, and needs."

Key things to know when using this technique

It is important to know that a focus group must have a clear plan that outlines the purpose of the group, the location, the logistics, and who the participants will be, including identifying a moderator and recorder. It is also important to define the outcomes and specify the budget and timeframe that the focus group will be active.

As with any group facilitation, it is key to provide structure to the group's agenda and roles. This will help keep the group focused and ensure a successful outcome.

When should you apply this technique?

This technique is used in a few different business analysis tasks in some knowledge areas in the BABOK® v3 guide. These tasks include the following:

Task	The reason this technique is used
Conduct elicitation	To help get an understanding of the ideas and attitudes in a group
Analyze the current state	To generate feedback from stakeholders or customers about the current state
Define the change strategy	To bring people together to get their input on the potential change strategy for an initiative

Analyze the potential value and recommend a solution	To get an understanding of what design options might be most suitable in terms of meeting the requirements
Measure the solution performance	To get subjective insight into and perceptions of a solution's performance
Recommend actions to increase the solution value	To help identify opportunities for solution performance

Focus groups are an effective way of learning about people's attitudes and opinions on a given subject. This technique can be facilitated both in person or remotely on an online platform. With an online focus group, the group can be recorded and opinions and views can be shared with a wider group for analysis.

The next technique you need to include in your preparation is functional decomposition.

Functional decomposition

When you learn about functional decomposition, you need to make sure you are well versed in their primary purpose. You need to know what they entail and be able to explain when (that is, in what types of scenarios related to business analysis tasks) it is relevant to apply this technique.

Let's consider the purpose of this technique.

What is the purpose of this technique?

According to the BABOK® v3 guide, the purpose of functional decomposition is "to help manage complexity and reduce uncertainty by breaking down processes, systems, functional areas, or deliverables into their simpler constituent parts and allowing each part to be analyzed independently."

Key things to know when using this technique

The reason functional decomposition is such a strong technique is that it breaks down a complex concept into smaller, logical groupings or components that are easy to understand, analyze, and control.

Functional decomposition is a general technique that can be applied to many different contexts and for many different purposes. Some of these include measuring and managing specific factors that contribute to a result and analyzing and designing functions, processes, concepts, or problems. It can also be used to break large pieces of work into smaller and more manageable work products.

Functional decomposition breaks something complex down into a variety of different output formats. These formats include processes, business outcomes, work to be completed, functions, business units, products and services, and much more.

Functional decomposition can be applied by utilizing different diagrams, including, but not limited to, tree diagrams, nested diagrams, use case diagrams, flow diagrams, cause-effect diagrams, mind maps, decision trees, and so on.

It is, therefore, important to understand the overall purpose of this technique and have an understanding of the different ways it can be applied.

When should you apply this technique?

This technique is used in a few different business analysis tasks in some knowledge areas in the BABOK® v3 guide. These tasks include the following:

Task	The reason this technique is used
Plan a business analysis approach	To break down the business analysis deliverables and processes into smaller, more manageable concepts or activities to include in the business analysis approach.
Trace the requirements	To help break down high-level scope items into lower-level components. This is also used to help break down requirements into usable and trackable components.
Maintain the requirements	To help identify requirements that could be reused by breaking requirements down into useable components.
Analyze the current state	To help simplify concepts by breaking them down into smaller parts when analyzing the current state.

Define the future state	To help simplify concepts by breaking them down into smaller parts when defining the future state.
Define the change strategy	To break the solution down into smaller parts when defining the change strategy.
Specify and model the requirements	To model the requirements in a way that shows the different parts of a more complex business process or function.
Define the requirements architecture	To break down products, business functions, or other larger concepts into smaller logical components.

This technique is a powerful way of breaking a complex topic or system down into smaller, understandable parts. It provides the framework for creating a common understanding of a potentially complex situation.

The next technique you need to include in your preparation is a glossary.

Glossary

When you learn about glossaries, you need to make sure you are well versed in their primary purpose. You need to know what they entail and be able to explain when (that is, in what types of scenarios related to business analysis tasks) it is relevant to apply this technique.

Let's consider the purpose of this technique.

What is the purpose of this technique?

According to the BABOK® v3 guide, the purpose of a glossary is "to define key terms relevant to a business domain."

Key things to know when using this technique

It is important to develop a glossary when a business domain has unique terms that have a specific meaning. It is often also used when the same term has different meanings in different contexts; so, clarifying the meaning of the word with a glossary is important.

When should you apply this technique?

This technique is used in a few different business analysis tasks in some knowledge areas in the BABOK® v3 guide. These tasks include the following:

Task	The reason this technique is used
Specify and model the requirements	To document and keep track of the meaning of specific key business terms in the context of requirements

This technique promotes a common understanding of the business area that is under analysis. It supports the consistency of language used within an organization or initiative and is a good reference point for any team member or stakeholder who gets involved in an initiative after an extended period of time.

The next technique you need to include in your preparation is interface analysis.

Interface analysis

When you learn about interface analysis, you need to make sure you are well versed in its primary purpose. You need to know what it entails and be able to explain when (that is, in what types of scenarios related to business analysis tasks) it is relevant to apply this technique.

Let's consider the purpose of this technique.

What is the purpose of this technique?

According to the BABOK® v3 guide, the purpose of interface analysis is "to identify where, what, why, when, how and for whom information is exchanged between solution components or across solution boundaries."

Key things to know when using this technique

Interface analysis describes any type of interface between different solution components. These components can be between people, user interfaces, business processes, or specific technology solutions. Ultimately, this technique defines these interfaces in terms of the input, transformations or validations, and output that is described. Descriptions include the who, what, when, where, why, and how factors of each part of the interface that is described.

When should you apply this technique?

This technique is used in a few different business analysis tasks in some knowledge areas in the BABOK® v3 guide. These tasks include the following:

Task	The reason this technique is used
Conduct elicitation	To understand the interaction and the specific characteristics of the interaction between two components. This can be between two people, two systems, or even between two organizations.
Assess the requirement changes	To help identify any changes that may be required in the interactions between entities when requirements change.
Specify and model the requirements	To model inputs, outputs, and any validations or transformations that occur between entities.

Performing interface analysis provides a clear specification of the interfaces of a system or a collection of systems. It assists in providing a reference or guide for further analysis and can focus analysis efforts on only the areas required to avoid over-analysis.

The next technique you need to include in your preparation is interviews.

Interviews

When you learn about interviews, you need to make sure you are well versed in their primary purpose. You need to know what they entail and be able to explain when (that is, in what types of scenarios related to business analysis tasks) it is relevant to apply this technique.

Let's consider the purpose of this technique.

What is the purpose of this technique?

According to the BABOK® v3 guide, the purpose of the interview technique is to carry out "a systematic approach designed to elicit business analysis information from a person or group of people by talking to the interviewee(s), asking relevant questions, and documenting responses. The interview can also be used for establishing relationships and building trust between business analysts and stakeholders in order to increase stakeholder involvement or build support for a proposed solution."

Key things to know when using this technique

Interviewing as a technique is used by all business analysts at various stages of the requirements life cycle. There are two main types of interviews:

- **Structured interviews**: This is when the interviewer has a predefined set of questions that they ask the interviewee.
- **Unstructured interviews**: This is when the interviewer doesn't have a predefined set of questions and the conversation is based on the responses the interviewee provides.

In most cases, the business analyst will use a combination of structured and unstructured interview techniques.

You will notice that the interview technique is applied to all of the business analysis BABOK® v3 guide tasks and often, this is done in a very general way. For the exam, keep in mind that interviews are flexible and applicable to almost every context.

Every interview should have a clear goal, potential interviewees, interview questions, planned logistics, and a formal interview flow. These aspects are based on common meeting practices that should be adhered to when applying this technique.

When should you apply this technique?

This technique is used in a few different business analysis tasks in some knowledge tasks in the BABOK® v3 guide. These tasks include the following:

Task	The reason this technique is used
Plan a business analysis approach	To help build the business analysis approach and plan within a small group or individually
Plan stakeholder engagement	To help find out more information about stakeholders and stakeholder groups
Plan business analysis governance	To help identify potential decision-making, prioritization, approval, or change control approaches within a small group or individually
Plan analysis information management	To help a small group identify their information management requirements
Identify business analysis performance improvements	To gather subjective assessments of business analysis performance from different individuals or small groups

Prepare for elicitation	To gather input into preparation activities for elicitation from individuals or small groups
Conduct elicitation	To ask stakeholders questions to elicit their business needs and requirements
Confirm the elicitation results	To confirm that the elicitation results are accurate
Communicate business analysis information	To have individual conversations with stakeholders about business analysis information
Prioritize the requirements	To understand the basis for prioritization of an individual or small group
Assess the requirement changes	To gain an insight into the impact a change might have
Analyze the current state	To gain a deeper understanding of the current state
Define the future state	To gain a deeper understanding of the needs for the desired future state
Assess the risks	To gain an understanding of what risks there might be
Define the change strategy	To discuss the stakeholders' ideas for a change strategy
Define the requirements architecture	To collaboratively define the requirements structure
Define the design options	To help identify improvement opportunities and design options
Analyze the potential value and recommend a solution	To gain an insight into what the stakeholders believe will be a valuable solution option
Analyze the performance measures	To get an understanding of the perceived performance of a solution in the context of the perceived value
Assess the solution limitations	To help analyze problems
Assess the enterprise limitations	To identify concerns or organizational gaps

Interviewing is an effective way of establishing strong relationships with stakeholders and building rapport. It is a simple and direct approach to obtain elicitation results in a short period of time.

The next technique you need to include in your preparation is item tracking. This technique is covered in the next chapter of this guide.

Once you have understood the purpose and key aspects of each technique and you are able to apply the technique within the context of each relevant business analysis task, you know you are performing your role in an optimal and effective manner.

In the next chapter, we will cover the remaining BABOK® v3 guide techniques to ensure you have the complete set of techniques in your repertoire of skills and knowledge.

Summary

You now have a comprehensive understanding of the purpose, key aspects, and application of every business analysis technique covered in this chapter. You are able to situate each technique in the context of relevant business analysis tasks and you understand when each technique is used in practice.

In this chapter, we covered the acceptance and evaluation criteria, backlog management, balanced scorecard, benchmarking and market analysis, brainstorming, business capability analysis, business cases, business model canvas, business rules analysis, collaborative games, concept modeling, data dictionary, data flow diagrams, data mining, data modeling, decision analysis, decision modeling, document analysis, estimation, financial analysis, focus groups, functional decomposition, glossary, interface analysis, and interview techniques.

In the following chapter, we will cover the remaining business analysis techniques that are applied to business analysis tasks in practice.

14
Techniques (Part 2)

This chapter discusses the remaining BABOK® v3 guide techniques that support the successful execution of business analysis tasks in the workplace. It outlines the purpose of each technique and what it entails, as well as the tasks that use each technique to achieve a particular goal.

By the end of this chapter, you will know what these techniques are and understand the main purposes of each technique in the context of practical business analysis tasks.

More specifically, we will cover the following important techniques in this chapter:

- Item tracking
- Lessons learned
- Metrics and key performance indicators
- Mind mapping
- Non-functional requirements analysis
- Observation
- Organizational modeling
- Prioritization
- Process analysis
- Process modeling
- Prototyping
- Reviews
- Risk analysis and management
- Roles and permissions matrices
- Root cause analysis
- Scope modeling
- Sequence diagrams
- Stakeholder lists, maps, or personas
- State modeling

- Surveys or questionnaires
- SWOT analysis
- Use cases and scenarios
- User stories
- Vendor assessments
- Workshops

You will learn when to apply each of these techniques in the context of real-world scenarios.

Ensure you understand each technique's purpose and key aspects and when each one can be applied in practice. Visualize your own practical experience of business analysis and apply each technique in that context to bring it to life. This will help you gain a deeper comprehension, and therefore a stronger ability to answer the scenario-based exam questions.

Let's now start by understanding each technique in terms of its primary purpose and applicability to everyday business analysis tasks.

Item tracking

When you learn about item tracking, you need to make sure you are well versed in its primary purpose. You also need to know what it entails and be able to explain when (that is, in what types of scenarios related to business analysis tasks) it is relevant to apply this technique.

Let's consider the purpose of this technique.

What is the purpose of this technique?

According to the BABOK® v3 guide, the purpose of item tracking is "*to capture and assign responsibility for issues and stakeholder concerns that pose an impact to the solution.*"

Key things to know when using this technique

The items that a business analyst tracks can include actions, assumptions, constraints, dependencies, defects, enhancements, and issues.

These are captured in a structured way and are typically described using a unique identifier, a summary description, a category and type, the date the item was identified and who it was identified by, the impact, the priority, the resolution date, the owner, the person who is responsible for resolving or actioning the item, the strategy that was agreed on, the status, updates, and an escalation matrix.

Each of these items must be tracked until it is closed or resolved by the team.

When should you apply this technique?

This technique is used in a few different business analysis tasks in some knowledge areas of the BABOK® v3 guide. These tasks include the following:

Task	How is this technique applied?
Plan a business analysis approach	To track items raised when planning the business analysis approach
Plan business analysis governance	To track items raised when planning the governance approach
Plan analysis information management	To track any issues relating to information management practices
Identify business analysis performance improvements	To track any issues that relate to or are identified during performance improvement activities
Prioritize the requirements	To track issues raised during prioritization
Assess the requirement changes	To track issues or conflicts identified during the assessment of requirement changes
Approve the requirements	To track issues raised during the approval process
Analyze the current state	To track issues discovered when analyzing the current state
Verify the requirements	To manage and resolve any issues identified during verification activities
Validate the requirements	To manage and resolve any issues identified during validation activities
Assess the solution limitations	To track issues that relate to why a solution may not meet the potential value
Assess the enterprise limitations	To manage and resolve any issues identified during the enterprise limitations assessment

This technique ensures that any stakeholder concerns are tracked and resolved in a structured and controlled manner. It also provides the option for stakeholders to rank the items in order of importance.

The next technique you need to include in your preparation is lessons learned.

Lessons learned

When you learn about lessons learned, you need to make sure you are well versed in its primary purpose. You also need to know what it entails and be able to explain when (that is, in what types of scenarios related to business analysis tasks) it is relevant to apply this technique.

Let's consider the purpose of this technique.

What is the purpose of this technique?

According to the BABOK® v3 guide, the definition of the purpose of lessons learned is "*to compile and document successes, opportunities for improvement, failures, and recommendations for improving the performance of future projects or project phases.*"

Key things to know when using this technique

The lessons learned technique is also referred to as a retrospective. This means identifying improvements to business analysis processes and recognizing any particular processes that work well. Retrospectives should be conducted regularly during an initiative to ensure the team has the opportunity to continuously improve.

When should you apply this technique?

This technique is used in a few different business analysis tasks in some knowledge areas of the BABOK® v3 guide. These tasks include the following:

Task	How is this technique applied?
Plan a business analysis approach	To review any lessons previously learned to define a business analysis approach for an enterprise
Plan stakeholder engagement	To review any lessons previously learned to plan stakeholder engagement for an enterprise
Plan business analysis governance	To review any lessons previously learned to plan business analysis governance for an enterprise
Plan business analysis information management	To create a source of information to refer to when analyzing information management approaches for business analysis information
Identify business analysis performance improvements	As a source of information for any recommended changes that need to be made to processes, templates, and other related assets to improve business analysis delivery in the future
Manage stakeholder collaboration	To understand stakeholders' level of satisfaction or dissatisfaction with their business analysis engagement and activities
Analyze the current state	To inform the team of previous successes and failures in order to assist in finding opportunities for improvement of the current state
Define the future state	To determine which opportunities for improvement will be addressed in the future state
Assess the risks	To help inform the team of the potential risks of the initiative (by referring to past issues)
Define the change strategy	To inform the team of what went wrong in previous (similar) changes to help avoid repeating the same mistakes
Define the design options	To help identify opportunities for improvement with design options.
Assess the solution limitations	To help identify what could have impacted the solution's potential to deliver more value
Assess the enterprise limitations	To help identify opportunities for improvement within the enterprise

This technique is a great way of identifying opportunities for ongoing improvement and providing recognition for well-performed work. It helps reduce risk because it encourages the identification of issues and inefficiencies in an organized way.

The next technique you need to include in your preparation is metrics and **Key Performance Indicators** (**KPIs**).

Metrics and Key Performance Indicators (KPIs)

When you learn about metrics and KPIs, you need to make sure you are well versed in its primary purpose. You also need to know what it entails and be able to explain when (that is, in what types of scenarios related to business analysis tasks) it is relevant to apply this technique.

Let's consider the purpose of this technique.

What is the purpose of this technique?

According to the BABOK® v3 guide, the purpose of metrics and KPIs is "*to measure the performance of solutions, solution components, and other matters of interest to stakeholders.*"

Key things to know when using this technique

The term "metric" refers to the quantifiable levels of an indicator that is used to measure progress, whereas the term "indicator" identifies a specific numerical measurement that shows the degree of progress toward achieving a specific goal or outcome:

- A KPI is an indicator that measures progress toward a strategic goal.

- An indicator shows the result of a measure used to address specific concerns about needs, value, output, or activities. A well-formulated indicator demonstrates six characteristics—clear, relevant, economically useful, adequate, quantifiable, and credible.

- A metric—or rather, a target metric—is an objective that should be reached within a specified timeframe. *For example, an indicator could be defined as the number of website visitors per day and a target metric might be set to between 200 to 250 visitors per day.*

Part of this technique includes defining a way to collect the data and reporting on the key performance indicators and metric results.

When should you apply this technique?

This technique is used in a few different business analysis tasks in some knowledge areas of the BABOK® v3 guide. These tasks include the following:

Task	How is this technique applied?
Identify business analysis performance improvements	To define the metrics required for assessing business analysis performance as well as to determine how best to track this information
Analyze the current state	To assess the performance of the current state as well as to determine how best to track this information
Define the future state	To assess the performance of the future state and determine when the organization has achieved its objectives
Verify the requirements	To define what to track and to measure the quality of the requirements
Validate the requirements	To define what to track and measure for a solution or a solution component
Analyze the potential value and recommend a solution	To define and evaluate the measures used to define the value of a solution
Measure the solution performance	To measure the solution performance
Analyze the performance measures	To analyze the solution performance

This technique aligns indicators and metrics to the organizational objectives, solutions, and resources and promotes organizational alignment.

The next technique you need to include in your preparation is mind mapping.

Mind mapping

When you learn about mind mapping, you need to make sure you are well versed in its primary purpose. You also need to know what it entails and be able to explain when (that is, in what types of scenarios related to business analysis tasks) it is relevant to apply this technique.

Let's consider the purpose of this technique.

What is the purpose of this technique?

According to the BABOK® v3 guide, the purpose of mind mapping is "*to articulate and capture thoughts, ideas, and information.*"

Key things to know when using this technique

This technique uses images, words, and colors to show information, ideas, or thoughts in a visual, non-linear way. A mind map has a central primary topic or idea and branches and sub-branches that elaborate on or refine each topic or category of ideas and thoughts.

When should you apply this technique?

This technique is used in a few different business analysis tasks in some knowledge areas of the BABOK® v3 guide. These tasks include the following:

Task	How is this technique applied?
Plan stakeholder engagement	To map out all the stakeholders that need to be engaged and show the relationships between them
Plan business analysis information management	To help identify all the different categories of business analysis information that need to be managed
Prepare for elicitation	To help the team collaboratively identify the requirements sources and plan which techniques to apply during elicitation activities
Conduct elicitation	To help the stakeholders generate ideas, content, and considerations in a short period of time using a visual and creative method
Analyze the current state	To explore relevant aspects of the business needs in the current state
Define the future state	To explore ideas for the future state and indicate relationships that might exist between ideas
Assess risks	To identify potential risks and indicate the relationships that might exist between risks
Define the change strategy	To help generate ideas for different change strategies
Define the design options	To help identify potential design options

Mind mapping is an effective visual tool that promotes collaboration and creative thinking. It summarizes complex topics in an easy-to-understand way. It also provides a clear link between topics and their related subtopics.

The next technique you need to include in your preparation is non-functional requirements analysis.

Non-functional requirements analysis

When you learn about non-functional requirements analysis, you need to make sure you are well versed in its primary purpose. You also need to know what it entails and be able to explain when (that is, in what types of scenarios related to business analysis tasks) it is relevant to apply this technique.

Let's consider the purpose of this technique.

What is the purpose of this technique?

According to the BABOK® v3 guide, the purpose of non-functional requirements analysis is *"to examine the requirements for a solution that define how well the functional requirements must perform. It specifies criteria that can be used to judge the operation of a system rather than specific behaviors (which are referred to as the functional requirements)."*

Key things to know when using this technique

Non-functional requirements are also referred to as quality attributes or quality-of-service requirements.

Non-functional requirements are most effective when they are expressed in textual descriptions and include measurable qualities. Measurements can be expressed as percentages or numerical values or in time (such as seconds or minutes).

The most common non-functional requirements categories include availability, compatibility, functionality, maintainability, performance efficiency, portability, reliability, scalability, security, usability, certification, compliance, localization, service-level agreements, and extensibility.

When should you apply this technique?

This technique is used in a couple of different business analysis tasks in some knowledge areas of the BABOK® v3 guide. These tasks include the following:

Task	How is the technique applied?
Specify and model the requirements	To define and analyze the quality attributes of a solution
Measure the solution performance	To define the expected characteristics of a solution

The non-functional requirements describe the constraints that a solution operates in. They outline measurable ways of how well the functional requirements of a solution must perform.

The next technique you need to include in your preparation is observation.

Observation

When you learn about observation, you need to make sure you are well versed in its primary purpose. You also need to know what it entails and be able to explain when (that is, in what types of scenarios related to business analysis tasks) it is relevant to apply this technique.

Let's consider the purpose of this technique.

What is the purpose of this technique?

According to the BABOK® v3 guide, the purpose of observation is "*to elicit information by viewing and understanding activities and their context. It is used as a basis for identifying needs and opportunities, understanding a business process, setting performance standards, evaluating solution performance, or supporting training and development.*"

Key things to know when using this technique

This technique is also referred to as job shadowing. There are two basic approaches to applying observation as a technique:

- **Active/noticeable**: This approach allows the observer to ask questions as and when they observe something that is either unclear or prompts an idea for a business need.
- **Passive/unnoticeable**: This approach doesn't allow the observer to interrupt the person or people being observed while a process or activity is performed. Any questions must be asked at the end of the observation period.

It is important to carefully prepare for the observation activity and conduct the observation as agreed by the stakeholders or relevant parties. Once the observation is complete, it is important to record and confirm that the information captured during the observation is accurate and is a true reflection of what was observed.

When should you apply this technique?

This technique is used in a few different business analysis tasks in some knowledge areas of the BABOK® v3 guide. These tasks include the following:

Task	How is this technique applied?
Identify the business analysis performance improvements	To observe and take note of the business analysis performance
Conduct elicitation	To gain an insight into and information on how the work is currently performed
Analyze the current state	To gain an insight into potential new business needs by observing how the work is currently performed
Measure the solution performance	To provide feedback on solution performance once it's observed
Analyze the performance measures	To observe the performance in action and analyze the results
Assess the enterprise limitations	To observe or witness a solution or enterprise interactions in order to identify impacts

This technique provides real-world, practical insight into the everyday workings of a process, role, or system, which provides a deeper understanding of business issues and needs. This enables the business analyst to make recommendations that are in line with the actual issues experienced in the operational aspects of a process, topic area, or system.

The next technique you need to include in your preparation is organizational modeling.

Organizational modeling

When you learn about organizational modeling, you need to make sure you are well versed in its primary purpose. You also need to know what it entails and be able to explain when (that is, in what types of scenarios related to business analysis tasks) it is relevant to apply this technique.

Let's consider the purpose of this technique.

What is the purpose of this technique?

According to the BABOK® v3 guide, the purpose of organizational modeling is "*to describe the roles, responsibilities, and reporting structures that exist within an organization and to align those structures with the organization's goals.*"

Key things to know when using this technique

An organizational model is a visual representation of the structure of an organization or business unit. It defines the boundaries of a group, the formal relationships between group members, the functional role of each person, and any interdependencies between groups.

There are three primary organizational models that exist. These are as follows:

- **Functionally oriented**: This is when a group is categorized based on the available skill sets and areas of expertise. For example, organizing an organization into sales, marketing, and finance departments.
- **Market-oriented**: This is when a group is categorized to serve a specific segment, geography, process, or projects in a way that is not based on the skills and expertise of individuals.
- **Matrix**: This is when there is a manager for each functional area and another manager for a product or service. Functional managers might be responsible for performance whereas product- or service-based managers are only concerned with the delivery of products and services for their area.

It is important for the business analyst to determine what organizational model exists and the potential for changing the model in the future state.

When should you apply this technique?

This technique is used in a few different business analysis tasks in some knowledge areas of the BABOK® v3 guide. These tasks include the following:

Task	How is this technique applied?
Plan business analysis governance	To help understand the roles and responsibilities within an organization
Analyze the current state	To help understand the roles and responsibilities within an organization
Define the future state	To help define the roles and responsibilities that will exist in a future organization
Define the change strategy	To help define the roles and responsibilities that are required for a change and which are part of the scope of the solution
Specify and model the requirements	To help model the roles and responsibilities within an organization
Define the requirements architecture	To help understand the roles and responsibilities within an organization in order to understand different viewpoints
Assess the enterprise limitations	To ensure all changes to the organization's structure have been addressed
Recommend actions to increase the solution value	To visually depict any changes to the organization's structure

This technique is easy to relate to and is a common tool applied to all organizations. It clearly shows the roles and relationships that exist within a project or organization.

The next technique you need to include in your preparation is prioritization.

Prioritization

When you learn about prioritization, you need to make sure you are well versed in its primary purpose. You also need to know what it entails and be able to explain when (that is, in what types of scenarios related to business analysis tasks) it is relevant to apply this technique.

Let's consider the purpose of this technique.

What is the purpose of this technique?

According to the BABOK® v3 guide, the purpose of prioritization is *"to provide a framework for business analysts to facilitate stakeholder decisions and to understand the relative importance of business analysis information."*

Key things to know when using this technique

Prioritization is about determining the relative importance of business analysis information, such as the requirements.

There are four main prioritization approaches that you should be aware of:

- **Grouping**: This is when a business analyst facilitates a discussion where business analysis information is grouped based on categories such as high, medium, and low.

- **Ranking**: This is simply when the business analysis information is ranked from the most important to the least important. This is often applied as part of the prioritization of a product backlog.

- **Timeboxing/budgeting**: This is when business analysis information is prioritized based on a fixed allocation of a resource. This is most commonly based on how much work can be delivered within a specified time period with the resources available.

- **Negotiation**: This is when a consensus between stakeholders must be obtained to determine which requirements should be prioritized as more important to implement at any given point during the project's life cycle.

In some cases, a combination of these general prioritization approaches is applied.

When should you apply this technique?

This technique is used in a couple of different business analysis tasks in some knowledge areas of the BABOK® v3 guide. These tasks include the following:

Task	How is this technique applied?
Prioritize the requirements	To prioritize the requirements
Recommend actions to increase the solution value	To assist in determining the relative value of different actions that could help increase the solution value

Prioritization as a technique is effective in identifying, agreeing, and negotiating trade-offs, and building consensus. This helps to ensure that the initiative's objectives and timelines are met optimally.

The next technique you need to include in your preparation is process analysis.

Process analysis

When you learn about process analysis, you need to make sure you are well versed in its primary purpose. You also need to know what it entails and be able to explain when (that is, in what types of scenarios related to business analysis tasks) it is relevant to apply this technique.

Let's consider the purpose of this technique.

What is the purpose of this technique?

According to the BABOK® v3 guide, the purpose of process analysis is "*to assess a process for its efficiency and effectiveness, as well as its ability to identify opportunities for change.*"

Key things to know when using this technique

Process analysis is most commonly used to identify gaps in current processes or between current and future state processes, to recommend process improvement areas, to understand where technology and people fit into a process, and to understand the impacts of a change on a process.

A key element of process analysis is to identify gaps and areas that require improvements. Once these gaps or areas of improvement have been determined, it is important to analyze these areas to understand the root cause of any inefficiencies or gaps identified. This way, you can be sure you are solving any problems related to the process.

Common methods for applying process analysis in a structured way include using a SIPOC (which originates from the Six Sigma methodology) and value stream mapping (used in Lean methodologies).

When should you apply this technique?

This technique is used in a few different business analysis tasks in some knowledge areas of the BABOK® v3 guide. These tasks include the following:

Task	How is this technique applied?
Identify the business analysis performance improvements	To analyze existing processes and find opportunities for improvement when analyzing business analysis performance
Conduct elicitation	To understand and analyze existing processes and find opportunities for improvement when conducting elicitation
Analyze the current state	To understand and analyze existing processes and find opportunities for improvement in the current state
Assess the enterprise limitations	To find possible opportunities for improvement in an enterprise
Recommend actions to increase the solution value	To identify opportunities for improvement in relatable processes

This technique is effective as it helps address issues correctly with solutions and minimize potential waste. There are many different ways of applying process analysis, which gives business analysts a lot of flexibility in how to apply this technique.

The next technique you need to include in your preparation is process modeling.

Process modeling

When you learn about process modeling, you need to make sure you are well versed in its primary purpose. You also need to know what it entails and be able to explain when (that is, in what types of scenarios related to business analysis tasks) it is relevant to apply this technique.

Let's consider the purpose of this technique.

What is the purpose of this technique?

According to the BABOK® v3 guide, the purpose of process modeling is "*to provide a standardized graphical model to show how work is carried out and is a foundation for process analysis.*"

Key things to know when using this technique

A process model, in its most basic form, includes a trigger event, a sequence of activities, and a result. More complex interpretations of a process model can include elements such as data stores, input and output descriptions, and call-out descriptions that supplement the visual diagram.

Some of the common notations for process modeling include flow charts and value stream mapping, data flow diagrams, **Unified Modelling Language (UML)** diagrams, **Business Process Modelling Notation (BPMN)**, integrated **DEFinition (DEF)** notation, **Input, Guide, Output, and Enabler (IGOE)** diagrams, SIPOC, and value stream analysis.

A process model typically contains the following types of elements:

- **Activity**: This describes the activity of a specific task that is being performed.
- **Event**: This is a zero-time occurrence that either triggers (initiates), interrupts (timers), or terminates (ends) the flow in a process model.
- **Directional flow**: This is the part of the diagram that shows what direction the sequence of activities is flowing in.
- **Decision point**: This is the element that indicates whether a decision needs to be made about whether the outcome will affect the directional flow of the diagram.
- **Link**: This is an element that indicates whether there is a link to another process model diagram.
- **Role**: This element shows who is performing particular activities.

All these elements are essential to a process model, regardless of the notation or method you choose to apply.

When should you apply this technique?

The technique applications are as follows:

Task	How is this technique applied?
Plan a business analysis approach	As a visual way of defining and documenting an approach
Plan stakeholder engagement	To see which business processes and systems support which stakeholders
Plan business analysis governance	To document the processes that govern the business analysis
Plan business analysis information management	To document the processes that define information management
Identify the business analysis performance improvements	To document the business analysis processes and find opportunities for the improvement of those processes
Conduct elicitation	To elicit business process information from stakeholders in order to better understand their needs
Maintain the requirements	To help find the processes and requirements that might be suitable for reuse
Define the future state	To define how work can be performed in the future state
Define the change strategy	To describe the process of how work is carried out during the change or as a part of the scope of the solution
Specify and model the requirements	To describe the steps or activities that are performed when executing a particular business process
Assess the enterprise limitations	To describe the current business processes that need to change in order to achieve potential value or change

This technique is a great way of illustrating the sequential nature of the activities that are performed for a particular process. Most stakeholders are familiar with the concepts of a process diagram and find them easy enough to follow.

The next technique you need to include in your preparation is prototyping.

Prototyping

When you learn about prototyping, you need to make sure you are well versed in its primary purpose. You also need to know what it entails and be able to explain when (that is, in what types of scenarios related to business analysis tasks) it is relevant to apply this technique.

Let's consider the purpose of this technique.

What is the purpose of this technique?

According to the BABOK® v3 guide, the purpose of prototyping is "*to elicit and validate stakeholder needs through an iterative process that creates a model or design of requirements. It is also used to optimize user experience, to evaluate design options, and as a basis for development of the final business solution.*"

Key things to know when using this technique

A prototype is used to demonstrate a model or a limited- or non-working version of a product to stakeholders with the intention of validating that it meets their requirements. It is used to solicit more requirements or to alter any requirements that may have changed or been miscommunicated to designers.

The two common types of prototyping are throw-away and evolutionary (or functional) prototyping. The first approach discards the prototype once it is used for demonstrative or requirements elicitation purposes, whereas the latter approach uses an initial version of a product that is evolved and improved on.

Some examples of different forms of prototyping include the following:

- **A proof of concept model:** This type of prototype models the design of a system and doesn't show the workflow, visual aspects, or materials used.
- **A form study**: This type of prototype only illustrates the look and feel but doesn't include any of the functionality.
- **A usability prototype**: This type of prototype is designed to allow you to see how a user interacts with it.
- **A visual prototype**: This type of prototype is used to only show the visual aspects of a solution and does not include any functionality.
- **A functional prototype**: This type of prototype includes the functionality, workflow, and qualities of a system in development.

Any of the preceding forms of prototyping can be applied to elicit, validate, or explore requirements with stakeholders.

Some examples of commonly used methods for prototyping are as follows:

- **Storyboarding**: This shows the sequence of activities of a solution in a visual and textual pictorial format.
- **Paper prototyping**: This is drawing a process or user interface with a pencil and paper.
- **Workflow modeling**: This shows a sequence of steps (usually human-centric).
- **Simulation**: This demonstrates a solution or components of a solution (for feedback).

These methods of prototyping are used in either a formal or informal manner to expedite and complete the requirements elicitation activities.

When should you apply this technique?

This technique is used in a few different business analysis tasks in some knowledge areas of the BABOK® v3 guide. These tasks include the following:

Task	How is this technique applied?
Conduct elicitation	To elicit requirements through an iterative process to create a model of the requirements and designs
Define the future state	To help model some future state options and value propositions
Specify and model the requirements	To help stakeholders see or visualize what a solution or design might look like once it is complete
Measure the solution performance	To help simulate a new solution so that performance measures can be determined or collected

Prototyping provides a visual representation of a future state or part of a future solution. This is a highly effective method for obtaining real and accurate feedback on a solution in development.

The next technique you need to include in your preparation is reviews.

Reviews

When you learn about reviews, you need to make sure you are well versed in their primary purpose. You also need to know what they entail and be able to explain when (that is, in what types of scenarios related to business analysis tasks) it is relevant to apply this technique.

Let's consider the purpose of this technique.

What is the purpose of this technique?

According to the BABOK® v3 guide, the purpose of reviews is *"to evaluate the content of a work product."*

Key things to know when using this technique

Reviews are concerned with evaluating a work product, not the skills or participants who created the product. When performing or planning a review, it is essential to define the objective as well as decide how the review will be completed and who will participate in the review.

Reviews come in different forms and different techniques can be applied to carry them out. Common review techniques that can be applied are inspections, formal walkthroughs, single-issue reviews (technical reviews), informal walkthroughs, desk checks, and a pass-around.

A review session may include an author (of the working product under review), a reviewer, a facilitator (if a formal walkthrough is conducted), and a scribe.

When should you apply this technique?

This technique is used in a few different business analysis tasks in some knowledge areas of the BABOK® v3 guide. These tasks include the following:

Task	How is this technique applied?
Plan business analysis governance	To review the proposed business analysis governance plan with the stakeholders involved
Identify the business analysis performance improvements	To identify potential changes to processes or deliverables that could be incorporated into future business analysis work
Confirm the elicitation results	To review and confirm elicitation results with stakeholders
Communicate the business analysis information	To provide stakeholders with the opportunity to review and provide feedback related to any relevant business analysis information
Approve the requirements	To review and approve the requirements
Verify the requirements	To review the requirements for their level of quality
Validate the requirements	By stakeholders to review the requirements and confirm whether their business needs are accurately and completely reflected.

Reviews help a team identify defects or issues with deliverable quality early on in the initiative. This can prevent excessive rework and also acts as an engagement method to get stakeholders more involved.

The next technique you need to include in your preparation is risk analysis and management.

Risk analysis and management

When you learn about risk analysis and management, you need to make sure you are well versed in its primary purpose. You also need to know what it entails and be able to explain when (that is, in what types of scenarios related to business analysis tasks) it is relevant to apply this technique.

Let's consider the purpose of this technique.

What is the purpose of this technique?

According to the BABOK® v3 guide, the purpose of risk analysis and management is "*to identify areas of uncertainty that could negatively affect value, it analyses and evaluates those uncertainties, and develops and manages ways of dealing with the risks.*"

Key things to know when using this technique

This technique is about identifying, analyzing, and evaluating risks that exist within the scope of an initiative. This includes defining and agreeing on controls for risks that do not yet have any controls in place.

The steps in risk analysis and management include identifying the risks and recording them in a risk register. Once a risk is identified, it is analyzed in terms of its impact level on a variety of aspects, such as (but not limited to) the scope, quality, cost, effort, duration, reputation, and social responsibility.

Risks are prioritized based on their level of impact and can be expressed in terms of a function of probability and its impact.

Risks are then evaluated by comparing the risk analysis results with the potential value of the solution implemented. Then, the team has to decide how to treat the risk. Here are some common solution options to consider:

- **Avoid the risk**: Change plans to avoid the risk completely or remove the source of the risk.
- **Transfer the risk**: The liability of the risk is either shared or moved to a third party.
- **Mitigate the risk**: Actions can be taken to reduce the probability of the risk occurring.
- **Accept the risk**: This is a decision to accept the risk as it stands. If it occurs, the project will find a solution.
- **Increase the risk**: A decision is made to increase the risk in order to increase an opportunity.

Every organization has its own variation of these treatment options and the business analyst should bear this in mind in order to work effectively.

When should you apply this technique?

This technique is used in a few different business analysis tasks in some knowledge areas of the BABOK® v3 guide. These tasks include the following:

Task	How is this technique applied?
Plan stakeholder engagement	To identify any risks that occur due to stakeholder attitudes or inability to participate in an initiative
Identify the business analysis performance improvements	To identify risks to the initiative as a consequence of stakeholders' inability to participate or their attitudes in relation to their participation in an initiative
Prepare for elicitation	To help identify any risks that could disrupt or prevent the success of the elicitation activities
Manage stakeholder collaboration	To identify and manage the risks that relate to stakeholder participation, involvement, or engagement
Prioritize the requirements	To help understand any risks in the context of requirement prioritization activities
Assess the requirement changes	To determine the level of risk associated with a change introduced by an initiative
Analyze the current state	To identify any risks in relation to the current state
Assess the risks	To identify and manage any risks in the context of an initiative
Validate the requirements	To identify any risks that could prevent a requirement from delivering the anticipated value
Analyze the potential value and recommend a solution	To identify and manage any risks that could affect the potential value of a requirement
Analyze the performance measures	To identify and analyze risks by developing plans to help modify risks and/or manage them on an ongoing basis
Assess the solution limitations	To identify and manage any risks that could affect the potential value of a solution
Assess the enterprise limitations	To consider risks relating to technology, finance, and business where these risks could affect the potential value from being delivered to the enterprise
Recommend actions to increase the solution value	To evaluate different outcomes under specific conditions (in the context of risks)

This technique provides a way of recording, managing, and planning for strategic, operational, and initiative risks in a formal way. It can also be a useful source of information for future initiatives where similar risks might occur and, therefore, mitigation activities used in the past can potentially be reused in the future.

The next technique you need to include in your preparation is a roles and permissions matrix.

Roles and permissions matrix

When you learn about roles and permissions matrices, you need to make sure you are well versed in their primary purpose. You also need to know what they entail and be able to explain when (that is, in what types of scenarios related to business analysis tasks) it is relevant to apply this technique.

Let's consider the purpose of this technique.

What is the purpose of this technique?

According to the BABOK® v3 guide, the purpose of a roles and permissions matrix is *"to ensure coverage of activities by denoting responsibility, to identify roles, to discover missing roles, and to communicate results of a planned change."*

Key things to know when using this technique

This technique outlines all the roles and solution activities associated with each role when using a particular solution.

To simplify this technique, let's look at an everyday practical example of some common solution roles.

Administrator, **Staff**, and **Support** roles can each perform different functions in a system. For example, the **Administrator** role can perform all of the functions in a solution whereas the **Staff** role can only update and create new staff records using the system. When a new user gets access to the system, they are assigned a role. Depending on their role in the system, they are able to perform different types of functions using this system.

A business analyst will often identify the required roles for a solution by considering the organization models, procedural manuals, and/or job descriptions. Once the types of roles are identified, the next step is to define which functions are controlled by the permissions protocols. These functions can be discovered by performing a functional decomposition.

The last step in defining the permissions matrix is assigning authority levels. These can include authorities such as write access, read access, delete access, and so on. The last concept to understand is that each level of access can be defined to inherit the authority attributes from the level above it. For example, if a role has the authority to write to a record, it will also be able to read a record.

When should you apply this technique?

This technique is used in one business analysis task in a knowledge area of the BABOK® v3 guide. This task is as follows:

Task	How is this technique applied?
Assess the enterprise limitations	To identify the roles and permissions for stakeholders who will be the users of a new solution

Using roles and permissions matrices is a structured way of ensuring procedures are implemented and data is secured effectively and correctly. They also provide a team with documented roles and responsibilities in the context of the solution activities.

The next technique you need to include in your preparation is root cause analysis.

Root cause analysis

When you learn about root cause analysis, you need to make sure you are well versed in its primary purpose. You also need to know what it entails and be able to explain when (that is, in what types of scenarios related to business analysis tasks) it is relevant to apply this technique.

Let's consider the purpose of this technique.

What is the purpose of this technique?

According to the BABOK® v3 guide, the purpose of root cause analysis is "*to identify and evaluate the underlying causes of a problem.*"

Key things to know when using this technique

This technique is about performing a systematic and structured analysis of a problem by delving into the problem's origin and uncovering its true cause.

A root cause analysis can be used to perform a reactive analysis. A reactive analysis is when a problem occurs and a solution is needed. A root cause analysis is used to identify what caused the problem in the first place.

On the other hand, a root cause analysis can also be applied as a preventative measure to try and identify problem areas and their causes. This way, preventative action can be taken.

Two common root cause analysis methods are as follows:

- **The fishbone diagram:** This diagram starts by describing the effect and then builds up categories of potential causes of the problem. This can be broken down even further into more detailed causes per category.
- **The five whys method:** This is about asking the question "why" numerous times based on the problem and its previous answers. This method delves deeper into the causes of the problem and provides clarity on what the causes are.

When should you apply this technique?

This technique is used in a few different business analysis tasks in some knowledge areas of the BABOK® v3 guide. These tasks include the following:

Task	How is this technique applied?
Identify the business analysis performance improvements	To help understand any causes of failure or any difficulties in the business analysis work that is performed or delivered
Analyze the current state	To help understand the cause of any problems that may exist in the current state, which could assist in further understanding the business needs
Assess the risks	To help uncover the underlying problems that cause a risk to occur
Specify and model the requirements	To model the causes of a problem to outline a rationale for its occurrence
Define the design options	To help identify problems and their associated causes to better be able to find an appropriate solution to help address them

Analyze the performance measures	To assist with identifying the cause of performance-related issues
Assess the solution limitations	To identify the causes and factors that contribute to a solution not reaching the potential value intended
Assess the enterprise limitations	To see whether an underlying cause of a problem relates to an enterprise limitation

This technique helps stakeholders and teams determine the true causes of issues and business problems in a structured, logical fashion. It creates a visual representation of the issues at hand and provides a tool for preparing solution options.

The next technique you need to include in your preparation is scope modeling.

Scope modeling

When you learn about scope modeling, you need to make sure you are well versed in its primary purpose. You also need to know what it entails and be able to explain when (that is, in what types of scenarios related to business analysis tasks) it is relevant to apply this technique.

Let's consider the purpose of this technique.

What is the purpose of this technique?

According to the BABOK® v3 guide, the purpose of scope modeling is *"to define the nature of one or more limits or boundaries and place elements inside or outside those boundaries."*

Key things to know when using this technique

A scope model is most often used to define the boundaries of control or change, a solution, or a business need. In most cases, a scope model will show items that are either in scope or out of scope. It can also show both in-scope and out-of-scope items.

A business analyst is mostly concerned with the elements that are part of in-scope items; however, they also need to be clear on which items are out of scope and what the broader context of this is.

The level of detail when defining scope boundaries is important as the scope model should contain enough detail to be meaningful but not be too detailed and cause a situation where "analysis paralysis" slows down the initiative's progress. Any assumptions made at the time of defining the scope model must be expressed and maintained. The scope model can be described using text or diagrams, or a combination of both.

When should you apply this technique?

This technique is used in a few different business analysis tasks in some knowledge areas of the BABOK® v3 guide. These tasks include the following:

Task	How is this technique applied?
Plan stakeholder engagement	To show stakeholders which elements fall outside the scope of a solution but are still relevant and in context
Analyze the current state	To describe the boundaries of the current state that is being analyzed
Define the future state	To describe the boundaries of the future state in the context of the solution
Define the change strategy	To describe the boundaries of the solution and areas where changes will occur
Specify and model the requirements	To illustrate the scope using a visual representation
Define the requirements architecture	To describe the boundaries of the requirements architecture

Scope modeling is versatile and has multiple uses. It is used to facilitate vendor contract discussions and stakeholder expectation management and provides a guide for the entire team on what is in scope and what is out of scope. It is a very good technique to help with resource planning and effort estimates, as well.

The next technique you need to include in your preparation is sequence diagrams.

Sequence diagrams

When you learn about sequence diagrams, you need to make sure you are well versed in its primary purpose. You also need to know what it entails and be able to explain when (that is, in what types of scenarios related to business analysis tasks) it is relevant to apply this technique.

Let's consider the purpose of this technique.

What is the purpose of this technique?

According to the BABOK® v3 guide, the purpose of sequence diagrams is *"to model the logic of usage scenarios by showing the information passed between objects in the system through the execution of the scenario."*

Key things to know when using this technique

This technique shows how processes or objects interact with each other in the context of specific scenarios.

There are three key notational elements:

- **A life line:** A life line demonstrates the life span of an object that is modeled for a scenario.
- **An activation box:** An activation box shows the time period that an operation is executed in.
- **A message**: A message shows the interaction between two objects.

This technique shows the sequence of actions in the order that they occur and is a great visual way to ensure that a logical and accurate process is followed.

When should you apply this technique?

This technique is used in one business analysis task in a knowledge area of the BABOK® v3 guide. This task is as follows:

Task	How is this technique applied?
Specify and model the requirements	To show how processes and objects interact with each other and what sequence this occurs in

This technique shows the interaction between objects in a system in a chronological and visual way. This technique is a clear way of communicating the steps that are performed for any given business or solution scenario.

The next technique you need to include in your preparation is stakeholder lists, maps, or personas.

Stakeholder lists, maps, or personas

When you learn about stakeholder lists, maps, or personas, you need to make sure you are well versed in their primary purpose. You also need to know what they entail and be able to explain when (that is, in what types of scenarios related to business analysis tasks) it is relevant to apply this technique.

Let's consider the purpose of this technique.

What is the purpose of this technique?

According to the BABOK® v3 guide, the purpose of stakeholder lists, maps, or personas is *"to assist the business analyst in analyzing stakeholders and their characteristics."*

Key things to know when using this technique

With these techniques, the most important stakeholder characteristics that are analyzed include aspects such as the level of authority and attitudes toward the initiative, as well as the business analysis efforts and their level of decision-making authority.

There are a few different ways of analyzing stakeholders, which can be categorized as follows:

- **Stakeholder lists**: These are lists of all the stakeholders that have a part to play in an initiative. This could range from stakeholders that are impacted indirectly to stakeholders who have direct decision-making authority within the initiative.
- **Stakeholder maps**: A stakeholder map is a representation of the stakeholders and groups categorized in terms of their relationship to an initiative.

  The most common maps you can apply include creating a stakeholder matrix, which defines the level of influence against the level of stakeholder impact. The other method is an onion diagram, which ensures that all the levels of stakeholders are included. These levels start from the immediate project team members to the external vendors, suppliers, and regulators. An onion diagram ensures all types of stakeholders are considered.

- **Responsibility (RACI) matrices**: This method demonstrates the level of responsibility that a stakeholder or stakeholder group may have in relation to an initiative.

- **Personas**: This method of performing stakeholder analysis is about formulating descriptions of typical characters that interact with the solution. These are fictional character descriptions that help teams understand the type of person who will use a solution and what their needs are in terms of the solution.

When should you apply this technique?

This technique is used in a few different business analysis tasks in some knowledge areas of the BABOK® v3 guide. These tasks include the following:

Task	How is this technique applied?
Prepare for elicitation	To help identify who should be consulted when preparing for the elicitation activities, as well as who should be part of the elicitation and what their roles might be
Manage stakeholder collaboration	To work out who should be involved and to what degree they should be involved in the business analysis work
Specify and model the requirements	To identify and understand the stakeholders' needs in more detail

This technique is used to identify the specific people required for requirements elicitation and helps with the planning of collaboration, communication, and any facilitation activities that need to be performed. It is also an effective way of getting to know your stakeholders (and some specific people) in order to get a deeper understanding of their business needs.

The next technique you must include in your preparation is state modeling.

State Modeling

When you learn about state modeling, you need to make sure you are well versed in its primary purpose. You also need to know what it entails and be able to explain when (that is, in what types of scenarios related to business analysis tasks) it is relevant to apply this technique.

Let's consider the purpose of this technique.

What is the purpose of this technique?

According to the BABOK® v3 guide, the purpose of state modeling is "*to describe and analyze the different possible states of an entity within a system, how that entity changes from one state to another, and what can happen to the entity when it is in each state.*"

Key things to know when using this technique

Each entity has a life cycle that has a beginning and an end.

Let's look at the following real-world example to bring the state modeling technique to life.

A gift card can have an inactive, active, blocked, or canceled status.

A state model describes the different states that an entity can be in, how each transition between the states occurs, and the conditions that change the entities' states.

A **state** is described by a name and the actions that are valid for an entity when in a specific state. In some cases, an entity can be in more than one state at a time.

If we consider our gift card example, the gift card (the entity)'s state is inactive, which means the card cannot be used for transactions but it can be assigned to a particular customer record.

A **state transition** is the conditions and/or actions that cause an entity to change from one state to another. In our example of the gift card, once the customer registers their inactive gift card on the cardholder portal, the status changes from inactive to active. Now, the gift card can also carry out transactions.

A **state diagram** shows the entire life cycle of an entity, from its very first state to the last state it can be in. It also shows the direction of flow between states. An alternative way of depicting a state model is to use a table. You simply start with the beginning state, describe the action that transforms the state, and then describe the next state. The last state then becomes the beginning state in the next row of the table.

State modeling is a good technique to apply if a business analyst wants to define business rules and attributes of information.

When should you apply this technique?

This technique is used in one business analysis task in a knowledge area of the BABOK® v3 guide. This task is as follows:

Task	How is this technique used?
Specify and model the requirements	To specify the different states of the entities described as well as outline the events that transform the entities from one state to another

This technique helps describe the different states of an entity as it passes through an activity or scenario. It shows how and when an entity transforms from one state to another and is an effective technique to identify business rules as part of elicitation activities.

The next technique you need to include in your preparation is surveys or questionnaires.

Surveys or questionnaires

When you learn about surveys or questionnaires, you need to make sure you are well versed in their primary purpose. You also need to know what they entail and be able to explain when (that is, in what types of scenarios related to business analysis tasks) it is relevant to apply this technique.

Let's consider the purpose of this technique.

What is the purpose of this technique?

According to the BABOK® v3 guide, the purpose of survey and questionnaires is "*to elicit business analysis information - including information about customers, products, work practices, and attitudes - from a group of people in a structured way and in a relatively short period of time.*"

Key things to know when using this technique

There are two types of questions to include in a survey—open-ended and close-ended. As the terms imply, a close-ended question is when a question expects a specific, pre-defined answer (such as yes or no) and an open-ended question is when the question invites an open answer that elaborates on and describes a response in more detail.

A survey or questionnaire requires careful planning in terms of the objective of the survey, the questions, the type, the audience (including a sample group), the timeline, the distribution methods, the testing of questions, and so on. Once the survey has been conducted, the results should be documented and the data should be captured in a meaningful way. Wherever relevant, the survey results should be shared with the stakeholders.

When should you apply this technique?

This technique is used in a couple of different business analysis tasks in some knowledge areas of the BABOK® v3 guide. These tasks include the following:

Task	How is this technique applied?
Plan stakeholder engagement	To identify the shared characteristics of stakeholder groups
Plan business analysis governance	To help identify different aspects of governance
Plan business analysis information management	To ask stakeholders to contribute to defining the business analysis information management approach
Identify the business analysis performance improvements	To solicit feedback from stakeholders on the business analysis performance
Conduct elicitation	To gain insight into the needs of the stakeholders in order to identify and define the requirements
Analyze the current state	To help get an understanding of the current state from a wide group of stakeholders
Define the future state	To help get an understanding of the needs and wants of the future state from a wide group of stakeholders
Assess the risks	To gain an understanding of what the stakeholders believe are the risks to an initiative
Define the design options	To help identify opportunities for improvement or design options
Analyze the potential value and recommend a solution	To gain an understanding of which design options best meet the stakeholders' needs, as well as what their expectations are in terms of the value delivered
Measure the solution performance	To obtain the stakeholders' opinions about a solution's performance
Analyze the performance measures	To understand what the expectations are in terms of a solution's performance

Assess the solution limitations	To assist in obtaining feedback as part of problem analysis activities
Assess the enterprise limitations	To obtain the stakeholders' opinions and concerns or identify organizational gaps
Recommend actions to increase the solution value	To gain insight from a wide spectrum of stakeholders in terms of their expectations of the value delivered

This technique is an inexpensive way of asking a wide range of stakeholders a common set of questions. It is a relatively easy way of soliciting the feedback of a large group and can provide a significant amount of information in a relatively short period of time.

The next technique you need to include in your preparation is SWOT analysis.

SWOT analysis

When you learn about SWOT analysis, you need to make sure you are well versed in its primary purpose. You also need to know what it entails and be able to explain when (that is, in what types of scenarios related to business analysis tasks) it is relevant to apply this technique.

Let's consider the purpose of this technique.

What is the purpose of this technique?

According to the BABOK® v3 guide, the purpose of SWOT analysis is "*to evaluate an organization's strengths, weaknesses, opportunities, and threats to both internal and external conditions.*"

Key things to know when using this technique

SWOT analysis describes pertinent factors that relate to an organization using the following categories:

- **Strengths**: This includes the internal aspects of the organization that are considered key strengths. Some examples could be its reputation, people, or products.

- **Weaknesses**: This includes the internal aspects of the organization that are considered a current weakness or something that is not done well by the organization. Some examples could be a poor reputation for quality products.
- **Opportunities**: This is about the opportunities that exist outside the organization that they could potentially take advantage of to grow. An example is online commerce.
- **Threats**: This is about the external threats that add stress to the organization on different levels. Some examples could be their competitor's products being superior to their own or disruption to the industry in terms of how services are delivered or being charged for.

This technique is valuable for applying at a strategic level to understand the internal and external environmental factors that an organization operates with.

When should you apply this technique?

This technique is used in a couple of different business analysis tasks in some knowledge areas of the BABOK® v3 guide. These tasks include the following:

Task	How is this technique applied?
Analyze the current state	To evaluate the strengths, weaknesses, opportunities, and threats of the current state of an organization
Define the future state	To evaluate the strengths, weaknesses, opportunities, and threats that could be changed or avoided in the future state
Define the change strategy	To help form the decisions around which change strategy is the most suitable for the organization
Analyze the potential value and recommend a solution	To evaluate the strengths, weaknesses, opportunities, and threats that could affect the solution value
Assess the enterprise limitations	To show how to maximize strengths and reduce weaknesses in order to define strategies to address enterprise-wide limitations

SWOT analysis is a valuable tool to use when analyzing an organization's internal and external environment in the context of the organization's current situation.

The next technique you need to include in your preparation is use cases and scenarios.

Use cases and scenarios

When you learn about use cases and scenarios, you need to make sure you are well versed in its primary purpose. You also need to know what it entails and be able to explain when (that is, in what types of scenarios related to business analysis tasks) it is relevant to apply this technique.

Let's consider the purpose of this technique.

What is the purpose of this technique?

According to the BABOK® v3 guide, the purpose of use cases and scenarios is *"to describe how a person or system interacts with the solution being modeled to achieve a goal."*

Key things to know when using this technique

A use case describes how a primary actor interacts with a system. It also shows any interactions between use cases or secondary actors (such as timers or external system triggers).

Use cases are illustrated in a use case diagram that consists of the following notational elements:

- **Use cases**: The functionality of a solution.
- **Actors**: The users that interact with the solution in different ways.
- **Relationships**: Show how the actors interact with the different use cases shown in the diagram.

  There are two types of relationships between use cases—namely the following:

- **Include**: This relationship shows that the use case will always include the functionality of another as part of its execution.
- **Extend**: This relationship shows that a use case will extend to use the other use case's functionality as part of its own when certain conditions are met.

Each use case that is identified in a use case diagram is supported by a detailed use case description. Each use case description includes information including the title of the use case, any conditions that the use case has to meet before it can be activated or used, the sequence of activities that are performed during its execution, and any exceptions that may exist.

The use case's description also includes information about which actors use it, what the trigger for it to execute is, and the overall purpose of its existence.

When should you apply this technique?

This technique is used in a couple of different business analysis tasks in some knowledge areas of the BABOK® v3 guide. These tasks include the following:

Task	How is this technique applied?
Maintain the requirements	To identify a part of the solution that can be used by more than one part of the solution
Specify and model the requirements	To model the behavior of a solution by describing the use cases and the actors and their relationship
Measure the solution performance	To help define the expected outcomes of a solution

A use case diagram is used to summarize the scope of a solution by showing the actors and primary use cases or functions to the reader. It also shows interactions between the actors and use cases, which provides an easy-to-understand visual representation of how a new solution will be used. Supporting use case descriptions provide the necessary detail to the delivery and implementation teams in order to bring the solution to life.

The next technique you need to include in your preparation is user stories.

User stories

When you learn about user stories, you need to make sure you are well versed in their primary purpose. You also need to know what they entail and be able to explain when (that is, in what types of scenarios related to business analysis tasks) it is relevant to apply this technique.

Let's consider the purpose of this technique.

What is the purpose of this technique?

According to the BABOK® v3 guide, the purpose of user stories is "*to represent a small, concise statement of functionality or quality needed to deliver value to a specific stakeholder.*"

Key things to know when using this technique

This is a technique that uses straightforward short sentences to describe the needs of a stakeholder. A user story also includes where the value in the feature it describes lies by including a reason for the requirement or need. The goal of user stories is to encourage simplicity and further conversation between members of the delivery team.

A user story will always include information about who the feature is for, what function the feature performs, and why it is of value to the user. A common way to formulate a user story is "as a [role], I need to [what], so that [why]."

Another format that is sometimes used is called the Gherkin format, which follows a "Given…, when…, then …." format.

User stories are an effective way of getting teams to understand the essence of a user's needs and acts as an effective trigger for further discovery and development.

When should you apply this technique?

This technique is used in a few different business analysis tasks in some knowledge areas of the BABOK® v3 guide. These tasks include the following:

Task	How is this technique applied?
Maintain the requirements	To identify the requirements that could be suitable for reuse
Specify and model the requirements	To describe the requirements as a small statement in terms of who needs the requirement, what the requirement needs, and why a requirement is needed.

User stories are succinct and easy to understand for stakeholders and team members. They focus on the value it brings to a stakeholder and can be used across many different elicitation activities and methodology frameworks.

The next technique you need to include in your preparation is vendor assessments.

Vendor assessments

When you learn about vendor assessments, you need to make sure you are well versed in their primary purpose. You also need to know what they entail and be able to explain when (that is, in what types of scenarios related to business analysis tasks) it is relevant to apply this technique.

Let's consider the purpose of this technique.

What is the purpose of this technique?

According to the BABOK® v3 guide, the purpose of vendor assessments is "*to assess the ability of a vendor to meet commitments regarding the delivery and the consistent provision of a product or service.*"

Key things to know when using this technique

This technique is about ensuring that an organization follows the correct procedures to assess a potential new vendor in terms of the following categories of capabilities:

- The vendor's knowledge and expertise
- The licensing and pricing models
- The vendor's market position
- The terms and conditions
- The vendor's experience, reputation, and stability

By following these steps of assessing vendors, the organization safeguards itself by increasing their chances of developing a productive and fair relationship with a suitable and reliable vendor.

When should you apply this technique?

This technique is used in a few different business analysis tasks in some knowledge areas of the BABOK® v3 guide. These tasks include the following:

Task	How is this technique applied?
Analyze the current state	To help ensure that the vendors that are used as part of the current state meet the commitments
Define the future state	To help assess whether a potential vendor's solution meets the value expectations
Define the change strategy	To determine whether vendors are a part of the change strategy or solution implementation
Define the design options	To help assess whether a potential vendor's solution is viable and meets the value expectations
Measure the solution performance	To help identify which of the vendor's performance measures should be included in the solution performance assessment.

This technique helps guide an organization in establishing well-rounded vendor relationships by asking the right questions. It acts as a basis for supporting the organization in establishing strong, long-term vendor relationships.

The next technique you need to include in your preparation is workshops.

Workshops

When you learn about workshops, you need to make sure you are well versed in their primary purpose. You also need to know what they entail and be able to explain when (that is, in what types of scenarios related to business analysis tasks) it is relevant to apply this technique.

Let's consider the purpose of this technique.

What is the purpose of this technique?

According to the BABOK® v3 guide, the purpose of workshops is *"to bring stakeholders together in order to collaborate on achieving a predefined goal."*

Key things to know when using this technique

In the context of business analysis information, workshops are used to elicit, clarify, validate, and prioritize information in a collaborative, group format. When a business analyst facilitates any workshop, the roles of a sponsor (if available), a facilitator, a scribe, a timekeeper, and the participants must be accounted for.

Just as with any other elicitation activity, it is essential to prepare for a workshop, be professional when conducting it, and, after the workshop, always follow up with the results.

When should you apply this technique?

This technique is used in a few different business analysis tasks in some knowledge areas of the BABOK® v3 guide. These tasks include the following:

Task	How is this technique applied?
Plan the business analysis approach	To help build an approach in a collaborative team setting
Plan stakeholder engagement	To help learn more about the stakeholder groups in a collaborative way
Plan business analysis governance	To solicit information about governance aspects in a collaborative way
Plan business analysis information management	To help discover the business analysis information management needs in a team setting.
Identify the business analysis performance improvements	To facilitate ideas and opportunities for performance improvement in a team setting
Conduct elicitation	To elicit business analysis information in a team setting
Confirm the elicitation results	To facilitate a formal review of the elicitation results in a group setting
Communicate the business analysis information	To give a group of stakeholders the opportunity to provide feedback, collaborate, and approve requirements in a group setting
Prioritize the requirements	To help understand the basis for prioritization from a group of stakeholders
Assess the requirement changes	To help understand the impacts of a change or resolve any changes required in a group setting
Approve the requirements	To help facilitate obtaining the approval of requirements

Analyze the current state	To engage stakeholders in a group to describe the current state and their business needs
Define the future state	To engage stakeholders in a group to describe their desired future state
Assess the risks	To engage stakeholders in a group to describe what risks they have identified and which risk factors need consideration
Define the change strategy	To engage stakeholders in a group to develop a change strategy together
Define the requirements architecture	To define the requirements architecture in a group setting
Define the design options	To engage stakeholders in a group to collaboratively identify opportunities for improvement and design options
Analyze the potential value and recommend a solution	To engage stakeholders in a group to get their input on which design options best meet their needs, as well as to understand their value expectations
Assess the enterprise limitations	To engage stakeholders in a group to understand their concerns or identify any organizational gaps

Workshops are one of the most popular and effective means for eliciting business analysis information from a group. This technique is an efficient way of engaging with a group of people who share a common goal.

You have now learned all about the different techniques that a business analyst can apply to everyday business analysis tasks. These techniques cover a broad spectrum of business analysis activities and should be skillfully applied to achieve each technique's intended purpose and function. Although you may not be an expert in every technique covered in the BABOK® v3 guide, you should aspire to master each technique to a degree that will add value to your work as a business analyst.

Summary

You now have a comprehensive understanding of the purpose, key aspects, and application of every business analysis technique covered in this chapter. You can now consider each technique in the context of relevant business analysis tasks and you understand when each technique is used in practice.

The techniques we covered in this chapter include item tracking; lessons learned; metrics and KPIs; mind mapping; non-functional requirements analysis; observation; organizational modeling; prioritization; process analysis; process modeling; prototyping; reviews; risk analysis and management; roles and permissions matrices; root cause analysis; scope modeling; sequence diagrams; stakeholder lists, maps, or personas; state modeling; surveys or questionnaires; SWOT analysis; use cases and scenarios; user stories; vendor assessments; and workshops.

Now that you have learned the purposes, key things to know, and when each technique is applied in practice, it is time for you to learn about the different perspectives of business analysis. In the next chapter, you will find a summary of the key perspectives described as part of the BABOK® v3 guide. These perspectives should be considered as different ways that business analysis knowledge and skills can be applied across a variety of specialisms.

Mock Exam Questions: Case Studies

This chapter contains four short case studies that are based on real-world **Business Analysis** scenarios. Each case study contains a series of multiple-choice questions that you must answer after interpreting the case study and its context.

By the end of this test, you will have an idea of how well you can interpret case-study scenarios in the context of Business Analysis concepts and facts. This is a good way to prepare yourself for the actual exam, and it is also a great way to test your study progress. Good luck!

The case studies are as follows:

- Case study 1: Global online platform
- Case study 2: Offender management system
- Case study 3: Health and fitness app
- Case study 4: Business case for a retail company

Let's get started by reviewing the first case study, detailed next.

Case study 1 – Global online platform

You are on a brand new project. No requirements exist yet; the initiative is still at an idea stage. The idea is to implement an online storefront similar to the Amazon platform, but with the main difference of selling services rather than products. You are part of a global organization with offices in 13 countries. As part of your elicitation activities, you have to elicit requirements from stakeholders across all offices. You have a limited budget and only have 2 months to finish all the elicitation activities required, as well as getting stakeholder requirements approved.

Questions

Question 1

Considering the provided case study, which elicitation technique should be the first technique you employ?

Select the correct choice from the following options:

    A. Interviews

    B. Workshops

    C. Document Analysis

    D. Observation

Question 2

Considering the provided case study, which of the following analysis techniques should be the least likely elicitation technique to be used, and hence should not be included as part of your Business Analysis approach?

Select the correct choice from the following options:

    A. Interviews

    B. Workshops

    C. Surveys

    D. Document Analysis

Question 3

Considering the provided case study, which of the following general elicitation approaches would be the most credible approach to follow?

Select the correct choice from the following options:

    A. Run elicitation workshops for every country and elicit their requirements.

    B. Develop a base of requirements using Document Analysis in some selective countries, and then run requirements validation sessions with all countries remotely.

C. Simply copy all requirements and features from Amazon and apply them to your context. Present the requirements for approval.

D. Perform interviews with a key person in each country and confirm they agree with your requirements.

Question 4

Considering the provided case study, which additional activities should be included in your Business Analysis approach?

Select the correct choice from the following options:

    A. Stakeholder analysis

    B. Roles and responsibilities

    C. Change control process

    D. Requirements session agendas

Case study 2 – Offender management system

You are part of a third team that is attempting to implement an organization-wide offender management system for the Queensland Department of Justice. The first two teams who attempted to implement the offender management system have never passed the design stage of the project before it was canceled. Your stakeholders have been engaged many times in elicitation activities (and are quite fatigued), and you have a lot of business analysis information available from previous attempts to implement this system. This time, it will be different—there is a new sponsor who has given a top-down mandate to "make it happen". You have to minimize stakeholder elicitation sessions but ensure requirements are valid and comprehensive.

Questions

Question 1

Considering the provided case study, you decide to approach one of the key stakeholders directly about requirements. They reply to your request for an elicitation interview request with: "I already provided these requirements to Person A 6 months ago!" What should be your response?

Select the correct choice from the following options:

A. I have those requirements with me and would love to validate them with you.

B. Those requirements are out of date—we need to start again.

C. We have a mandate to engage with you, and hence we must do this session.

D. Don't shoot the messenger—I just want to help!

Question 2

Considering the provided case study, you discover during document analysis that some requirements are missing in a particular section. Knowing that the stakeholders are fatigued from requirements elicitation activities, what would be the best approach to elicit the requirements for the missing section?

Select the correct choice from the following options:

A. Tell stakeholders the missing requirements are not your fault and they must give you time to finish it off.

B. Build a rapport with stakeholders, share what you discovered, and ask how they would prefer to be engaged to fill out the missing section.

C. Prepare "made-up" requirements for the missing section and ask stakeholders to validate your suggestions.

D. Just leave the gap in requirements and see if it is noticed during implementation.

Case study 3 – Health and fitness app

You are on a team that has been assigned to work as part of a brand new initiative in a health insurance company. The initiative is about introducing a new health and fitness app that customers can use to keep fit and healthy. The company has never developed an app before and has never thought about helping its customers to stay healthy! This is a brand new mindset, and it is therefore at the forefront of the company's strategy for growth and development. Everyone in the organization wants to participate in this initiative and wants to have an opportunity to say what they think would be the top requirements for this new app! Everyone is excited, and the spotlight is on your team to deliver. The chief executive officer (CEO) has provided some direction in terms of wanting your team to ensure the app is the best of the breed, and they have made a significant budget available for the project. The primary constraint for your team is that you must deliver this solution within the next 6 months.

You have an unlimited budget and unlimited interest from stakeholders. In order for you to develop best-of-breed requirements within your limited timeframe, you must ask your CEO (who is your sponsor) to allow you to embark on an experimental path where you can test out competitor products and observe results in the form of volunteer participants, who use the products and provide their feedback on specific features.

Questions

Question 1

Considering the provided case study, which one of the following analysis techniques would be the most suitable to apply when researching the best-of-breed competitor products?

Select the correct choice from the following options:

A. Personas

B. Business Model Canvas

C. Benchmarking and Market Analysis

D. Prototyping

Question 2

Considering the provided case study, you and your team have decided to build a prototype app to use during requirements elicitation activities. The idea is to use this prototype to build a solution over a period of time. Which form of prototyping are you employing?

Select the correct choice from the following options:

A. Functional prototyping

B. Throwaway prototyping

C. Experimental prototyping

D. User-engagement prototyping

Question 3

Considering the provided case study, you reach a point where you believe you have all the stakeholder requirements documented. You request a colleague to review your requirements for usability. Which one of the following Business Analysis tasks are you performing?

Select the correct choice from the following options:

A. Validating requirements

B. Desk checking

C. Verifying requirements

D. Maintaining requirements

Question 4

Considering the provided case study, you reach a stage in requirements analysis where you need to confirm a specific user scenario with stakeholders about the steps they believe the app should follow once a new user has registered to start using the app. Which combination of techniques could be the most appropriate to use to achieve this goal?

Select the correct choice from the following options:

A. State model and/or process diagram

B. Use case and/or sequence diagram

C. Persona and/or prototype

D. User story and/or persona

Question 5

Considering the provided case study, you are tasked to review the backlog. The team asks you to first elaborate on the user stories that are listed as a top priority on the backlog. Where do you start looking to find these user stories?

Select the correct choice from the following options:

A. User stories listed as urgent

B. User stories at the top of the backlog

C. User stories not yet on the backlog

D. User stories that look like they need elaboration

Question 6

Considering the provided case study, you discover a white-label app solution in the market that is customizable for your specific company. Your sponsor is interested but would like to know what the return on investment (ROI) would be if the company decides to use this white-label app solution instead of building one in-house. Which of the following options describes the type of information you need to acquire to determine the ROI for this solution?

Select the correct choice from the following options:

A. Total costs, discount rate, and total benefits

B. Total benefits and cost of investment

C. Total benefits, cost of investment, and discount rate

D. **Present value (PV)** and total benefits

Question 7

Considering the provided case study, your sponsor is asking you to determine the expected costs of buying the app off the shelf. Which are some of the types of costs you should include in this estimation?

Select all the correct choices from the following options:

A. The effort, operational costs, and physical resources

B. The initial cost to acquire

C. Department operational expenses

D. Implementation costs

Question 8

Considering the provided case study, the app has been in production for about 6 months and the sponsor of the initiative is now asking to understand how well the solution is performing for the organization. Which of the following aspects should you consider when you start collecting some performance measures to answer the sponsor's inquiry about solution performance?

Select the correct choice from the following options:

A. You should consider sample size and frequency of taking measures, and give preference to more recent measurements.

B. You should consider sample size (frequency is not relevant) and give preference to more recent measurements.

C. You should be guided by what is available and provided by the solution vendor only.

D. You should only consider whether customers are using the app or not.

Question 9

Considering the provided case study, which of the following Business Analysis tasks would be relevant for you to do to establish who your stakeholders for this project are? Choose the most relevant Business Analysis task.

Select the correct choice from the following options:

A. Manage stakeholder collaboration

B. Communicate Business Analysis information

C. Plan stakeholder engagement

D. Plan Business Analysis governance

Question 10

Considering the provided case study, you decide to create a diagram to demonstrate to the stakeholders how the app will interact with some of the backend systems in the organization. Which two underlying competencies are you demonstrating by doing this activity?

Select the correct choice from the following options:

A. Analytical thinking and problem solving

B. Conceptual thinking and visual thinking

C. Visual thinking and system thinking

D. Systems thinking and conceptual thinking

Case study 4 – Business case for a retail company

You are asked to assist a business by making a strategic decision on a solution to support their future business growth.

Problem statement

A Melbourne-based boutique clothing store that has been selling upmarket evening wear for the last 50 years has recently decided it is time to modernize their sales processes in order to have a wider reach. They currently don't have an online presence, and they serve a niche, small Melbourne market. However, due to economic pressures in the retail sector, they are forced to join the online world of e-commerce and grow the business in order to survive. They have a strong product catalog and a strong recognizable brand in the Melbourne market.

Desired outcome

However, they want to embrace the personalization trend and offer an ability for their customers to customize their orders. They want to remain a niche boutique with an impeccable reputation for quality and customer service.

They are considering the following broad options but need your help to assess these alternatives in more detail:

- **Option 1**: Establish themselves on the Etsy (or similar) online marketplace and grow from there.
- **Option 2**: Develop their own custom e-commerce solution in-house and from the ground up.
- **Option 3**: Buy an off-the-shelf e-commerce solution with the intent to not do any customization.
- **Option 4**: Set up a regular website (without online ordering capability) but increase their reach through online advertising only.
- **Option 5**: Do nothing and try to weather this economic slowdown.

Option		Year 0 Initial Investment	Year 1 Net Benefits	Year 2 Net Benefits	Year 3 Net Benefits	Year 4 Net Benefits
	Discount Rate`		2.1%	2.3%	2.5%	2.55%
1		$60000	$45000	$45000	$45000	$50000
2		$500000	$150000	$208000	$300000	$350000
3		$250000	$150000	$165000	$270000	$390000
4		$50000	$80000	$130000	$130000	$170000

Options outlined for years 0 to 4, showing financial initial investment and net benefits and discount ratios

Questions

Question 1a

Considering the provided case study, you are asked to help work out the financials for this business case. You should calculate the following financial ratios *for each provided solution* option:

- ROI
- PV
- Net Present Value (NPV)

Question 1b

Considering the case study and the financial ratio results you calculated, make a recommendation for which of the following solutions you believe provides the best ROI in relation to the initial investment required:

A. Option 1

B. Option 2

C. Option 3

D. Option 4

Question 1c

Considering the case study and the financial ratio results you calculated, make a recommendation for which of the following solutions you believe provides the best overall value to the organization:

A. Option 1

B. Option 2

C. Option 3

D. Option 4

Answers

This section contains the answers to each of the four case study-based test questions.

Answers – Case study 1 – Global online platform

Question	Answer
1	C. You will use Document Analysis because you have access to the Amazon platform, which is where you can source a baseline of features and requirements to validate with real stakeholders. This is a great time saver and a low-budget option.
2	A. You will not have the time or budget to conduct individual interviews with stakeholders. You can run some workshops, send surveys, and perform document analysis.
3	B. You have a lot of information available to develop a base set of requirements that you can validate with all countries in virtual workshops. This way, you engage everyone with the opportunity for input and achieve time and budget constraints.
4	A, B, and C. The requirements session agendas are not relevant for the Business Analysis approach deliverable.

Answers – Case study 2 – Offender management system

Question	Answer
1	A
2	B

Answers – Case study 3 – Health and fitness app

Question	Answer
1	C
2	A
3	C
4	B
5	B
6	B
7	A, B, D
8	A
9	C
10	C

Answers – Case study 4 – Business case for a retail company

Question	Answer									
1a	Option		Year 0 Initial Investment	Year 1 Net Benefits	Year 2 Net Benefits	Year 3 Net Benefits	Year 4 Net Benefits			
		Discount Rate		*2.1%*	*2.3%*	*2.5%*	*2.55%*	**ROI**	**PV**	**NPV**
	1		$60000	$45000	$45000	$45000	$50000	208%	$180722	$120722
	2		$500000	$150000	$208000	$300000	$350000	102%	$984218	$484218
	3		$250000	$150000	$165000	$270000	$390000	290%	$951922	$701922
	4		$50000	$80000	$130000	$130000	$170000	920%	$498034	$448034
1b	D									
1c	C									

Mock Exam Questions: Theory

16

This chapter contains a multiple-choice mock test, specifically focusing on the **Business Analysis Body of Knowledge (BABOK®)** Guide v3, as discussed in Chapter 13, *Techniques (Part 1)*, and Chapter 14, *Techniques (Part 2)*.

There are 50 test questions, and it should take you no more than 60 minutes to complete.

By the end of this test, you will have an idea of how well you understand and can recall techniques related to concepts and facts. This is a good way to prepare yourself for the actual exam, and it is also a great way to test your study progress. Good luck!

Questions

Question 1

When a Business Analyst develops a change control process, which of the following attributes should be considered for inclusion as part of the definition of the change request?

Select all the correct choices:

A. Benefits

B. Risks

C. Stakeholder influence

D. Cost estimates

Question 2

As a Business Analyst, when you are preparing criteria to be used to assess a set of requirements in order to choose between multiple solutions, which type of criteria are you developing?

Select the correct choice:

A. Acceptance criteria

B. Evaluation criteria

C. Acceptance and evaluation criteria

D. Solution assessment criteria

Question 3

As a Business Analyst, when you are preparing criteria to be used to define the conditions that must be met by a solution in order for the solution to be accepted by stakeholders, which type of criteria are you developing?

Select the correct choice:

A. Acceptance criteria

B. Evaluation criteria

C. Acceptance and evaluation criteria

D. Solution assessment criteria

Question 4

When you are working as an analyst in an environment where there is a backlog of work items and requirements, how do you know which items in the backlog represent the highest business value and the highest priority?

Select the correct choice:

A. The item has a score on the card.

B. The item is at the top of the backlog.

C. The item is assigned to a developer.

D. The item is listed on the left of the backlog.

Question 5

Which one of the following techniques is an effective technique to apply when a Business Analyst has to measure business performance beyond the normal financial measures?

Select the correct choice:

    A. Business Case

    B. Business Process Modeling

    C. Business Model Canvas

    D. Balanced Scorecard

Question 6

Which of the following options describes the activity involved when a Business Analyst researches which products and services customers need or want?

Select the correct choice:

    A. Benchmark studies

    B. Research

    C. Observation

    D. Market Analysis

Question 7

You are invited to go and visit another organization that is deemed the best in class when it comes to selling cheap flights online. Your role is to learn what they do to be so successful in the arena. Which analysis technique are you performing by visiting this organization?

Select the correct choice:

    A. Benchmarking

    B. Market analysis

    C. Observational studies

    D. Best practice analysis

Question 8

Which four dimensions does the Balanced Scorecard technique use to express business value?

Select the correct choice:

A. Learning and Growth, Business Process, Customer, and Financial

B. Learning and Growth, Business Process, Customer, and Strategy

C. Learning and Growth, Business Perspective, Customer, and Strategy

D. Learning and Growth, Business Perspective, Customer, and Financial

Question 9

As the Business Analyst on a project team, you are asked to run a session with a number of business stakeholders to establish their key objectives for the initiative you are working on. Everyone is quite new to the initiative, and no formal objectives have been set. Which one of the following techniques can be a good way to generate ideas within the group?

Select the correct choice:

A. The five whys

B. Brainstorming

C. Interviewing

D. Workshops

Question 10

When the business has to capture the rationale for making a change to a business area, process, or existing solution, which analysis technique will you advise them to apply?

Select the correct choice:

A. Business process analysis

B. Financial ratios

C. Business case

D. Scope modeling

Question 11

Which of the following terms best describes the following definition:

"A potential problem that may have an adverse effect on a solution"?

Select the correct choice:

    A. Assumption

    B. Constraint

    C. Risk

    D. Issue

Question 12

The business model canvas technique describes how an enterprise creates, delivers, and captures value for and from its customers. Which of the following options include some of the building blocks that describe how an organization intends to deliver value?

Select all the correct choices:

    A. Key activities, key partnerships

    B. Value proposition, revenue streams

    C. Customer segments, key resources

    D. Competitors, economy

Question 13

As a Business Analyst, during a conversation with a stakeholder, the stakeholder tells you that their division's policy says that only customers who have been with the company for more than 3 years are considered long-term customers. You need to know how to define a "long-term customer" as part of your requirements analysis. Which of the following terms best describes the Business Analysis information you have received from this stakeholder?

Select the correct choice:

  A. Definitional business requirement

  B. Definitional business rule

  C. Behavioral business requirement

  D. Behavioral business rule

Question 14

What is the primary purpose for a Business Analyst applying a form of collaborative games during a group workshop?

Select the correct choice:

  A. To establish a common understanding of a problem or solution

  B. To let the stakeholders get to know each other better

  C. To make work more fun

  D. To get people to share their opinions more freely

Question 15

As a Business Analyst on a project, you are faced with a very specialized and complex business domain. Which analysis technique will you apply to define and organize the knowledge, definitions, and vocabulary of this domain?

Select the correct choice:

  A. Terms and definitions

  B. Data dictionary

  C. Terminology matrix

  D. Concept model

Question 16

When you are building a data dictionary, you must define each data element in terms of its primitive data elements. Which of the following attributes listed here is an example of a primitive element?

Select the correct choice:

    A. Value

    B. Sequence

    C. Priority

    D. Number

Question 17

The Gane-Sarson Notational context diagram is an example of which type of analysis diagram?

Select the correct choice:

    A. Process diagram

    B. Process flow diagram

    C. Data flow diagram

    D. Data repository diagram

Question 18

In the context of data models, when we refer to a destination external to the system under discussion, we can use which one of the following terms?

Select the correct choice:

    A. Source

    B. Sink

    C. Target

    D. Element

Question 19

When you analyze data with the intention to find patterns that provide useful information about the data, you are performing a type of which one of the following general techniques?

Select the correct choice:

    A. Data mining

    B. Data patterning

    C. Data analysis

    D. Data relationships

Question 20

This type of data model is an abstraction of the conceptual data model that incorporates rules of normalization to formally manage the integrity of the data and relationships. It is associated with the design of a solution.

Which type of data model are we referring to here?

    A. Conceptual data model

    B. Logical data model

    C. Physical data model

    D. Real data model

Question 21

As part of your role as a Business Analyst, you are asked to assist in determining the best way to make a decision about a number of potential vendor solutions being considered by the business. They would like to be able to compare the features in a way that allows them to indicate and give more value to features that are more important to the business. Which one of the following decision analysis techniques would you recommend they apply to achieve the desired outcome?

Select the correct choice:

    A. Weighted decision matrix

    B. Simple decision matrix

    C. Feature decision matrix

    D. Decision tree

Question 22

A decision model shows how repeatable business decisions are made. Which one of the following options describes two ways in which a decision model can be illustrated?

Select the correct choice:

    A. Decision matrix and decision tree

    B. Decision table and decision tree

    C. Decision table and trade-off

    D. Decision matrix and trade-off

Question 23

As a Business Analyst who is responsible for eliciting requirements both directly from engaging with stakeholders and indirectly through other means, which one of the following elicitation techniques can be described as an indirect elicitation technique in this context?

Select the correct choice:

    A. Interviews

    B. Observation

    C. Document Analysis

    D. Workshops

Question 24

Which analysis technique uses the following methods—Top-down, Rolling Wave, Delphi, and Program Evaluation and Review Technique (PERT)—to express itself?

Select the correct choice:

    A. Data mining

    B. Interface analysis

    C. Metrics and key performance indicators

    D. Estimation

Question 25

When you want to determine the potential value of a solution, you add the cost to acquire the solution, the cost of using the solution, and the cost of supporting the solution for the foreseeable future. What is this financial metric referred to as?

Select the correct choice:

    A. The total cost of ownership

    B. The total cost of value

    C. The total cost of benefit

    D. The total cost of the solution

Question 26

Which financial metric term do we use to refer to when we take the predicted expected total benefits and we subtract (minus) the expected total costs?

Select the correct choice:

    A. Cost-benefit analysis

    B. Return on investment

    C. Present value

    D. Net Future value

Question 27

As a Business Analyst, you have been tasked with working out the Return on Investment (ROI) for one of the solution options that your project is considering. You know the following about this solution:

- Year 1 Benefits = $30,000
- Year 2 Benefits = $40,000
- Initial Cost of the Investment = $35,000

What is the ROI?

Select the correct choice:

A. 25%

B. 75%

C. 100%

D. 10%

Question 28

In order to objectively compare the effects of different rates and time periods when comparing different solution approaches, you have to calculate the Present Value (PV) for each solution approach being considered. Your task is to calculate the PV for one solution, and you have the following information available:

- Year 1 Benefits = $80,000
- Year 2 Benefits = $93,000
- Year 3 Benefits = $87,000
- Discount Rate Year 1 = 2.2%
- Discount Rate Year 2 = 1.9%
- Discount Rate Year 3 = 2.3%

What is the PV?

Select the correct choice:

> A. $254,587.82
>
> B. $230,845.90
>
> C. $101,981.01
>
> D. $33,844.23

Question 29

When we present the Net Present Value (NPV), we have to take the PV and consider the cost of investment.

Is this statement true or false?

> A. True
>
> B. False

Question 30

Which of the following techniques is used to manage the complexities of business areas, domains, and systems by breaking it down into simpler parts of processes, systems, functional areas, or deliverables?

Select the correct choice:

> A. Functional Requirements
>
> B. Functional Decomposition
>
> C. Sub Components
>
> D. Sub Decomposition

Question 31

When a Business Analyst uses the Interface Analysis technique, they can apply this technique to different types of interfaces. Select all the types of interfaces that could be specified when applying this technique.

Select all the correct choices:

    A. User interfaces

    B. Business process

    C. Data interfaces

    D. Project interfaces

Question 32

There are two basic types of Interviews that a Business Analyst can use during requirements elicitation activities. Choose which option describes these options accurately.

Select the correct choice:

    A. Formal, Informal

    B. Open, Closed

    C. Structured, Unstructured

    D. Planned, Unplanned

Question 33

Which of the following techniques is used to capture and assign stakeholder concerns in an organized way?

Select the correct choice:

    A. Interviews

    B. Item Tracking

    C. Reviews

    D. Walkthroughs

Question 34

When you perform a SWOT analysis, you assess the organization's internal and external environments by considering four dimensions. What are those four dimensions called?

Select the correct choice:

    A. Strengths, Weaknesses, Opportunities, Threats

    B. Strengths, Weaknesses, Obstacles, Threats

    C. Strengths, Weaknesses, Obstacles, Time

    D. Strengths, Weaknesses, Opportunities, Time

Question 35

Which one of the following analysis techniques would be the most appropriate to use when working with your team to find opportunities for improvement, failures, and making recommendations for future improvements?

Select the correct choice:

    A. Lessons Learned

    B. Optimization

    C. Review

    D. Survey

Question 36

A key performance indicator (KPI) is one that measures progress toward a strategic goal or objective. A good indicator has six characteristics.

Select the choice that includes all six characteristics:

    A. Clear, Relevant, Economical, Adequate, Qualifiable, Trustworthy/Credible

    B. Clear, Relevant, Economical, Accepted, Quantifiable, Trustworthy/Credible

    C. Clear, Relevant, Economical, Accepted, Qualifiable, Trustworthy/Credible

    D. Clear, Relevant, Economical, Adequate, Quantifiable, Trustworthy/Credible

Question 37

When you have generated ideas and information around a particular topic, which one of the following non-linear diagram techniques is the most appropriate to apply?

Select the correct choice:

    A. Brainstorming

    B. Mind Mapping

    C. Focus Groups

    D. Workshops

Question 38

Which one of the following types of requirements describes the criteria that can be used to judge the operation of a system rather than specific behaviors?

Select the correct choice:

    A. Functional requirements

    B. Quality of service requirements

    C. Business requirements

    D. System requirements

Question 39

When you apply the technique called Observation while performing elicitation activities, and you don't interrupt the person you are observing during the work process, you are performing a certain type of observation. Choose the type of observation you are performing.

Select the correct choice:

    A. Unnoticeable observation

    B. Active observation

    C. Engaged observation

    D. Unengaged observation

Question 40

When you develop an organizational model and you choose to group staff together based on shared skills or areas of expertise, as well as acknowledging a standardized way of working within that area, you are showing a particular type of organizational model. Select the type of organizational model you are illustrating.

Select the correct choice:

A. Market-oriented

B. Skills-oriented

C. Functionally oriented

D. Matrix model

Question 41

Which process analysis method involves the diagramming and monitoring of inputs and application points for processing those inputs, starting from the frontend of the supply chain?

Select the correct choice:

A. Process mapping

B. Process modeling

C. Value stream mapping

D. Value stream modeling

Question 42

Which one of the following options describes a key difference between a flowchart and a Unified Modeling Language (UML) activity diagram?

Select the correct choice:

A. One employs synchronization bars to show parallel processing.

B. One employs swim lanes to show roles.

C. One employs notation to show tasks or activities.

D. One employs decision nodes/notational elements.

Question 43

What methods can be applied to prototyping?

Select all the correct choices:

A. Storyboarding

B. Paper prototyping

C. Simulation

D. Conversation

Question 44

What methods can be applied to reviews?

Select all the correct choices:

A. Inspection

B. Pass around

C. Critique analysis

D. Read and revise

Question 45

Choose whether the following statement is true or false when assessing risks: "To avoid a risk by removing the source of the risk, can be used as a risk treatment option."

A. True

B. False

Question 46

Which of the following diagrams is often used to illustrate the results of a root-cause analysis?

Select the correct choice:

    A. PESTLE diagram

    B. Fishbone diagram

    C. Use case diagram

    D. Problem diagram

Question 47

Which of the following diagrams is often used to illustrate the logic of usage scenarios by showing the information passed between objects in a system through the execution of the scenario?

Select the correct choice:

    A. Use case diagram

    B. Activity diagram

    C. State diagram

    D. Sequence diagram

Question 48

When you describe a fictional character or archetype that shows the typical way that a user interacts with a solution, you are creating a _____.

Complete the sentence by selecting the correct choice:

    A. Character

    B. Persona

    C. User definition

    D. Profile

Question 49

Which one of the following techniques is an effective elicitation technique used to question a large number of stakeholders in a uniform way?

Select the correct choice:

A. Survey

B. Workshop

C. Interview

D. Document Analysis

Question 50

When you apply the SWOT analysis technique and you define the strengths of the organization, which environment are you analyzing?

Select the correct choice:

A. External environment

B. Internal environment

C. Economic environment

D. Asset environment

Answers

Questions	Answers
1	A, B, D
2	B
3	A
4	B
5	D
6	D
7	A
8	A
9	B

10	C
11	C
12	A, B, C
13	B
14	A
15	D
16	A
17	C
18	B
19	A
20	B
21	A
22	B
23	C
24	D
25	A
26	A
27	C ROI = (($30,000+$40,000) - $35,000)/$35,000 X 100 = 100%
28	A PV = ($80,000/(1 + 2.2%) + ($93,000/(1+1.9%) + ($87,000/(1+2.3%) = $80,000/1.022 + $93,000/1.019 + $87,000/1.023 = $78,277.88 + $91,265.95 + $85,043.99 = $254,587.82
29	A
30	B
31	A, B, C
32	C
33	B
34	A
35	A
36	D
37	B
38	B
39	A
40	C
41	C

42	A
43	A, B, C
44	A, B
45	A
46	B
47	D
48	B
49	A
50	B

17
Your Future with a Success Mindset

This chapter is written for the *new future you*, where you are already a certified **Certification of Competency in Business Analysis (CCBA®)** or **Certified Business Analysis Professional (CBAP®)** professional.

"Life shrinks or expands in proportion to one's courage."

- Anais Nin

Now that you have achieved the CCBA® or CBAP® designation, it is time for you to also consider working toward achieving your next goal. I am guessing this might be an increase in earnings, and I would like to assist you with some ideas around this to ensure you reach this next stage of your career fast and successfully. This chapter shares some ideas for what you should keep in mind when planning to achieve this goal, and provides some practical advice on how to execute your plans for reaching this goal, with the following topics:

- Planning your next salary increase
- Understanding the process

Let's now dive into how you can go about achieving this future career goal.

Planning your next salary increase

The CCBA® and CBAP® qualifications make for a powerful opening statement when you start the process of planning your next salary increase...

People get increases, not qualifications

Just as there is no get-rich-quick scheme that actually works, there is no get-an-instant-massive-increase scheme that works either. This chapter is not about how to get an instant or undeserving increase that is demanded by you as the worker. No—this chapter is about planning and executing a reasonable and goal-oriented strategy to ensure you get the most return out of your contribution to your organization every day so that you can feel great about your earnings and the extra benefits it can bring into your life.

So, now that is clear, let's just say a few more words about this chapter.

You might have noticed that I said *the process of planning your salary increase* in the first paragraph, rather than the one conversation about your salary increase. There is a reason for that. You will learn what that is in this chapter.

Another word that we will redefine here is *asking*. Asking in this context describes all the activities you perform on your journey to getting the increase you deserve, and we simply use the term "asking" to capture all these activities—and, of course, this is also the polite term to use.

But I am getting ahead of myself. I will start by telling you a little about what I have learned and observed both from the employee perspective as well as the employer's side when it comes to increased earnings. Let's start with the employee.

The employee viewpoint

The employee perspective is sometimes (but definitely not always) that of fear. The employee focuses on what they could lose if they didn't have the job they are currently in. They worry about their worth and whether another employer would employ them, let alone pay as much as they currently earn.

The employee sometimes suffers from the comfort-zone factor as well (a very common human condition), where they are "happy enough" with the salary they get for what they are doing… nothing wrong with that, except the employee with that mindset, will never get a salary increase, certainly not one worthy of what they could get if they were willing to improve their mindset (and value).

So, let's assume that you have gone through the process of getting your CCBA® or CBAP® designation. Is this because you were fearful of what might happen to your career and self-worth if you didn't get the CCBA® or CBAP® designation, or because your expectation is to either get an increase in your current role—or perhaps you want to pursue a better-paying role elsewhere?

Regardless of how you are thinking of going about gaining an increase, you are already halfway there, and this chapter will make it easier and more financially rewarding for you when you finally achieve the goal of higher earnings.

For those of you who are fearful of losing what you already have and feeling fearful of "sticking your neck out" by asking for a salary increase, join this journey anyway and see whether this could help you change your perspective and learn that you are in fact in the driver seat of your career, even more so now that you have your CCBA® or CBAP® designation under your belt.

Understanding the employer's point of view

Let's look at the perspective of the employer when it comes to salary increases. You may have heard this saying: "You are only paid enough to keep you in the role you are in…", or something along those lines. This tells me that it is all about your perception of your own value that you bring to the organization (and not that of the employer). The employer will not offer you a higher salary than what you are willing to work for, regardless of their personal opinion about your value to the organization. If you don't believe you are worth more, no one will believe that. That applies to any situation in life, not just this scenario.

But don't blame the employer. It makes good business sense to keep your costs as low as possible and revenue as high as possible. If they didn't follow this principle as a rule in business, not many businesses would survive.

So, where does this leave you? We will get to that later in this chapter.

However, before you start worrying about how you will go about getting a salary increase, let's first understand the deeper reasons: your personal "why" you want a salary increase.

Why do you want an increase?

Who doesn't want to be paid more, right? It is, however, very important to do a bit of introspection and really find those specific reasons why you want to earn more, such as the following:

- What will be different when you earn more?
- What could you do then that you cannot do today?
- What else would be possible?

Some of you will have reasons such as *My kids will be able to get a better education*, or *I can give them something they have been asking for*, or *I can take my family on a more luxurious holiday every year*. All of these reasons are very good as long as they also include a reward for you, and *only* you!

The reason you must find a strong reason that moves you personally into a feeling of intense happiness, contentment, joy, and fulfillment when you think about getting an increase in earnings is that without that reason, you will EITHER not get an increase OR you will settle for less than what you are worth and deserve.

The "What if?" game

A great game to play with yourself while you are working out what is that deeper reason for wanting to ask for a salary increase is the "What if?" game. Here is how it works:

Pick something you enjoy doing. Let's say you love to travel but currently, due to budgetary limitations, you have to plan your holidays to be local and within a strict budget.

With this game, you could simply ask yourself the following question:

- What if I could go on an overseas holiday every year with my family when I earn X% more as a CBAP® professional?

Or, perhaps you want to study something again but just don't feel you can justify the expense of joining university again. You could, therefore, ask yourself the following question:

- What if I can start studying part-time again when I earn X% more as a CBAP® professional?

I know the "What if?" question seems very basic and even obvious, but how often do you stop and think about your life like that? We tend to block things out and just power on through every routine day, doing what we believe is the right thing to do … and very seldom do we question the status quo.

This chapter, in conjunction with your new CCBA® or CBAP® designation, is questioning the status quo of your current career situation. Let's now explore the options for something better to strive toward.

Understanding the fear of failure

Now, the fear-of-failure factor has been very well documented in almost every personal development book, and therefore I will keep it brief here. To get to the bottom of the fear-of-failure factor, we just need to quickly understand some basic things every human being does (because we are human!). We all make up stuff as we go through life and we tell ourselves that it is true. So, we believe the stuff we make up, and we even justify those beliefs we have with whatever events created them. The bottom-line fact of this matter is that we make stuff up in order to make sense of our internal and external worlds. Each one of us decides what we believe is true about ourselves in terms of who we are, what we can do, and what we deserve. This often has boundaries, and this is often the bottom-line reason why we earn what we earn.

On a more personal note, I woke up to this fact one day, realizing this about my beliefs and the more disturbing fact that I simply made up my own beliefs and stuff based on my perceptions of things as they have happened around me in the last 40+ years or so. If I say I woke up to this, I actually just mean that I became aware of this. It didn't suddenly open up my world to a whole new belief system about things; I have been "practicing" to believe my beliefs for so long that it is a bit harder to change some of those beliefs than it is to just become more aware of them. However, being aware is a great first step toward changing the beliefs that are not supporting us to get ahead in our lives.

What does this have to do with salary increases?

Well, I touched on this before when I said we have a belief of what we think we should be paid. We make up this belief by looking at the market averages, our skills and our knowledge (based on our perception of this), and a myriad of other reasons (which I have personal experience of listening to when speaking with countless CBAP® professionals and Business Analysts alike). This is how and why we settle for a salary that we can live with.

This chapter is telling you the following:

- You made up those rules and limitations about your salary.
- There are likely a whole host of attributes about the value you bring to an organization you haven't tapped into at all yet.
- You are a CCBA® or CBAP® professional now, and that is valuable in itself.

So, to get back to how to deal with the fear-of-failure factor, it is to reprogram a few things in your brain; but let's summarize what the outcome of this reprogramming should do for us, as follows:

- Know that everyone has a fear of failure. It is much worse in your mind than the actual event of failure ever is.
- What is the worst thing that could happen if you fail? Most people who fail end up with either a life lesson that brings them ultimate joy and fulfillment or an unexpected door opens that would never have opened if they hadn't failed.

So, try to keep these two factors at the front of your mind whenever you feel that pang of fear in your gut when we touch on the topic of money.

Understanding the process

So, we've been tap dancing with a few peripheral concepts that often sit under the hood of our entire psyche around money, but in this chapter, we will get down to the mechanics of what you should do, what you need to know and appreciate, and some ideas of how to approach your individual salary-increase conversations.

Before you ask for an increase

There are actually a lot of things that you should do before you ever raise the topic of a salary increase. Right at the start of this chapter, I said: "People get increases, not qualifications." This is very true and is the backbone principle of maximizing your value to the organization.

Being of value

Let's take a step back and consider this analogy. Imagine you are the customer of a small coffee shop down the street. You go past there every morning to get your coffee and your smile from the barista every morning. Technically, you only pay for the coffee, yet you go to that coffee shop because of the extra free smile you get when you pick up your coffee. It makes you feel good. The barista smiles because he loves his customers and the service he provides; he feels proud of his coffee and the freedom his business gives him. So, he smiles easily. It is not fake or insincere at all.

One day you get to the office and a colleague tells you that he went to get his coffee at this same small coffee shop but realized only after the coffee was made that he forgot his money. The barista laughed and said: "No problem. You pay me next time," and laughed some more. Your colleague said it was unexpected, and the barista changed an embarrassing situation into a beautiful moment of trust. Your colleague told everyone else in the office too.

The barista understands the true meaning of giving value—sincerely. An indirect benefit of doing this one good deed would have made so many more workers aware of the barista's existence, and they would have flocked to his coffee shop as a result.

As a Business Analyst who now has a CCBA® or CBAP® designation, you must start your journey toward a pay increase with the sincerity and perspective of the barista. You should do your job plus more, and you should trust and build relationships without expecting more. This should be your baseline position before anything else.

There is a right way to brag

Now, I am (like many Business Analysts) not a huge fan of blowing my own trumpet. I like to do my work quietly and well. On top of that, I am not a big talker, as I would much prefer being quiet and left by myself to dwell on my thoughts. Not all Business Analysts are like that, of course (hopefully not, because it comes with a host of challenges!).

One of those challenges is being effective at getting the message out to the people who need to know what you can and have achieved.

I have a story of when I was running a Business Analysis practice a few years ago. One of my team members came to see me every morning for a 5-10-minute chat about everyday things. We would start the conversation talking about the cats she was fostering or her commute that morning—just a bit of small talk. Then, we would move on to what she did the previous day and any issues she might be having. She almost never directly asked for assistance or anything like that; she just made sure that I knew exactly what she was doing, achieving, or having challenges with. Anytime there was a challenge she mentioned, she would assure me that I didn't need to do anything about it—she just wanted to mention it.

She made sure I knew the good things she was doing, in a subtle and friendly way. We did this short routine every day and I never felt she was bragging or pushing herself for anything, yet I found myself promoting her over others. Why? Because I knew what she was doing and what she was achieving, and it was really that simple. Others had great things to say about her too, because of the same reason. She communicated enough to make sure people knew (plus, the right people knew) what she was doing, without having the reputation of being insincere, or bragging, or constantly chatting.

On the other hand, I had another team member who would also come and talk to me almost every day. The conversations almost never had a clear point, and they were always negative and about problems. I found myself trying to avoid this person just because I didn't feel like having these pointless ongoing negative conversations—it was draining.

So, who would you think ended up receiving not only a huge increase but also a bonus?

There were other great members in my team but all I knew of them was that they were too busy to make time to update me, and there was zero proactivity in terms of my relationships with those people. It was always me initiating and driving any conversations with them; they never took the initiative in any way to be proactive with anything that I was aware of. Where did they end up when it came to increases? Sadly, they ended up with good increases but not GREAT increases. The irony is that they probably worked harder than the person who came for a 5-10-minute chat every day or so.

Is that fair?

Look—I'm not talking about fair or unfair; I'm simply talking about a process that works and a process that doesn't work very well. From a manager's perspective (and a human-nature perspective), the easier a team member makes it for me to know what they are doing, achieving, or struggling with makes it so much easier to be a manager for them than for the team member who is also doing a good job but expecting me as the manager to figure that out for myself.

So, the moral of this story is this:

- Talk to your manager frequently with good news, neutral news, and personal news. Neutral news could be a challenge or a problem but always come with a solution to discuss. Always remember your manager is a person as well: someone probably overworked and who would appreciate a personal touch by building a real relationship with them.
- Don't hide or think that others will blow your trumpet for you. It doesn't work reliably like that, unfortunately. Go and tell people the good things you have done, and also make sure to listen to their news and achievements.
- Avoid just approaching your manager with bad news or problems. The manager is there to always help and support you, but bringing a solution (or even just an idea or two) will go a long way to not only help the manager deal with your problem but will increase your value in your manager's eyes.

So, I think you get the point that once you have set yourself a baseline of always giving value without expecting anything in return and being a good communicator without being a bragger, these are two fundamental ingredients to build on as strongly and vigorously as you can before doing anything more direct to achieve your desired salary increase.

But let's now look at some more specific approaches to follow to ensure you get the salary increase you deserve.

Making your intentions clear

Now that you know that you should take the position of adding value beyond what is expected and communicate that value consistently to those who have influence over your earnings, it is time that you make sure your goals are defined and communicated.

Many organizations have a performance management process where certain objectives are agreed that you as an employee should meet. This is all good and gives you a great starting point, but this is the normal, the average, and the general path that is predefined for you. If you do well with this performance management process by following the steps the organization asks you to follow, you will receive your share of an average increase. This chapter is not about the average increase or this basic process. This chapter is about going above and beyond this process and making sure you set your intentions for your goals and expectations to yourself first, and then to your manager.

So, what does this mean?

You have achieved your goal of becoming a CCBA®- or CBAP®-certified Business Analyst. That is awesome and a great achievement. However, what is your goal now that you are certified? More specifically, what is your measurable goal for a salary increase?

If you are like many, it will be a fluffy statement such as *I will ask my manager next time we speak if this will play a part in my increase*; or you might say something such as *I will now look for another contract or role outside my organization and hopefully earn more.*

Defining your goal

Only you will know your exact situation and goal. Write it down in a specific and measurable way. Set a timeframe and an amount—for example, I will earn X% more in X months from today.

Once you have a specific goal, you can start working backward to work out what you need to do to achieve the goal.

Knowing the rules of the game

Now that you know the specific earnings goal you have set for yourself, you need to work out what you need to do to ensure you reach this goal. It is important that you define the steps you need to take clearly because just setting the goal and hoping it will just happen is not a good approach.

It is like baking a cake—*you must know the ingredients and the recipe to be successful at baking a cake. This is about finding all the right ingredients and following a proven recipe.*

But first, does your manager want you to bake a cake?

Sometimes, it is worth having a friendly conversation (after following the first two basic principles of adding value and communicating effectively for a while) with your manager about your intention to reach certain career goals, one being a salary increase. Ask your manager what they would suggest you do to place yourself in a position to have a discussion with them about an increase in 3, 6, or 12 months (depending on your goal). Ask them what they would expect from you in the discussion in order for this to result in a successful increase.

You can start this conversation in the following way:

"...as you know, I have recently passed the CCBA® or CBAP® exam, which means I am now internationally recognized as a professional business analyst. I am very proud and excited to have achieved this designation and look forward to making an even bigger contribution to our team with my new knowledge and skills.

Today, I would like to discuss your thoughts on what you think would be some milestones for me to reach in order to have a successful salary increase discussion with you in the near future. I am ready to take my career to the next level and would appreciate your guidance and advice on how best to pursue this..."

If you are asked about what percentage you are interested to pursue as a salary increase, simply tell the manager that the average salary for a CBAP®-certified business analyst is 16% (refer to the study posted on the home page of the **International Institute of Business Analysis (IIBA®)**, published by Randstad Canada) above uncertified Business Analysts. You can express a higher percentage based on any additional responsibilities or other factors—it is up to your discretion.

This conversation can be very powerful. You are setting your intention by having this conversation upfront, and you are providing the manager with the opportunity to provide you with their view of what is required. Once you have this conversation, you can close the conversation by asking the manager if it will be OK if you put together a career progression plan based on the input they gave you, and whether you could have regular follow-up meetings with them to ensure you remain on track with this goal.

By approaching this first intention of setting up a meeting with your manager, you are including them in a collaborative and consultative way, whereby you are demonstrating proactively that you are focused, career-driven, and willing to do what it takes to achieve your goals. The key is that you follow this up as per your agreement and that you are the driving force behind whatever this career progression plan sets out for you to do.

Note: Sometimes, this meeting will make it clear to you whether you should pursue this career goal with the organization. If you leave this meeting with a negative outcome, firstly do some introspection and determine the truthful answers to the following questions:

- Is there something you can do to improve the situation by demonstrating a change in your behavior or attitude within the team?
- Are you being reasonable with your expectations? Have you built a strong reputation and delivered outstanding and provable value, and do you have the track record of an individual that deserves a salary increase?

- Is the organization perhaps undergoing a transformation or stagnation that has affected the culture in a negative way? Are you better off making a bigger change by finding an alternative job at the salary level you deserve?

You need to be honest with yourself and address the true answers to these questions. Only you will know what they are.

Why your employer is likely to give you an increase when you ask

There are some good reasons why an employer will most likely agree to a salary increase for you when you ask, assuming everything we have discussed thus far is well established and things are going steady in your role as a Business Analyst.

Here are the reasons:

- **Direct cost of replacing you:** If we assume that your employer would need to replace you if you decided to leave the organization, then it is worth realizing that the cost of replacing you is very high—likely, much higher than the salary increase you are after. This is why an employer will most probably be willing to give you an increase if asked in the right way.

 Note that some organizations might not see this cost easily, and hence may make the costly decision to not give you an increase when you ask for one, but any organization that is switched on and likes having you around will most likely oblige.

- **Indirect cost of replacing you:** Finding a replacement Business Analyst not only takes time to find a suitable candidate but there are also all the intangible aspects such as knowledge, ramp-up time, and relationships that are lost when you leave and someone new has to take your place.

 However, be warned that some employers are quite stubborn and don't take kindly to employees asking for salary increases without being able to demonstrate their own personal and professional value in a sound business case. This is to be expected, so don't ask before it makes sense.

It is important for you to make an assessment of whether or not your approach to asking your employer for an increase is done at the right time, in the right way, and when you have the best chance of success.

Summary

Now that you have achieved the CCBA® or CBAP® designation, you are ready to start looking further forward into your career. One primary goal should be to look at ways to effectively increase your earnings.

Readers will now have skills for gaining an increase, which is neither a quick nor a passive process. Remember that the fear of failure we all foster is elaborated in our minds, and should not prevent you from taking action to realize your life's dreams. You first need to work on providing more value, building open lines of communication between you and your manager, and actively pursuing this goal in collaboration with your management and organization. You now understand the perspective of your employer and direct line manager, which enables you to create a clear milestone-based plan to achieve your goals more effectively.

And, finally, all the best for the next stage of your career, and well done for being successful in achieving your CCBA® or CBAP® designation.

Other Books You May Enjoy

If you enjoyed this book, you may be interested in these other books by Packt:

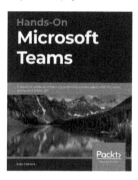

Hands-On Microsoft Teams

João Ferreira

ISBN: 978-1-83921-398-4

- Create teams, channels, and tabs in Microsoft Teams
- Explore the Teams architecture and various Office 365 components included in Teams
- Perform scheduling, and managing meetings and live events in Teams
- Configure and manage apps in Teams
- Design automated scripts for managing a Teams environment using PowerShell
- Build your own Microsoft Teams app without writing code

Learn Power BI
Greg Deckler

ISBN: 978-1-83864-448-2

- Explore the different features of Power BI to create interactive dashboards
- Use the Query Editor to import and transform data
- Perform simple and complex DAX calculations to enhance analysis
- Discover business insights and tell a story with your data using Power BI
- Explore data and learn to manage datasets, dataflows, and data gateways
- Use workspaces to collaborate with others and publish your reports

Leave a review - let other readers know what you think

Please share your thoughts on this book with others by leaving a review on the site that you bought it from. If you purchased the book from Amazon, please leave us an honest review on this book's Amazon page. This is vital so that other potential readers can see and use your unbiased opinion to make purchasing decisions, we can understand what our customers think about our products, and our authors can see your feedback on the title that they have worked with Packt to create. It will only take a few minutes of your time, but is valuable to other potential customers, our authors, and Packt. Thank you!

Index

Automatic Teller Machines (ATMs) 90

B

BABOK v3.0 Guide
  about 34
  business analysis 55
  business analysis information 56
  business analysis key concepts 35
  core content 34
  design 56
  enterprise 56
  extended content 34
  knowledge areas 36
  organization 56
  perspectives 37
  plan 57
  requirement 57
  risk 57
  techniques 37
  underlying competencies 37
  using, as reference guide 12, 13
BACCM™ , applying to business analysis
  about 51
  change 53
  context 54
  need 53
  solution 53
  Stakeholder 54
  value 54
BACCM™, applying to Business Analysis Planning
  and Monitoring
  about 79
  change 79
  context 82
  need 80, 81
  solution 81
  Stakeholder 82
  value 82
BACCM™, applying to Elicitation and Collaboration
  about 117
  change 117
  context 120
  need 118
  solution 118
  stakeholder 119

  value 119
BACCM™, applying to Requirements Analysis and
  Design Definition
  about 238
  change 238
  context 241
  core 239
  solution 239
  stakeholder 240
  value 240
BACCM™, applying to Requirements Life Cycle
  Management
  about 155
  change 155, 156
  context 158
  need 156
  solution 156
  stakeholder 157
  value 157
BACCM™, applying to solution evaluation
  about 286
  Change 286
  Context 288
  Need 287
  Solution 287
  Stakeholder 287
  Value 288
BACCM™, applying to strategy analysis
  change strategy 194
  concepts 194
  context 196
  need 195
  solution 195
  stakeholder 195
  value 196
backlog management
  applying 361
  purpose 361
  using, considerations 361
balanced scorecards
  about 362
  applying 363
  purpose 362
  using, considerations 362
baseline day 18

C